COGNITIVE APPROACHES TO CULTURE
Frederick Luis Aldama, Patrick Colm Hogan, Lalita Pandit Hogan, and Sue Kim, Series Editors

Permissible Narratives

The Promise of Latino/a Literature

Christopher González

THE OHIO STATE UNIVERSITY PRESS / COLUMBUS

Copyright © 2017 by The Ohio State University.
All rights reserved.

Library of Congress Cataloging-in-Publication Data
Names: González, Christopher, author.
Title: Permissible narratives : the promise of Latino/a literature / Christopher González.
Other titles: Cognitive approaches to culture.
Description: Columbus : The Ohio State University Press, [2017] | Series: Cognitive approaches to culture | Includes bibliographical references.
Identifiers: LCCN 2017020891 | ISBN 9780814213506 (cloth ; alk. paper) | ISBN 0814213502 (cloth ; alk. paper)
Subjects: LCSH: American literature—Hispanic American authors—History and criticism. | American literature—Mexican American authors—History and criticism. | Narration (Rhetoric)
Classification: LCC PS153.H56 G66 2017 | DDC 810.9/868073—dc23
LC record available at https://lccn.loc.gov/2017020891

Cover design by Thao Thai
Text design by Juliet Williams
Type set in Adobe Minion Pro

♾ The paper used in this publication meets the minimum requirements of the American National Standard for Information Sciences—Permanence of Paper for Printed Library Materials. ANSI Z39.48–1992.

9 8 7 6 5 4 3 2 1

To my grandfather, Tomás

CONTENTS

Acknowledgments		ix
INTRODUCTION		1
CHAPTER 1	Brown Buffalos and New Mestizas: Consciousness and Readership in Chicano/a Literature	32
CHAPTER 2	Translingual Minds, Narrative Encounters: Reading Challenges in Piri Thomas's *Down These Mean Streets* and Giannina Braschi's *Yo-Yo Boing!*	66
CHAPTER 3	In Graphic Detail: Challenges of Memory and Serialization in the Storyworlds of Gilbert Hernandez	107
CHAPTER 4	Paratextual Play: Intertextual Interventions in Sandra Cisneros's *Caramelo* and Junot Díaz's *The Brief Wondrous Life of Oscar Wao*	145
CONCLUSION	The Narrative Possibilities of Latino/a Literature	177
Works Cited		183
Index		190

ACKNOWLEDGMENTS

I HAVE A cherished memory that serves as my initiation to the power of narrative. When I was a young boy, my mother purchased a subscription to a specialty press that published variations or continuations of well-known stories and fairy tales. What made these books different, and in my eyes special, was the publisher's ability to incorporate specifics from a child's life into the story. My mother had provided the company with my name, the name of family members and pets; the city in which I lived, Lubbock, Texas; and my address, all unbeknownst to me. And yet, when I read my name and other family details blended into the story, when I saw my name in print, it felt like a kind of magic. I was *in* the story! I was reading about things I had done in an alternate universe—adventures with Mother Goose and Humpty Dumpty. For a time I received similar books in the mail featuring me in various adventures, and I was always eager to get the next one. I loved them because it was simple to imagine myself in the story. I was fortunate to still be at an age when children accept storytelling as a wondrous thing and not the work or potential drudgery it can often be in later years.

When I was in middle school, I discovered the Choose Your Own Adventure books—a more substantive if less specific variant of the books I found so enchanting as a preschooler. Again, the conceit of the books—me as protagonist of the story—attracted me. Some of the details were incongruous with those in my life to be sure, but I played along, deciding based on the choices in the narrative presented to me and turning to the appropriate page to discover how I fared. Often these books ended with the fictional version of me in some embarrassing or horrible situation within the story, and I'd begin again as if it were a video game. Though the choices I had to make in reading these books were part of the fun, the greater appeal for me was that I could imagine myself in the story with little effort.

At some point, it became harder and harder to imagine myself within the literature that often served as my English homework. In the sixth grade I remember selecting an age-appropriate biography of Roberto Clemente during a mandated period of "free" reading time. I believe it was the first time I had ever read anything in an English class that concerned a Latino. By the time I attended high school in the early 1990s, I wondered why none of the novels or stories I was reading—was *required* reading—in my English classes was written by a Latino/a author. While I noticed the lack of such short stories or novels, it never occurred to me that I could ask my teachers why we never read stories by Latinos. And so I never did.

Though I did not realize it then, many factors worked to exclude so many Latino/a authors from my English classrooms. The secondary school language arts classroom is conservative by nature, and textbook publishers, state school education boards, and school administrators direct teachers to present to students only those stories vetted over decades, if not centuries. I saw this firsthand when I was a high school English teacher for several years. Teachers and administrators often deem literatures of more recent times as riskier and potentially controversial. They would rather err on the side of not angering parents and the community.

To be honest, works of Latino/a literature are often ignored for many reasons: the entrenchment of teaching methods proffered by New Criticism; the evaluation of literature written by Latinos as a special case without being treated as literature; the suspicion of narratives of cultural expression that are seen as radical or subversive to the well-established traditions of in-school patriotism and nationalism. It turns out I have been thinking about the possibilities of Latino/a narratives for most of my life. The resulting pursuit of an answer has led me to write this book.

My dedication is to the memory of my grandfather, Tomás González, whose life placed him in a time and place where he could not receive a formal education beyond elementary school because he was born in Seguin, Texas, and grew up on a farm in San Marcos, Texas. The value of his work capacity on a farm took precedent over his formal education in a school. Though he was functionally illiterate as an adult, his was a brilliant mind that matched his tenacity and determination. I remember once he was alone at home and someone had called. The message had been important, and he had attempted to write it down. When I arrived, he grew frustrated that I could not decipher his message, for he had already forgotten the message itself. His frustration morphed into tears, and it was the only time I ever heard him say, "I can't read." For a man who was like a father to me, it shocked me to see him so exposed and vulnerable on that day. I am still rattled by it.

My mind often turns to him when I consider the processes of reading and writing, the significant role of storytelling, and the lives of Latino/a men and women. I like to think he would be proud of me as a writer, teacher, and academic. I am convinced I could not have written this book had he not been my grandfather. The story of how he met Buddy Holly will remain for another time. But it, too, serves as a point of inspiration for me.

Many more people deserve my thanks and appreciation than are shown here, but I am constrained by word count and my own fallible memory. At Texas A&M University-Commerce, M. Hunter Hayes was the first professor to tell me I should pursue a PhD, and I value that life-changing bit of advice. At The Ohio State University, I was blessed with such terrific mentors as these: Adéléké Adéẹ̀kọ́ who taught me the power of proverbs; Frederick Luis Aldama, who showed me what was possible; David Herman, who always improved my writing and my sense of humanity; Pranav Jani, who showed me what determination and courage look like; Brian McHale, whose ability to find a weakness in argumentation was beyond measure; Manuel Luis Martinez, who showed me that criticism and creativity go hand in hand; James Phelan, who helped me see narrative as a communicative act; Elizabeth Renker, who showed me why rigor in scholarship matters; and Robyn Warhol, who helped me find confidence in my critical voice. They have all proved to be exemplars of so many good things. Theresa Rojas and Samuel Saldívar III are friends who continue to give me words of encouragement that often sustain me when I need them most.

Special thanks go to Gilbert Hernandez and Jaime Hernandez for always treating me with kindness every time I have asked them for their time or insight into visual/verbal storytelling. They are as gracious as they are talented. Fantagraphics Books aided me with the images that appear with permission in chapter 3, and I appreciate very much the staff for their attentiveness and willingness to help. Portions of chapter 4 first appeared in *Reading Junot Díaz*, published in 2015 by the University of Pittsburgh Press, and they appear here in revised form.

At The Ohio State University Press, I am grateful to the editors of the Cognitive Approaches to Culture series: Frederick Luis Aldama, Patrick Colm

Hogan, Lalita Pandit Hogan, and Sue J. Kim for their support and guidance. Kristen Elias Rowley, Editor-in-Chief, has put up with my questions, requests, and suggestions throughout the process with such patience, and I am filled with gratitude.

Family members who helped out in many forms too often to count: Robert González and his wife, Linda, who are among my best of friends; Grady Mobley, for being a kind father-in-law; Jeff Elbel, who teaches me something every time I see him; Linda Spoehrer, whose passion for the Dallas Cowboys makes us natural friends and allies; Irene, Elva, and Chencia, three women whom I adore and respect beyond measure; Ruth, who left us much too soon but whose spirit never seems far away; Tomás Jr., the greatest trickster figure I ever knew.

My daughters are evidence I am the beneficiary of some cosmic lottery. Olivia is my favorite artist and fellow lover of Studio Ghibli films. Emilia is a mighty girl who sticks up for friends and stands up to bullies. I'm glad she is on my side!

None of this happens without my wife, Ginger González. A mere five months after I graduated from high school, we met by chance. The process of becoming such steadfast friends and loving companions, however, has not been accidental. This, too, makes me think of the cosmic lottery I must have won. Whatever the explanation, I remain indebted to her for her accountability, love, honesty, and willingness to be my partner in life.

INTRODUCTION

THE OFT-CITED METAPHOR that the United States is a melting pot might also be applied to the literary production of U.S. authors. Part of what lends such vitality to literatures of the United States is that they are composed of disparate but related histories and cultural practices. With so many rich literary and storytelling traditions from the various social and identity positions of the U.S. citizenry, the tempering of the U.S. literary tradition over time yields a literature of borrowing where literary traditions, narrative devices, and cultural themes reveal themselves in new and interesting ways. Literatures of the United States are enriched and strengthened because of this strenuous process of borrowing.

Yet this process also means losing a vital part of one's self in this e pluribus unum way of looking at American literature. Certain historically marginalized groups in the United States resist this metaphor of the melting pot because they feel they have not had an opportunity for the same level of self-expression as the dominant group. Political movements that have arisen out of the struggle for civil rights—such as the Chicano movement, the First Wave Feminism movement, the Gay movement, and others—all desire to be heard from an equal platform. They do not want to lose their sense of self by removing specific markers of identity, which often happens through the process of assimilation.

If we adopted a similar understanding in terms of Latino/a literary production, we would see that some proponents of Latino/a literature desire that such narratives be considered equally valid as other literary forms by hegemonic groups in the United States without losing that unique sense of Latinoness within its literature. Equal access, in the sense of narrative design and production, means that authors—and with this book, Latino/a authors—have the same gamut of narrative devices at their disposal when crafting their storyworlds as writers from dominant groups have. However, Latino/a authors, indebted to their predecessors who have helped establish a rich, albeit nascent, literary tradition, also risk being manacled to those earlier narrative forms. Thus, having the capacity to engage in many narrative designs often means moving away from what others expect of Latino/a literature. Readers' imaginations are where these expectations take root like weeds, the result of societal norms and traditions. But these limiting a priori expectations hold far too much sway, and authors of Latino/a literature must be relentless in how they contest these reader expectations at the site of reading comprehension. This site has everything to do with storyworld design and reconstruction, which raises the issue of narrative permissibility.

What is permissible when it comes to narrative form? The aim of narrative theory has been to determine how narratives are made, how they work, and how they are consumed. An author's syntagmatic and paradigmatic choices when creating a narrative reveal one type of narrative permissibility. Syntagmatic considerations in narrative are often more inflexible by definition, while paradigmatic considerations both create an expectation yet also provide the opportunity for upending expectations. While "the butler did it" may have once been a clunky paradigmatic (and thus formulaic) narrative choice, upsetting that paradigm creates a new opportunity for readers of the mystery genre.

For some cultural theorists, such examinations of narrative form are thought of as puerile, or worse, out of touch from material realities of the world. Why would it matter, for instance, whether it was the gardener rather than the butler who did it, when marginalized peoples continually experience racism and inequality on a daily basis? The answer goes far beyond the notion of representation; it is the consequence of the representational encounter that holds the promise of paradigmatic changes in narrative. Cultural critics may hold structuralist or formalist considerations with more than healthy skepticism, but some formalist considerations are very much relevant to larger, societal concerns, as I aim to show.

When I speak of paradigmatic considerations of narrative, I do not wish to confuse what I am saying with semiotic-based uses of the concept. Rather, I am concerned with paradigmatic changes to expected narratives when they are implemented by Latina/o writers. In short, such changes are consistently met with indifference and resistance by publishers, editors, and readers. If we give the benefit of the doubt and agree that the reason for such inhospitality is not a racist stance, then we must look to other explanations. Prominent examples arise in our popular culture with much more frequency. Why do some people resist the possibility that Idris Elba, a black British actor, could play James Bond? Why is it so revelatory to have Diego Luna play a major character with his heavy accent in the Star Wars universe? Why is it so notable to have Junot Díaz write a novel that is infused with science fiction, fantasy, and comic book lore? The answers suggest paradigmatic changes that reveal deeply entrenched expectations for certain narratives. In other words, it is as if certain filmmakers and writers do not have permission to alter narratives to which audiences have become habituated. I propose that we begin thinking about narrative permissibility, a conversation this book helps initiate.

CREATING A READERSHIP

In order for authors of Latino/a literature to venture into all aspects of narrative; that is, to have narrative permissibility there must be an audience willing to engage with a variety of Latino/a writing. While this is commonsensical on its face, audiences and publishers in the United States have had a myopic understanding of the potential and possibilities of Latino/a narrative. Manuel Martín-Rodríguez's *Life in Search of Readers* is one of the first works of scholarship to explore how a readership (and lack thereof) has been a significant impediment to Chicano/a literature. Part of Martín-Rodríguez's argument is that prior to the Chicano movement, Chicano/a authors wrote with two specific audiences in mind: the "realistic" audience that these authors understood as their likely audience, and a larger potential audience (9–10). *Life in Search of Readers* does an excellent job of exposing the material realities that affected Chicano/a literary production and its intended audience.

Martín-Rodríguez's study is an important source from which I launch this book. I wish to further explore works beyond those of Chicano/a literature (I examine, for example, works of Dominican American and Puerto Rican narrative) and include graphic narrative in my investigation of how Latino/a narrative design operates vis-à-vis its audience. Further, though I acknowledge early examples of Latino/a narrative—from María Amparo Ruiz de Burton to José Antonio Villarreal to John Rechy—my case studies fall within a four-decade stretch from 1967 to 2007, the year Junot Díaz published *The Brief Wondrous Life of Oscar Wao*. Thus, *Permissible Narratives* examines a range of narrative texts that have created challenging reading situations during the rise of Latino/a literature. These challenging reading situations often arise because an author decided upon a narrative strategy rarely associated with Latino/a literature.

Prior critical investigations of Latino/a literature have mostly followed a thematic, sociocultural, or political trajectory of inquiry. Sonia Saldívar-Hull's *Feminism on the Border* is a good example. Saldívar-Hull's book is expressly political, begun "in the late 1980s, when discussions of race, gender, sexuality, and class were under attack," hoping *Feminism* would "contribute to the destabilization of antifeminist prognostications" (vii). Saldívar-Hull could not have written this book without a deep exploration of the personal, as both a Chicana and an academic. As a Chicana Feminist reading the creative works of other Chicana Feminists, Saldívar-Hull highlights the power of these texts through the process of reading. Not only does she engage in astute close analyses of texts by writers such as Helena María Viramontes, Sandra Cisneros, and Gloria Anzaldúa, but she also exposes the tacit reality that the text can have a real and profound impact on its audience. So, while *Feminism* stands as a political work, the impetus for it lies in Saldívar-Hull's personal engagement with selected narrative prose and poetry. *Feminism* demonstrates how an overtly political text, enmeshed within sociocultural contexts, still pursues the fundamental cognitive and emotive transaction between author and audience via the text.

Except for Martín-Rodríguez's examination of readers of Chicano/a literature, the development and evolution of Latino/a literature vis-à-vis a flexible and understanding readership—how the changing demands of audiences influenced authorial narrative strategies and decisions—remain unexamined. Latino/a literature has placed complex and challenging demands upon audiences throughout its development, positioned as it is to complicate and expand the umbrella corpus of U.S. literature through thematic, linguistic, and formal contributions. However, a preponderance of scholarship on Latino/a literature has viewed challenges to undermine and destabilize hierarchical and hegemonic structures in the United States. The politics of representation is omnipresent in studies of Latino/a literature. For instance, Arturo J. Aldama's *Disrupting Savagism* exemplifies this sort of scholarly bent. Aldama frames his inquiry in a manner that positions certain narrative voices (e.g., Chicanos, Native Americans) as "talking back" to a power structure that may or may not hear them. Aldama's book and others that take a similar approach focus on the power dynamic between the subject who speaks (often a product of colonization) and the hegemony that has the cultural capital to listen and act but instead ignores. Again, such studies articulate a political struggle, but even in

Disrupting Savagism the crux of the issue rests in the authored text's ability to affect and influence an audience. Aldama's study is significant, but it elides the audience and concentrates on the larger ideopolitical structures of society. I set aside the question "How does the subject speak, and who hears it?" to ask "How does the text, as a creative work, seek to engage and move its specific audience?" This second question highlights the contrast between my work and much of the scholarship concerning Latino/a literature.

THE DEVELOPMENT OF LATINO/A LITERATURE

The publication trajectory of Latino/a literature, however, has not been without its own challenges, some of which originated in the publishing industry. Martín-Rodríguez has detailed the difficulties Chicano/a authors faced when attempting to find publishers for their works; major publishing houses were selective in the Latino/a novels they published. As a corrective to this, specialty publishers such as Quinto Sol Publications, Bilingual Review/Press, and Arte Público Press formed to fill this need. However, because these specialty presses often had a specific vision for the Latino/a literature they wanted to publish, Latinos were often the victims of their own success. If we consider three of the best-selling Chicano works from the 1960s to 1970s—Tomás Rivera's *. . . y no se lo trago la tierra*, Ernesto Galarza's *Barrio Boy*, and Rudolfo Anaya's *Bless Me, Ultima*—each resembles a bildungsroman and even a künstlerroman. Together with Piri Thomas's *Down These Mean Streets*, these works fostered a desire within specialty presses to publish similar works by Latinos because they saw them as marketable. Here was a market with which publishers could identify. While this development was a welcome opportunity for Latino/a authors, the success of these narrative forms soon proved a constraint on later Latino/a writers.

A similar observation resonates in the use of "magical realism" in Latino/a literature. Latino/a authors such as Anaya and Ron Arias used this literary technique made popular by Latin American writers such as Alejo Carpentier and Gabriel García Márquez, and so "magical realism" soon became a way to market Latino/a literature to Anglo audiences. As Martín-Rodríguez notes:

> The label "magical realism" routinely applied to most Chicano/a texts that enter the mainstream is, in fact, the single most important solecism currently haunting the marketing of Chicano/a texts, as it works to reduce these texts to a quaint, facile imitation of what was a booming, revolutionary literary movement a few decades ago. When used by non-Latinos/as, as the term

is mostly used, the label "magical realist" employed to define a Latino/a text suggests a reductionist approach to minority literature that actually works to make it meaningless and insignificant [...]. As such, the magical realism definition is now being used to exoticize the texts to which the term is applied, to make them foreign rather than a product of the U.S. literary arena. (125)

So potent is the "magical realism" label that even the current generation of Latin American writers such as Chilean author Alberto Fuguet, Bolivian author Edmundo Paz Soldan, and Mexican author Jorge Volpi have all tried to shake the magical realist designation. As Argentine Brazilian filmmaker Hector Babenco puts it, "Latin America is never remembered for having contributed anything to the world. Magical realism became our cultural export" (quoted in Margolis 52).

Thus, early successes by Latino/a authors have made it difficult for successive generations of Latino/a writers to write in a manner that differed from those well-established literary tropes. As a result, Latinos could now challenge readers anytime they broke from expectations of their work. Over time, these authors have nurtured and grown a readership by pushing beyond narrow conceptions of what Latino/a literature "looks like." In *Crowding Out Latinos,* Marco Portales contends that "Chicano literature has not yet made a discernible difference in the lives of millions of book-buying Americans" (12). Though Portales focuses on one subset of Latino/a authors and texts, his study demonstrates that the growth of a Latino/a literature readership has been agonizingly slow.

Although literary studies has only relatively recently acknowledged the surge of Latino/a writing as a proper literature, the fact is that Latinos have been a significant presence in the United States since the early nineteenth century—a presence that continues to grow and gain influence with each passing year. In fact, the Latino/a presence in the United States has grown steadily since as far back as the Treaty of Guadalupe Hidalgo in 1848, which almost doubled the geographic size of the United States overnight because of Mexico's ceding of half of its territory. Although this may have been the largest incorporation of Mexican-descended people at one time into the United States, the number of Latinos that comprise the U.S. population has flourished in the interim. Despite the significant number of Latinos post-1848, it was not until the latter part of the twentieth century, with advent of an educated, urban, Latino/a demographic eager for cosmopolitan experiences, that a low-, middle-, and high-brow Latino/a literature constituted itself—as an effort to satisfy this diversifying taste (Aldama, *Routledge Concise History* 4).

Since the late 1960s and early 1970s we have witnessed a greater prominence of Latinos as creators and consumers of art and pop culture. As Raphael Dalleo and Elena Machado Sáez explain in *The Latino/a Canon and the Emergence of Post-Sixties Literature,* "Within this context of canon formation a commonsense periodization has emerged for Latino/a literature, dividing the contemporary literary scene into a Civil Rights generation and what we refer to in our title as the 'post-Sixties' writers that have followed" (2). Dalleo and Machado Sáez encapsulate their project as supporting earlier claims viewing "a politics of social justice as incompatible with market popularity" (3). Specifically, Dalleo and Machado Sáez posit that

> rather than retreating from politics, or substituting what Nancy Fraser calls a "politics of recognition" for a "politics of redistribution," recent Latino/a literature imagines creative ways to rethink the relationship between a politics of social justice and market popularity—a combination that the critical reception denies by either rejecting one of these elements or articulating them as binary opposites. (3)

Scholars thus acknowledge a break in Latino/a literature that occurred around the time of and immediately subsequent to the Civil Rights movement. Dalleo and Machado Sáez see the initial book reviews of works of Latino/a literature as taking a preeminent role in shaping the market success of such texts, and they devote an entire chapter engaging two influential critics: Ilan Stavans and Gustavo Pérez Firmat. I disagree with the notion that reviewers have a meaningful and lasting influence on a text's interaction with its audience, though they do influence bookstores and book sales. My position is that the book reviewer has the potential either to drive readers to a text or to thwart them. Yet once a reader takes up reading comprehension, the reviewer is of minimal importance, serving only to confirm or reject the reader's own estimation of the book. So, while reviewers and their reviews can have an influence on a book's initial sales or readers' early orientation toward the work, such issues are outside my study.

But this notion of visibility as it concerns Latino/a literature signals how this body of Latino/a authored works has flourished since the Civil Rights era. This growth of Latino/a works is the obverse of what has happened to indigenous culture and native peoples of the United States: as their numbers shrink, their presence in art, culture, and academic works becomes disconcertingly small—and limited in range. The same might apply to other groups who have assimilated, such as Norwegian Americans or the German Americans who settled in the Texas Hill Country in the 1840s. At first blush, one might assume that the greater the prominence that Latinos gain as a demographic group, the more influence and control over the forms of artistic expression circulating within that community. However, just as a larger Latino/a demographic in the United States does not always translate into a similar demographic percentage in higher education, Latino/a authors do not comprise a similar percentage of U.S. authors published by, say, large presses that are the standard-bearers of the publishing industry. But it is undeniable that the Latino/a subpopulation in the United States has outpaced all other subpopulations in growth in the early part of the twenty-first century.

In comparison with the European immigrants of the late nineteenth and early twentieth century whose assimilation into U.S. culture also heralded a migration (both literal and figural) from their ancestral culture, Latino/a culture balances between Latin American and Anglo cultures, though often tipping toward one or the other. Often we see scholarship counterposing Latino/a literature with other literary traditions to identify Latino/a texts as being concerned with sustaining and negotiating a dual identity. This emphasis is evident in such works as Gloria Anzaldúa's *Borderlands/La Frontera*, Gustavo Pérez Firmat's *Life on the Hyphen*, Ilan Stavan's *Hispanic Condition*, and Ramón Saldívar's and José David Saldívar's explorations of the dialectical nature of the U.S.-Latino/a relationship in *Chicano Narrative* and *Dialectics of Our America*, respectively. This approach is so dominant in Latino/a literary scholarship that it is understandable why many of these scholars begin their examinations with questions of identity, leading them to examine Latino/a literature through the lens of identity politics. While an identity-oriented approach to Latino/a literature has borne some interesting and suggestive fruit, the dominance of this approach largely ignores how both formal features of a particular narrative and its built-in relationship to an ideal audience radically complicate any dual-identity model. These considerations bolster my contention that Latino/a literature has been (and still is) positioned to influence not only U.S. literature but *the audiences* of U.S. literature as well—but not in the a priori ways that have dominated in the past but in ways that emphasize an identity politics approach to examining Latino/a literature.

For most of its history of literature in America, scholars, bookstores, and audiences have viewed ethnic literatures of the United States through the lens of the author's identity. This is not an accusation: ethnic authors have historically written about matters of identity. Yet because the public comes to expect that, say, a Latino author like Tomás Rivera would write about the Chicano migrant experience, there is the tendency to adopt an a priori way of looking at all literature produced by Latinos. Conversely, there is not a similar, identity-based, a priori stance for engaging with non-ethnic literature in the United States. So, when I say my book eschews an a priori approach for examining the selected Latino/a works, I mean I am not foisting certain issues based on conventional expectations of Latino/a literature. Overwrought interpretations of Latino/a authors and their implied authors can become an a priori mode of engaging with a text that privileges the narrative based on the identity of the author or author construct. Inherent in this position is the central concern of this book, namely, that a priori ways of viewing Latino/a literature have tangible effects on the production and reception of Latino/a works. Two examples will illustrate this point.

John Rechy's breakthrough novel, *City of Night,* has, for most of its publication history, been largely ignored by the Latino/a community. *The Norton Anthology of Latino Literature* edited by Ilan Stavans points out that the success of *City of Night,* "based on a topic shied away from and condemned by macho Latino culture, was unacceptable to Chicano critics writing about traditional Mexican American lives" (1023). Conversely, the LGBTQ community has heralded Rechy's novel as an excellent work of gay literature. The lack of reception of *City of Night* by the Chicano community underscores the limitations of an a priori approach to Latino/a literature. Because Rechy's novel did not comport with established expectations for Chicano literature, many critics ignored the novel instead of viewing it as an example of the diversity and potential of Latino/a literature.

Another, more recent, example of a novel reveals how the identity of an author often relates to the subject of his or her novel in ways that confound readers and critics. Sesshu Foster's 2005 novel *Atomik Aztex* is a work of alternative history that posits a world in which it was the Aztecs that drove out the European colonizers from the Americas:

> Perhaps you are familiar with some worlds, stupider realities amongst alternate universes offered by the ever expanding-omniverse, in which the Aztek civilization was "destroyed." That's a possibility. I mean that's what the Europians *thot.* They planned genocide, wipe out our civilization, build cathedrals on **TOP** of our pyramidz, bah, hump our women, not just our women but the Tlazkalans, the Mixteks, the Zapoteks, the Chichimeks, the Utes, the Triki, the Kahuilla, the Shoshone, the Maidu, the Klickitat, the Mandan, the Chumash, the Yaqui, the Huicholes, the Meskwaki, the Guarani, Seminoles, endless peoples, decimate 'em with smallpox, measles and shit fits, welfare lines, workaholism, imbecility, enslave 'em in the silver mines of Potosí, the gold mines of El Dorado & Disneylandia, on golf courses & country clubs, *chingados,* all our brothers, you get the picture. (1)

Atomik Aztex is a highly imaginative novel that, despite its alternate universe conceit, deals frankly with what it means to be Latino/a in the United States. But in direct defiance of literary expectations, Foster is Asian American writing a novel built on Latino/a themes. Is this novel best categorized as Latino/a or Asian American or neither? The answer matters less than what occurs at the level of narrative design. To hold an a priori expectation on Foster's novel puts the work at risk of being ignored altogether.

My approach attends to the text, its relation to its narrative target, but especially to the way considerations of audience influence authorial decisions in creating a storyworld. Rather than claim that Latino/a authors (and they alone) have an essential capacity for writing a particular type of fiction, say, magical realism or a narrative of "borderland" consciousness, I suggest that attending to Latino/a literature itself—its use of narrative techniques in creating storyworlds—allows us to understand how it has developed vis-à-vis an ever-shifting reading demographic and a publishing industry that has pressured and constrained Latino/a writing to conform to an a priori expectation of what such writing should be like, what is marketable, and what it should aspire to achieve. If we are to understand how Latino/a literature has developed, we must adopt an a posteriori approach to examining this corpus, by letting the corpus itself indicate the questions we ask about it.[1] Doing so allows us not only to discern current trends but also to expect how Latino/a literature may develop in the years to come. Latino/a literature has posed different challenges to readers during the last forty years—challenges that *Permissible Narratives* aims to map out. It is important to remember that reading challenges from the late 1960s may no longer be a challenge in the 2000s, given the change in readership. Tracing this shifting set of challenges, and the way in which audiences approach these challenges, helps us understand how Latino/a literature as a "Literature" has developed.

Here it is useful to take stock of the primary readers and consumers of Latino/a literature. Although Latinos comprise a significant quotient of the readership, I pursue this study under the assumption that the large majority

---

1. I do not mean to suggest that my adopted approach allows me unique access to the text itself. On the contrary, a critic who examines, say, historical or political dimensions of the text may also allow such an investigation to be generated from the text itself. However, a standard criticism of more formalist approaches to ethnic literature is that they do not consider the social, historical, or political valences that are ingrained in such works. I did not set out to find examples of Latino/a texts that presented challenging reading situations to their audiences. Rather, I recognized that certain Latino/a texts share a common trait—a narrative design that challenges the audience—and I have investigated how that trait reflects in the publication and reception of Latino/a literature over the last forty years. In short, I have adopted an inductive approach in my project.

of the growing Latino/a literature readership is both English speaking and Anglo. I draw on the terms coined by Patrick Colm Hogan to denote how people in groups identify with others. In *Understanding Nationalism,* Hogan uses the terms *practical identity* (a person's set of representational and procedural structures) and *categorial identity* (any group membership that helps define a person) to differentiate the two forms of identity formation (25–29). Practical identity might be exemplified by two narrative theorists who might discuss the concept of the narratee. Categorial identity, however, rests in membership of a group based on the definition of self. Hogan calls categorial identity a "form of labeling" that "may be religious, ethnic, national, a matter of sex or sexual orientation, or something else" (29). I invoke Hogan's categorial identity specifically as a reminder that there is no such thing as a monolithic Latino identity. It is fluid along spectrums of nation of origin, linguistic capability, gender, sexuality, religion, political affiliation, and more.

Again, I make this distinction to focus my examination, not to create an artificial binary when the reality is not that simple (i.e., Latino/a readers vs. Anglo readers). Besides, I have already declared that I do not wish to pursue an identity-based examination of Latino/a literature. My interests lie, rather, in specific challenges presented by a Latino/a text in light of its audience. It is foolhardy to claim that all readers and audiences engage with any text in similar ways. Yet we can posit a certain reader based on examining the text and exploring how the author-text-reader relationship foregrounds differences of practical and categorial identity. What I aim to show is that reading challenges are not necessarily bound to differences in race or ethnicity; the challenges may arise from some other disparity having to do with either practical or categorial identity. For example, Richard Rodriguez's *The Hunger of Memory* presented a challenge to many Latinos because of his conservative stance on education—thus creating a conflict for practical identity, or rather for the way a range of practical identities intersects with a particular categorial identity.

Since its inception Latino/a literature has faced publication challenges born from matters of audience and reader expectation. This fact correlates with the viable narrative forms available to a Latino/a author's desire to have his or her work published by a major publisher with the distribution power to increase visibility and marketability of those works. With no readership receptive to an array of narrative forms by Latino/a authors, two consequences arose: (1) publishers foisted certain narrative conventions on Latino/a authors, and (2) an open-minded readership was required. Novels affected by similar writing constraints include José Antonio Villarreal's *Pocho* and Arturo Islas's *The Rain God* among others. Often misidentified as the first Latino/a novel, *Pocho* stereotypes Mexican Americans in California. *The Rain God* suffered from publishing delay after delay that carried on for years; Islas's publisher rejected his manuscript multiple times and pressured him to change certain key aspects of his novel.[2]

A 1996 *New York Times* article by Doreen Carvajal sheds light on the difficulties Latino/a authors face when trying to have their work published by major publishing houses. Authors Dagoberto Gilb and Demetria Martinez shared their respective experiences with the publishing industry. "My dream had always been to publish in New York," Gilb noted. "It wasn't that I thought I was wonderful. I thought I wasn't any worse than what they were publishing" (quoted in Carvajal). Similarly, Martinez remarked on her attempt to publish her novel, *Mother Tongue*: "One editor felt it was too middle-class and the character reflected too much on her inner life. The impression she was giving me was that I didn't write about someone picking lettuce in the field" (quoted in Carvajal). These comments by Gilb and Martinez suggest how publishing houses and editors may be prisoners of past successes of Latino/a works. A Latino may write a superb novel about someone picking lettuce, but that does not mean it is the only kind of novel a Latino may write.

While Latinos continue to experience resistance to publishing in all forms and all genres, Latino/a literary history has been fraught with lost texts. One of the key issues in growing a Latino/a body of literature is the lasting posterity of the books themselves. For example, Frances R. Aparicio has noted the difficulties encountered by scholars of Puerto Rican literature:

> Many factors have led to this "absent" state of affairs in criticism. First, the isolation and marginalized status of many U.S. Puerto Rican writers and critics within academia and in the literary market has created not just a metaphorical "invisibility" of literature, but a material, pragmatic one. With only

---

2. Frederick Luis Aldama chronicles Islas's difficulties in his attempts to publish what would later become *The Rain God*, a novel that "broke with the formulaic migrant-farmworker or out-of-the-ghetto mold. To this day, Chicano/a authors celebrate Islas's effort to challenge the mainstream publishers' stranglehold on 'ethnic' fiction" (xiii–xiv). Regarding the publishing obstacles Islas faced, Aldama writes, "But Islas's gay/straight, El Paso/San Francisco scenes made mainstream editors so uncomfortable that they refused to publish the novel. A mid-1970s New York publishing climate had not caught up with the change in the ethno-sexual climate. By the time Islas did publish a version of 'Día [de los muertos],' he had received letters of harsh rejection for over a decade. Those that overlooked the same-sex sexuality pointed to an overreliance on Spanish; in fact only a handful of Spanish words appear in this manuscript. Islas transformed 'Día de los muertos' into a more 'sanitized' *The Rain God* (published in 1984 by a small house, it achieved word-of-mouth success), but his borderland fictions continued to disconcert. Publishers also refused his second novel, *La Mollie and the King of Tears*. (It was rejected, ironically, by the very house that would publish it posthumously.) Islas made his breakthrough with *Migrant Souls*, a follow-up to *The Rain God* that William Morrow finally published in 1990" (*Dancing with Ghosts* xvi).

two main publishing houses, Arte Público Press and The Bilingual Press, catering to Latino writers, many publications are out of print and inaccessible for scholars and readers at large. (21)

Aparicio raises an important issue that affects not only Puerto Rican literature but also the whole of Latino/a literature. Many smaller presses that specialize in Latino/a literature have often served as a springboard for Latino/a authors striving to have their books published by large presses. Also, the growing numbers of Latinos in the United States made the potential reach of Latino/a literature much more likely. *The Norton Anthology of Latino Literature* (Stavans, ed.) encapsulates the demographic expansion of Latinos in this way:

> According to the U.S. Census Bureau, in 1980 there were approximately 14,600,000 Latinos in the country. That number increased by 53 percent in the 1980s to some 22,300,000 by 1990, and the growth continued unabated in the 1990s. By the early years of the twenty-first century, Latinos had become the largest ethnic group in the country, surpassing African Americans. In 2003, the Census Bureau predicted that by 2050 one of every four U.S. citizens would have a Latino ancestor. By 2006, the Latino population had reached 43,168,000. By 2009, it had surpassed 45 million, and more people of Puerto Rican descent lived on the mainland than in Puerto Rico! (1461)

But despite the growing Latino/a demographic in the United States, Helena María Viramontes reminds us that "there's a big difference between having numbers and power. Historically, the small presses have kept our work alive" (quoted in Anders). Richard Rodriguez believes we should not see Latino/a literature as distinct from American literature: "We Hispanics are not specimens of difference. We act as though we are separate. It's as though we don't live in the same country—and that is outrageous. I want to be on an American shelf" (quoted in Anders). Further, Rodriguez has stated that "when he submits material [to a publisher], he wants it to reach the biggest group of readers possible" (quoted in Anders). Rodriguez makes a strong argument, but it is an argument that meets with resistance among many Latino/a writers and critics.

María Herrera Sobek, for instance, considers Chicano/a canon formation and pushes for different evaluative measures for ethnic literatures:

> The vectors and parameters of minority literatures must of necessity be judged differently because they arise out of a different socio-cultural context, just as English literature emerged out of a particular socio-political context.

> Therefore, if the English had the right to formulate a canon for their own literature, Third World peoples have the right to formulate their own canon. ("Canon Formation and Chicano Literature" 217)

In her essay, Herrera Sobek targets works of Chicano/a literature that have been, as she claims, "marginalized, neglected or disdained by previous literary canons" (218). I agree that the recovery of forgotten works of Latino/a literature is crucial in understanding the totality of such a body of work. But I also maintain that publishers and public alike must receive Latino/a literature regardless of whether these works make use of the conventions established by its publication history. How will Latino/a literature ever evolve and develop otherwise if it is constantly bound to repeat what it has already done?

Latino/a literature is enmeshed with readership. In *Hispanic*, Ilan Stavans explains the complex history of Latino/a literature and its audience:

> Until the late 1980s, English-speaking Latino writers had received little attention from mainstream society. [. . .] A generation of perfectly fluent English speakers had to emerge for solid novels to break into the mainstream. Our audience was reduced to college professors and students. These works almost never ignited a global debate, or made it into the core curriculum, or enchanted more than a few initiated. (229–30)

Stavans's point about reducing the audience to "college professors and students" allows me to emphasize that the early breakout novels by Latino/a authors had a significant, albeit small, audience. But what Stavans identifies as "mainstream" society, what I take to mean as society-at-large, did not mirror the passion of these academically oriented audiences for Latino/a literature. The salient question here is why works of Latino/a literature had small, devoted followings—followings unlike the nonexistent followings of mainstream readers. Stavans, again, is insightful on this point:

> At least for the time being, the audience reading Cristina Garcia's *Dreaming in Cuban* and Victor Villaseñor's *Rain of Gold* may look as if it is mainly non-Hispanic, a white, genuinely democratic readership ready to give silence a voice, but a passionate, middle-class, English-speaking Latino readership, hidden in the shadows, is also active. The biggest Latino best sellers are Richard Rodríguez's *Hunger of Memory*; Rudolfo Anaya's *Bless Me, Ultima*, which, by 1993, more than two decades since its original appearance, had sold some 400,000 paperback copies; Oscar Hijuelos's *The Mambo Kings Play Songs of Love*, which sold over 220,000 copies in paperback after it received the

Pulitzer Prize; and Sandra Cisneros's *Woman Hollering Creek,* a critical and commercial success when it was published in 1991, which sold more copies than did Hijuelos's book in a little over twelve months. The effect has been tangible. After decades of silence, José Antonio Villarreal, Ron Arias, and others are being reprinted today by major publishers, their tales of discrimination, drug abuse, and economic hardship slowly reaching the core of the American Dream. Other authors like Junot Díaz, Esmeralda Santiago, and Ernesto Quiñones have also become commodities of major New York houses. Their work is read in college and influences the younger generation. [. . .] In any case, this new generation, already inspired, is happily aspiring to higher goals and preparing itself intellectually in ways that easily surpass its parents' education, which means that a larger readership is in the making. (*Hispanic* 232–33)

While Stavans concedes a mainly non-Hispanic readership for Latino/a literature, he also makes a compelling case for the rise of a Latino/a readership. That readership, he assures, is out there: "No doubt, the challenge for writers and editors is to find it" (233). Yet it is important to remember that a developing readership feeds off a developing tradition of writers, and vice versa. Latino/a writers read not only works of Latino/a literature, but they read works outside of this specific tradition. It only makes sense that Latino/a authors would want to emulate more than just the early examples of Latino/a literature.

A study of the Hispanic book market conducted by Sarah Alonso shows several key factors for how publishers conceive of readers of Hispanic literature, including the projection that the Hispanic market will be much more English based and will respond less to Spanish-language marketing strategies that as of 2005 were in use (49). Book publishers recognize the purchasing power of Hispanics—$653 billion in 2003, rising to over one trillion in 2007—thus making it a profitable endeavor to market to this group (52). However, Alonso's study also reveals that the "book publishing industry's response to the surge in the Hispanic population has been cautious" (56). One significant development, according to Alonso, is the move by major publishing houses to devote an entire division or imprint to Hispanic titles, such as HarperCollins's imprint, Rayo (56). Yet these imprints have one eye on Spanish-language readers, and, as Stavans noted above, publishers are still attempting to understand the readership Latino/a literature invites. Gustavo Arellano, author of the syndicated newspaper column *¡Ask a Mexican!,* uses humor to encapsulate what large publishers do not seem to understand:

> A common misperception among publishing houses is that Latinos will buy any *libro* so long as the author has a Hispanic surname, the cover features sombreros and the plot involves a talking burro. Sorry, kids: Latino readers don't want the publishing version of affirmative action—they demand quality. They want crisp writing, fresh stories, writers who can illuminate all the angles of Latino U.S.A. instead of ruminating for the umpteenth time about illegal immigrants and their tough-as-tamales lives. More Sandra Cisneroses, fewer *Dirty Girls Social Club* rip-offs, *por favor*. (98)

By showing how myopic publishers are, Arellano, in no uncertain terms, expresses the possibilities of what Latino/a literature can be.

Along with this troubled genealogy of Latino/a literature, the relationship between narrative form and issues of audience has largely gone unexamined in this tradition. As a result, early in the publication history of Latino/a fiction, publishers insisted that Latino/a writers foreground what were thought to be narrative attributes and themes endemic to Latinos themselves, while in more recent years publishers have placed more of a premium on immersive storytelling—on the telling of stories that have the power to capture, and retain, the imaginations of the broadest possible readership. Not that the publishing industry deliberately pressured Latinos to write in a prescribed fashion, as if it were all some vast conspiracy. Over time, however, it became evident that readers were interested in Latino/a literary production. One look at today's Latino/a literature shows it is not just about barrios and magical realism anymore.

For example, Michael Nava's best-selling Henry Rios mysteries focus on a gay public defender in San Francisco, while Eric Garcia has written everything from sci-fi (*The Repossession Mambo* [2009]—later adapted for the screen in a film called *Repo Men*) to a chick-lit spoof (*Cassandra French's Finishing School for Boys* [2004]) to a novel about con artists (*Matchstick Men* [2002]), and even the *Anonymous Rex* series of neo-noir novels (in which dinosaurs are not only not extinct; they have interbred with humans and have their own detective agencies!). Such novels show a greater freedom for the stories Latinos write and publish. Also, that these types of novels have been able to appear in print only in recent years and not, say, thirty or forty years ago reflects the changes in the sociopolitical climate. In the 1960s, in the midst of the Chicano movement, writings by Rodolfo "Corky" Gonzales and Tomás Rivera spoke to injustices these men witnessed and experienced. Progress and the social advancement of Latinos has been an integral aspect of the broadening of the Latino literary imagination in print. This assertion is at the center of this book, which explores the use of various narrative devices and strategies leading to the growth of an actual reading audience whose attributes, for Latino/a authors, are more like those of an ideal readership.

CHALLENGING READING SITUATIONS IN LATINO/A LITERATURE

In this book I foreground four kinds of narrative features—and discuss how those features pose challenges to readers of Latino literature vis-à-vis its ideal audience. I provide a brief sketch of those features here and will expand on each of them in later chapters. The first feature is the ontological blurring that occurs when fiction purports to be reality. In Latino/a texts that use this narrative strategy, the author adopts an authorial counterself in pursuit of self-understanding and as a method of exploring identity consciousness. The second narrative feature I explore is the use of more than one language by Latino/a authors that manifests as either code-switching or bilingualism. Language usage is a narrative feature that highlights the difference in cultural representation and reading across culture in Latino/a narratives. The third narrative feature I investigate involves the space-time configuration of storyworlds in graphic narratives and how that configuration bears on readers' ability to conceptualize and remember events narrated across different serial installments. Finally, I will also consider paratextual playfulness within more recent works of Latino/a literature—specifically, their use of intertexts and footnotes. These four characteristics of Latino/a narrative, examined as challenging reading situations, will not only help us understand the conditions under which Latino/a literature developed, but will also allow us to contemplate how the difference between the ideal readership and a willing readership affects the narratives Latino/a authors create.

Latino/a literary history and culture provide the foundation for my critical framework, along with developments in cognitive narratology. With Hogan's practical and categorial identities in mind, two narratological concepts lend a foundational structure to my study. The first of these is David Herman's formulation of how authors create storyworlds (i.e., narrative worldmaking) and how readers take the narrated storyworld and reconstruct it in their minds. Herman's analysis of the design and reconstruction of storyworlds provides a more rigorous understanding for what we commonly call *reading comprehension*. Herman further articulates the process as "storying the world" and "worlding the story" from his *Storytelling and the Sciences of the Mind* (16). "Worlding the story" is the process of storyworld reconstruction within the mind of the reader based on the inscribed text or narrative blueprint. "Storying the world" indicates the cognitive changes that occur within readers after having read a narrative that causes them to see their world anew and perhaps from a new, potentially altered view and sense-making of the world.

I support Herman's theorization of "storying the world" and "worlding the story" because they seem to capture best not only the immersive potential of narrative but also the consequent simulating a narrative world within one's mind. However, the cultural critic in me pauses at the action potential of "storying the world." It is not far afield from the idea that reading literature will make you a better person, whatever that means—or, perhaps worse, that reading narratives by and about marginalized communities will encourage understandings of that community, albeit in a limited and potentially harmful way. While I value Herman's ideas concerning the reconstruction of a storyworld and the effects of that reconstruction, I also feel compelled to underscore the reality that a vast majority of readers both "story the world" and "world the story" in ways that are highly imperfect. There is a gradient that must be observed in these processes. But, as I will show, comprehending a rhetorical communication and reconstructing a narrative storyworld are not the same thing. From a commonsense viewpoint, storyworld reconstruction requires a highly engaged imagination to apprehend the level of nuance as inscribed in a storyworld. We may recognize reading comprehension as a process of understanding the plot of a narrative. The plot, as an analogue to the chronological cause and effect that Seymour Chatman calls *story* (19), can often be recapitulated by a reader without taxing his or her cognitive abilities. In *Story Logic,* Herman establishes this difference and the advantages of thinking in terms of a storyworld:

> For one thing, the term *storyworld* better captures what might be called the ecology of narrative interpretation. In trying to make sense of a narrative, interpreters attempt to reconstruct not just what happened—who did what to or with whom, for how long, how often and in what order—but also the surrounding context or environment embedding existents, their attributes, and the actions and events in which they are more or less centrally involved. [. . .] More generally, *storyworld* points to the way interpreters of narrative reconstruct a sequence of states, events, and actions not just additively or incrementally but integratively or "ecologically"; [. . .] narrative understanding requires determining how the actions and events recounted relate to what might have happened in the past, what could be happening (alternatively) in the present, and what may yet happen as a result of what already has come about. The importance of such processing strategies in narrative contexts is part of what motivates my shift from story to *storyworld*. (14)

But I would push Herman's definition of storyworld further so that it recognizes the sensorial and emotional factors of not only building a storyworld but *inhabiting* a storyworld as well. Readers dwell within the storyworld even as they reconstruct it from the text. The positive residual of "storying the world" must not simply come from an intellectual engagement of a narrative but also from the emotional crests and valleys a reader navigates during the process of storyworld reconstruction.

If, as Herman suggests, narrative storyworlds are mentally projected, richly textured environments along dimensions of space and time, then Latino/a narratives are much more than articulations of identity or explorations of themes. The storyworld, as a dynamic construct bound only by the limitations of the author's imagination, ought to have the freedom to expand in ways its author sees fit. However, creating a storyworld is effectively limited by what an audience can recreate in its mind. Herman's description of what goes into creating a storyworld (i.e., an ecology) is a highly complex process. Any narrative device used by the author that exacerbates the complexity of the storyworld and the reconstruction of its ecology in the audience's mind will prove to be a significant challenge, if not a downright obstacle.

Thus, one impetus for my study is to reassess the concept of the storyworld as defined by Herman. Also, it is important to consider that the storyworld, while inert when a book is resting upon a shelf in a bookcase, is on a figurative journey that reaches its culmination within the mind of its audience. The storyworld is a product of the process of narrative worldmaking motivated by the author's imagination. But a storyworld does not reach the fulfillment of its promise until it is reconstructed within the mind of its audience. Unlike some theorists who proclaim that a narrative is co-created (by the author's text and the reader's reading), I agree with Patrick Colm Hogan who states:

> I do balk somewhat at the idea of readers being co-creators—though this view is widely accepted today. Like so much else, it depends on precisely what one means by the terms. On the one hand, it is certainly true that there is some sort of mental representation of the story in the reader's mind. Since the reader typically has some interest in getting things roughly "right" about the narrative, this mental representation is not simply fantasy. It is, rather, a matter of the reader's attempts to understand the narrative. We may use "co-creation" to refer to inference and imagination that try to accommodate themselves to some independent facts. If so, then it makes sense to refer to the reader's *mental representation* of a narrative as "co-created." But I would not refer to the narrative itself as co-created. Rather, the narrative itself is the

complex of independent facts to which the reader is trying to accommodate his or her inference and imagination. (Aldama and Hogan 7)

Hogan's acceptance of the plausibility that there is a mental representation of a narrative (or specifically, a storyworld) which is co-created in the reader's mind is arguably the point of reading narrative. When a reader discusses being enthralled at reading an engrossing narrative, not only is that reader reconstructing the storyworld; he or she is both an active participant in its creation and the primary observer of the mental images he or she is co-creating (according to the textual cues). This process, as a vivid, imagined simulation of a narrative storyworld, can help explain how printed words on a page can evoke real emotions within a reader, even when a reader knows the narrative is a work of fiction. The reconstructed storyworld is a simulation, but the reader's emotions are real.

The second narratological concept concerns the reader. A noteworthy aspect of my study, one that arises from my exploration of storyworlds in post-1960s Latino/a literature, is the idea that narratives can and do present challenges to their readerships. Scholars of literature can agree that narratives have this power over their readerships to a varying degree. These challenges link to one's ability to reconstruct a storyworld. If readers reconstruct or simulate narrative environments when reading, say, a novel, as Herman and Hogan suggest, then anything within the narrative's design (as a blueprint for simulating the storyworld within a reader's imagination) that impedes this process of reconstruction is a severe limitation. So a challenging reading situation is one in which a reader cannot easily or accurately reconstruct the storyworld according to the narrative blueprint.[3] I propose a narrative construct that facilitates my analysis of such challenging reading situations as the ideal readership.

Here I must articulate my choice of using "ideal readership" over similar reader constructs that have been developed. Narrative theory has richly theorized the receiving end of the text, from Gerald Prince's positing of the "narra-

---

3. David Herman and Frederick Luis Aldama often use the term *blueprint* in reference to the textual design of narrative. If the narrative can be said to encapsulate a storyworld, and if readers use the narrative to reconstruct the storyworld, then referring to the text as a blueprint is an apt choice. Herman states that "interpreters seeking to build a storyworld on the basis of a text will also take into account complexities in the design of the blueprint itself—complexities creating additional layers of mediation in the relationship between narrative and storyworld" (Herman 107). Aldama tends to use the phrase *narrative blueprint* to denote the same design quality of narrative that Herman identifies (*A User's Guide to Postcolonial and Latino Borderlands Fiction* 104; *Your Brain on Latino Comics* 29; *Multicultural Comics* 19). My use of the term *blueprint* comports with both Herman's and Aldama's usage as it relates to design aspects of storyworlds.

tee," to Jonathan Culler's "competent reader," to Umberto Eco's "model reader," to Wolfgang Iser's influential "implied reader," to Rabinowitz's "authorial audience." This sampling of reader constructs all have their particular nuances and do not suggest exactly the same thing. For instance, Prince's "narratee" is the oft-unseen interlocutor present within the storyworld who is the narrator's direct addressee. Iser's "implied reader" has a converse relationship to Wayne C. Booth's "implied author." Both concepts share that the text implies something about the entity responsible for and the entity best suited to reading the narrative. Though I do not use these terms in my study, I support how Booth's and Iser's concepts signal that these constructs do not correspond with actual living human beings. Rather, they are both projections of the creator and consumer of the narrative that emanate from the inscribed text, as are all reader constructs. The differences in these reader constructs is what each purports to do and how we as theorists arrive at each.

Of all reader constructs theorized by narratologists, perhaps Rabinowitz's "authorial audience" comes nearest to my use of "ideal readership." But Rabinowitz's term is part of a larger rhetorical theory of narrative, and I dislike using only one part of his rhetorical model, one later revised by James Phelan, who defines the authorial audience as "the hypothetical, ideal audience for whom the implied author constructs the text and who understands it perfectly. The authorial audience of fiction, unlike the narrative audience [. . .], operates with the tacit knowledge that the characters and events are synthetic constructs rather than real people and historical happenings" (*Living to Tell about It* 212). Phelan himself uses the term *ideal audience* to define *authorial audience*, but my use of ideal readership differs from Rabinowitz's and Phelan's authorial audience in one crucial way: my conception of the ideal audience is not dependent on authorial intent and, perhaps most significantly, it also considers the material implications of the publishing market. Phelan's definition posits that the author conceives of the authorial audience when the author constructs the text. My contention is that the text itself calls for a particular ideal readership, one where authorial intent is superfluous and the publishing market is a serious consideration. Attempting to divine the ideal readership by assuming the position and agenda of the implied author is one kind of a priori engagement with a narrative I wish to avoid. As Frederick Luis Aldama asserts in *A User's Guide to Postcolonial and Latino Borderland Fiction*:

> No detailed account of the author's biography (her life experiences; her social, political, economic, and historical circumstances; her gender and sexual orientation; her ethnic background and upbringing), accompanied by the most extensive account of the way the author has reacted toward every

circumstance she has experienced, will ever explain why [Zadie] Smith, for example, chooses to begin *White Teeth* with the character Archie about to commit suicide or why [Hari] Kunzru chooses to begin his novel *The Impressionist* with action aswirl in the middle of a great flood. (14–15)

Aldama recognizes the dangers in privileging the authorial side of a narrative written by a marginalized author. Doing so puts one on a precipice that overhangs identity politics to the potential detriment of the narrative itself. In a similar vein, I believe it is possible to assess and hypothesize an ideal readership without having to detour through the author, whether implied or biological. I think the reverse is true: the positing of the authorial construct by venturing through the ideal readership is a useful and markedly different process in its own right.

At any rate, without the context of how the rhetorical model situates the term *authorial,* the term *authorial audience* yokes together the author and audience, with the text as the implicit link between the two in terms that positions them as a unit, as coeval. Though I acknowledge the author as the creator of the narrative, and hence the audience the author has in mind, over time the text may suggest an ideal audience that is not what the author intended when constructing the narrative. In short, I wish to give primacy to the ideal readership as a means of exploring other aspects of narrative.

Therefore, I propose using the construct of the *ideal readership* as an a posteriori method for understanding the design of a narrative—and particularly narratives written by Latinos—by examining an ideal audience suggested by the text without an identity-based expectation that seeks to constrain Latino/a authors. Further, my understanding of this reader construct might be called the *ideally equipped readership,* meaning a readership ideally equipped (cognitively and emotively speaking) to simulate the storyworld within its mind. But this is an unwieldy term, and I hesitate to add yet another entry to the roll call of reader constructs in narrative theory. My use of *ideal readership* acts as a lens by which to investigate what types of knowledge and experiences an audience must have at its disposal to reconstruct the storyworld as the primary focus for literary investigation. And, as I will show in the chapters to come, there are many loci that serve as sites of challenge to actual readerships. We can identify these by understanding how the ideal readership navigates these sites in Latino/a literature and then posit how this process of navigation affects an actual readership, and, in turn, Latino/a literature post-1960s. I seek to identify the disparity between how the ideal readership is equipped to deal with the challenges within the narrative and how the actual audience may fall short. The locus of my initial excavation of the ideal readership is not vis-à-vis the implied author but rather the actual readership. The result of examining the affinities or disparities between ideal readership and actual readership may reveal that there is not a shortcoming in the Latino/a narrative in question at all. Instead, maybe the actual audience is unwilling, unprepared, or ill equipped to encounter the text on its own terms. Such an outcome would radically change the perception of Latino/a literature and narratives written by authors from other historically marginalized groups.

Further, while scholars often think of authors along such identity vectors as race, ethnicity, nationality, class, and so on, scholars of narrative tend to stay away from similar ascriptions to readers and audiences. In two notable exceptions, Brian Richardson and Peter Rabinowitz have examined multiple implied audiences and dual audiences, respectively.[4] As with previous examinations of reader constructs, rather than attempt to understand how indeterminate numbers of readers (all from different backgrounds) engage with Latino/a literature, I examine the ideal readership evoked by a given Latino/a storyworld itself, not by the implied author. Though an implied author can have the same category designations as biological authors (e.g., Latino, gay, upper-class education), the question arises whether the ideal audience can be similarly categorized. Can an ideal readership have a heterosexual Latino identity? Does the ideal readership have an identity at all? Can the ideal readership be said to have personhood? Does the ideal readership experience emotions?

These questions can make up their own study entirely. But what I wish to raise now in this introduction is that readers' conception of self as expressed through identity influences their ability to reconstruct the storyworlds inscribed in Latino/a narratives. If the ideal readership does have an affinity for a particular identity, say, a Chicana Feminist identity, the process of ideal storyworld reconstruction can happen only when the actual reader becomes more like a Chicana Feminist, just as the ideal readership does. Such an outcome seems to be the initial steps of Herman's "storying the world."

That a reader who is not a Chicana Feminist can hold a Chicana Feminist identity position, even temporarily, is a provocative statement, one I recog-

---

4. In "Singular Text, Multiple Implied Readers," Richardson examines the plausibility that some narratives have multiple implied audiences. Though he does acknowledge that many works of postcolonial literature are written with multiple audiences in mind, Richardson's analysis is mostly concerned with modernist literature's capacity to address multiple implied audiences. Similarly, Rabinowitz looks at the possibility of dual implied audiences by using Nella Larsen's *Passing* in his essay "'Betraying the Sender': The Rhetoric and Ethics of Fragile Texts." I differ from both Richardson and Rabinowitz in what they see as some narratives that suggest multiple audiences. The ideal readership, in my configuration, is the audience that can reconstruct the storyworld perfectly.

nize Chicana Feminists might denounce. They might maintain that a man who has reaped the benefits of male privilege cannot possibly know what it is like to be a Chicana, ever. And they would be right. But I am not arguing that reading a narrative suited for an ideal readership with the knowledge and experiences of a Chicana is the same as being a Chicana or a substitute for the Chicana experience. Rather, I propose that when a reader attempts to reconstruct a narrative as a certain ideal readership might, he or she is simulating a storyworld suited to a different identity position than he or she normally holds. If so, such a reading experience may help enrich Suzanne Keen's theory of narrative empathy.[5] Empathy, in its truest sense, means understanding the experiences of an individual who is distinct from oneself. What better way to achieve such a level of empathy, beyond experiencing the same life events as the person in question? Again, the implications of Herman's "storying the world" spring to mind.

However, several potential problems concerning the outcomes of narrative empathy and "storying the world" surface. First, moving to take on the identity traits of an ideal readership does not always make a reader either more empathetic or better able to empathize with actual persons with similar categorial or practical identities. Second, increased empathy and changes in a reader's engagement with the world because of "storying the world" prima facie seem idealistic and render the reader incapable of speaking or responding to a material reality. Third, there is the problem of a reader's believing, having now read a certain work of fiction, perhaps by a minority author, that his or her understanding of marginalized people is something close to complete. In fact, such readers would potentially be more informed, but more experiential knowledge of a marginalized group—both actual and via storyworld simulation—would be necessary to avoid stereotyping and prejudicing. These are all valid concerns, and I will now take up each of them in their turn.

As to the first issue, I do not claim that an actual readership will instantly or easily become more like certain groups when reading a given narrative, at least not in a long-term, verifiable way. Individuals accumulate those aspects that yield their sense of identity over the course of a lifetime, and it would be difficult to claim that reading one or several types of narratives would affect those salient traits of a reader's identity. In effect, my assertion is not that

---

5. Suzanne Keen's *Empathy and the Novel* theorizes the implications of empathy when reading the novel. Specifically, theory of narrative empathy maintains that the worldmaking properties of reading narrative might have the effect of empathy for readers. As Keen notes, "If novels can be considered a part of readers' environment, then fiction may elicit the expression of dispositional empathy, or it may cultivate the sympathetic imagination through the exercise of innate role-taking abilities" (4).

reading narratives or reconstructing storyworlds *will* change a reader into a different, perhaps more empathetic, person. Instead, I suggest that a willing readership that works to align itself with a narrative's ideal readership will simulate certain identity traits—a process that *may cause* a greater sensitivity to issues surrounding these identity traits.

The second issue I raised above suggests that simulating an identity position is not the same as experiencing life events related to that identity position. A white male who reads Richard Wright's *Native Son* cannot claim to understand what it is like to be an African American man in the pre-civil rights era United States, ever. Reconstructing Wright's storyworld—the one in which Bigger Thomas rages against himself and society—makes these issues of race, masculinity, and violence a part of the reader even if he or she has never had similar experiences in real life. Because the storyworld is a simulated ecology in a reader's imagination (per Herman) and is co-constructed in the reader's mind (per Hogan), the storyworld, along with the social, psychological, and other questions raised by it, has now become a part of the reader's experiential knowledge. This process of storyworld reconstruction and the vertical alignment of ideal and actual readerships at the very least opens the potential for the reader to experience empathy and, as a consequence, experience the world in a way he or she may not have before taking part in the reconstruction of the storyworld. Further, that a narrative is fiction does not minimize the emotional engagement—or entanglement—experienced by a reader. Not only are real emotions evoked and inculcated by fictional narratives, Hogan claims "story structures are fundamentally shaped and oriented by our emotion systems" (*Affective Narratology* 1).

Finally, the possibility that a reader may still essentialize a group of people after they have read a certain narrative does not undermine the position I put forth. Some readers may have an essentialist understanding of certain groups of people even before reading a work of fiction. And ending up with an essentialist notion of "Othered" members of society is always a possibility for some readers. Still, the possibility of essentialism does not diminish the possibility that when a willing readership works to align itself with the ideal readership, a narrative's potential to affect a reader's engagement with the world is at its greatest.

These two issues surrounding the storyworld and the ideal readership both have significant implications when understanding the development of Latino/a literature and its willing readership, especially the degree to which the ideal readership and the actual readership may or may not align. If an alignment of a willing readership with an ideal readership is a superordinate goal of the narrative, any aspect of the narrative that disrupts or prevents effective storyworld reconstruction is a challenging reading situation. And it is the challenge that is necessary if simplistic understandings of identity are ever to be overcome. The challenging reading situation, much like Viktor Shklovsky's *ostranenie,* or the translated neologism "enstrangement," allows readers to understand Latino/a literature in a new way and break with stereotypical, tired expectations of what narratives by and for Latinos look like. With this in mind, my book uses these aspects of narrative theory to construct a new framework for the study of Latino/a literature, even as it suggests, more broadly, how textual and paratextual features of literary works must be investigated in parallel with their implications for specific, historically situated readerships.

With all of the above in mind, it is crucial to emphasize that narrative experimentation by Latino/a authors is not a recent phenomenon in Latino/a literature; it is just that such early examples of narrative innovation initially experienced limited reception and inhospitable readerships. First, many of these more daring narratives have only recently found an engaged, willing readership.[6] To be sure, early Latino/a authors who wanted to explore the complexities of narrative form—complexities Anglo-American modernist writers were exploring fifty years earlier—were limited by both publishing and marketing expectations, and by the lack of a receptive, willing readership. Second, the wider reception and attention garnered by more recently published Latino/a texts shows change in readership since the late 1960s. What ultimately marks Latino/a literature's maturation is not its successive narrative innovations but rather its creation and education of a willing readership—fostering what Jorge Luis Borges called "the hospitable imaginations of the readers" (485). I assert that willing readers do not opt out of engaging with a storyworld just because the narrative does not fit with prior expectations about how the text is likely to be structured or styled—a prior expectation based, in this case, on the ethnic identity or even linguistic choices of an author. A willing readership strives to align neatly with the ideal readership.

Yet the passage of time has also influenced the development and reception of Latino/a literature. In *Toward an Aesthetic of Reception,* Jauss lays out the horizon of expectations to argue for the fluidity of a text's interpretation over time:

---

6. Some narratively challenging Latino/a texts, such as Isabella Ríos's *Victuum* and Oscar "Zeta" Acosta's *The Autobiography of a Brown Buffalo,* have suffered from a failed initial reception. But in a larger sense, Latino/a literature has often struggled with the issue of finding an audience. One has only to look Arte Público Press's "Recovering the U.S. Hispanic Literary Project"—an initiative to bring back into print works of Latino/a literature that have fallen out of print—as an example of the difficulty Latinos have in writing for readers who often have narrow expectations for Latino/a literature.

> A literary work, even when it appears to be new, does not present itself as something absolutely new in an informational vacuum, but predisposes its audience to a very specific kind of reception by announcements, overt and covert signals, familiar characteristics, or implicit allusions. It awakens memories of that which was already read, brings the reader to a specific emotional attitude, and with its beginning arouses expectations for the "middle and end," which can then be maintained intact or altered, reoriented, or even fulfilled ironically in the course of reading according to specific rules of the genre or type of text. (23)

Thus, not only is a text's historical context of significance, but also the audience's experience plays a crucial role in reading literature. Further, if, as Jauss maintains, readers must be within a text's horizon of expectations in order to be in a position to interpret the text properly (what I would call "restructuring the storyworld"), then what I mentioned above regarding the disparity between the ideal readership and the actual readership, largely rests on the horizon of expectations. In other words, the ideal readership lies well within the horizon of expectations, while the actual readership that is unable or unwilling to meet the text on its own terms lies outside the horizon of expectations. In *Aesthetic Experience and Literary Hermeneutics,* Jauss further articulates this phenomenon:

> In the analysis of the experience of the reader or the "community of readers" of a given historical period, both sides of the text-reader relation (i.e., effect as the element that is conditioned by the text and reception as the element of concretization of meaning that is conditioned by the addressee) must be distinguished, worked out, and mediated if one wishes to see how expectation and experience mesh and whether an element of new significance emerges. These two horizons are the literary one, the one the work brings with it on the one hand, and that of his everyday world which the reader of a given society brings with him on the other. Because it is derivable from the work itself, the construction of the literary horizon of expectation is less problematic than is that of the social one which, as the context of a historical life-world, is not being thematized. (xxxii)

While Jauss works out an excellent paradigm of expectation concerning the vectors of the literary and the experiential, his binary model does not account for a trajectory of identity within his horizon. An intervention to Jauss's horizon of expectation of including how practical and categorial identity positions affect reader engagement and readership reception might open explorations of marginalized literatures in the United States that go beyond just identity or just narrative structure. Jauss's invocation of reader experience has a direct effect on the Latino/a literary tradition and its development. Jauss maintains that reader experience shapes reader expectation, which is another way of saying that reader experience helps shape a reader's evaluative measure of narrative aesthetic. If Jauss's contention is in fact the case, then it is easy to understand why authors of Latino/a narratives have had such a difficult time in establishing the freedom to create works that differ in significant ways from audiences whose limited experience with Latino/a identity and culture has unduly shaped expectations when reading Latino/a literature.

OVERVIEW OF CHAPTERS

To examine the relationships among the development of Latino/a literature, its ideal readership, and its willing readership, I will concentrate my analysis on aspects of narrative that have comprised challenging reading situations in this specific textual tradition. My chapters consider works of Latino/a literature in light of concepts from cognitive narratology to explore how storyworld blueprints and other issues related to form present notable challenges in a willing readership vis-à-vis an ideal readership. These challenges for readers, as they take shape within the various narratives themselves, are also located within specific moments in history.[7]

Chapter 1, "Brown Buffalos and New Mestizas: Consciousness and Readership in Chicano/a Literature," examines two works by Chicano/a authors: Oscar "Zeta" Acosta's *The Autobiography of a Brown Buffalo* and Gloria Anzaldúa's *Borderlands/La Frontera: The New Mestiza*. This chapter takes a look at these two case studies that purport to seek a new consciousness, narratives that posed as Latino/a autobiographies and were published during the politically charged 1970s and 1980s (i.e., the Chicano movement and Chicana Feminist movement, respectively). Not only is my interest in uncovering how Acosta and Anzaldúa depict consciousness within their narratives; I am most concerned with how these works challenge the reader and how these challenges influenced the development of Latino/a literature over four decades, through narration and literary expectations. At the center of these works is

---

7. For example, Oscar "Zeta" Acosta's *The Autobiography of a Brown Buffalo* (1972) put itself in an indeterminate relationship with historical facts in a way that vexed many readers who expected a literal autobiography, including readers sympathetic to the Chicano movement of the late 1960s. It demonstrates how a text may challenge readers of differing categorial identities through narrative aesthetic choices as well as through the historical political climate.

the challenging nature of ontologies that arises when fiction poses as reality, in its supposed representation of lived experience, and, crucially, how the authors deploy those ontologies via narrative discourse. *The Autobiography of a Brown Buffalo* broke the mold for Latino/a narratives by creating an authorial counterself who uses history as a foundation for his satirical, self-serving mythopoesis. For a text so timely and relevant to the Chicano movement, *The Autobiography of a Brown Buffalo* was largely ignored as it struggled to find a readership. Conversely, *Borderlands*, a text that openly announces its aim to create a difficult reading experience, found an expansive readership, particularly in cultural studies. Like Acosta's novel, Anzaldúa's uses an authorial doppelgänger who takes up achieving a new state of consciousness or identity. However, despite the many similarities between the two works, along with the significant challenges they pose in reading, they each achieved vastly different receptions.

Building on chapter 1, chapter 2, "Translingual Minds, Narrative Encounters: Reading Challenges in Piri Thomas's *Down These Mean Streets* and Giannina Braschi's *Yo-Yo Boing!*" is concerned with how multiple languages create challenging reading situations. I explore not only how the English and Spanish languages (and their variants such as those found in Spanish) are combined in different ways via code-switching and bilingualism, but also how these languages are inextricably linked to race and culture in Latino/a literature. Thomas and Braschi serve as bookends of a thirty-year-period of Puerto Rican narrative. Not only are the two authors separated by three decades, but their engagements with race are different. (Thomas struggles throughout his narrative to understand his identity within the context of race and language, while Braschi's work and personal experiences do not reflect the same trepidation with her skin color or language.) In addition, the two authors are further distinguished by their socioeconomic class and level of education. Thomas grew up in Spanish Harlem, code-switching his way to a "formal" education in the penitentiary, while Braschi took her PhD in Spanish literature from Stony Brook University, SUNY.

The freedoms and constraints surrounding the usage of a code-switching technique of narrative by Thomas and Braschi had a direct effect not only on storyworld design but also on audience reception and formation of character. While Thomas was pressured to self-translate and contextualize his minimal use of Spanish and agree to the insertion of a glossary, Braschi moves fluidly between Spanish, English, and Spanglish with little apparatus to aid a monolingual English-language reader. Latino/a writers have increasingly opted to include Spanish-language material in their texts. This tendency appears to have a direct relation to Latino/a literature's changing readership. I hope to show how Latino/a literature continues to be both constrained and enabled by its need to engage with many practical and categorial identities. If actual audiences must rely on experience in order move within these texts' horizon of expectations, a part of that experience also includes experience with the Spanish language—experience that the ideal readership already has.

Chapter 3, "In Graphic Detail: Challenges of Memory and Serialization in the Storyworlds of Gilbert Hernandez," concentrates on serialization and memory to explore how the comics of Gilbert Hernandez have successfully grown a readership while continually presenting his readers with significant reading challenges. Comics, like other so-called minority literatures, have been viewed rather myopically throughout their development. However, unlike minority literatures, comics have had wide latitude in terms of form and content, in part because of underground and alternative modes of the comics genre. Further, unlike traditionally serialized narratives, Hernandez's comics place severe demands on the long-term and working memory of readers due to the extravagantly detailed storyworlds. These comics, through the use of specific narrative devices, challenge reader memory in substantial ways that at once draw upon the rich history of Latino/a culture but also reveal how Hernandez's works are more than just "Latino/a comics," urging readers to work in ways that few texts have done.

Chapter 4, "Paratextual Play: Intertextual Interventions in Sandra Cisneros's *Caramelo* and Junot Díaz's *The Brief Wondrous Life of Oscar Wao*," focuses on, among other paratextual features, the use of footnotes in fictional narratives—and how those footnotes function to controvert or supporting the main text. Junot Díaz's and Sandra Cisneros's profligate uses of intertexts and paratexts within their novels and, in particular, intertexts whose use and presence extends the thematic architecture of the novel's storyworld. Here again, a cognitive approach aids my analysis, for intertexts and footnotes require a deft reading protocol that causes "leaving" the narrative proper to engage with the texture that specific intertexts lend to the storyworld. A range of postmillennial Latino/a novels have used techniques associated with postmodern literature such as the use of intertexts and footnotes. In using so many intertexts and footnotes in order to texture their storyworlds, Cisneros and Díaz force the reader to traverse the textual boundary and move in and out of other storyworlds and space-time configurations, forcing us to ask whether we are at a technologically enabled turning point in our society that makes searching for an obscure intertext as easy as logging onto the Internet. Jauss claims that because readers' experiences help broaden their expectations, increasing the likelihood of entering a text's horizon of expectations, readers can now gain such experiences more easily because of the Internet. Still, despite the relative ease of locating an obscure intertext is much more convenient in 2017 than it was in, say, 1972, it does not mean that doing so is not a challenge. Not only would such a reader need to engage with the text at hand; he or she would need to read with access to other intertextual material. Thus, an examination of these authors' use of intertextuality and paratextuality helps Latino/a literary scholarship take stock of narrative worldmaking practices by Latino/a authors.

My conclusion, "The Narrative Possibilities of Latino/a Literature," highlights the significance of Latino/a authors and the cognitively demanding challenges they pose for their readerships. I suggest how my study provides a model for understanding how storyworlds invite readers to take up not just understanding Latino/a narratives but also participating in these richly textured worlds. Publishers play a pivotal role in allowing Latino/a authors the opportunity to stretch and tax their readerships in invigorating ways. In order for works of Latino/a or any other minority literature to go beyond a localized readership and gain wider exposure, they must cultivate their own readerships by always seeking to challenge publisher and reader expectations.

CHAPTER 1

Brown Buffalos and New Mestizas

Consciousness and Readership in Chicano/a Literature

SOME OF THE best known and most widely studied works of Latino/a literature feature narrators who adopt memoirist or (auto)biographer positions. Pre-twentieth and early-twentieth-century Latinos helped establish this strong tradition of documentary writing, from the accounts of fifteenth-century witnesses to colonization and exploration such as Fray Bartolomé de las Casas and Álvar Núñez Cabeza de Vaca; to the memoirs of Juan Seguín, who fought alongside the near-mythic founding fathers of Texas, Sam Houston and Stephen F. Austin; to Puerto Rican–born Arthur A. Schomburg and his tireless efforts to reconcile his Hispanic and African heritages. This drive of Latinos to document experience reached full bloom following World War II with the works of such figures as Bernardo Vega, Ernesto Galarza, Luis Leal, Américo Paredes, César Chavez, Piri Thomas, Richard Rodriguez, Esmeralda Santiago, Luis Alberto Urrea, and Luis J. Rodriguez, among others. And even in works of fiction—conjurations of sheer imagination—in the mid- to late twentieth century by Latino/a authors continued to subscribe to a narrative style that emphasized documenting experience through the lens of identity in the United States. Consider, for example, the acclaimed works of Rudolfo Anaya, Arturo Islas, Sandra Cisneros, Esmeralda Santiago, and Cristina García. All of these writers use narrators, fictional or otherwise, that take on the project of filtering their life experiences through the sieve of narrative, often to create a record that documents particular experiences to relate them for a reader's (or listener's) consumption. These narratives display a compulsion to document the experientiality of the self as a Latino/a.

In Chicana/o literature, such devotion to first-person narration arises, in part, from an oral tradition and folkloric forms such as the *corrido* and the *testimonio*.[1] That Chicano/a life writers structure their narratives around a framework of liminality allows them to cast their experience as a person from a marginalized community. Further, because these narrators allow readers significant access to their thoughts, feelings, and other intimations, a close examination of these highly personal narrations provides an excellent opportunity for understanding how these kinds of narratives have contributed to creating both a corpus of Latino/a works and a readership of Latino/a works. These authors, in designing their narrative blueprints, create storyworlds that are, in fact, carefully constructed representations of consciousness or mind. I am interested in this architecture of consciousness both from an authorial design stance and from the perspective of the reader's reconstruction of those designs—via a process of experiencing literary texts known as Theory of Mind, a cognitive psychological term that Lisa Zunshine describes as "our ability to explain people's behavior in terms of their thoughts, feelings, beliefs, and desires. Thus we engage in mind-reading when we ascribe to a person a certain mental state on the basis of her observable action. [. . .] Attributing states of mind is the default way by which we construct and navigate our social environment, incorrect though our attributions frequently are" (*Why We Read Fiction* 6). Zunshine's definition suggests that Theory of Mind is not simply two minds meeting; it is also a cognitive process that allows us to make sense of inaccessible minds in a *social environment*. I believe this to be a salient issue, for the bulk of Latino/a literature arises out of the social dynamic within the United States, relatively speaking. Because they have been a group that has struggled for equal treatment and civil rights, Latinos have written about this liminal position within U.S. society as a means of "talking back" to oppressive hegemony.

In considering the relationship between the text and reader, this chapter examines Latino/a texts whose narrators work to narrate experiences from their liminal position within society through their representations of consciousness. Specifically, the narrators selected as case studies in this chapter are uniquely positioned because they are authorial counterselves[2]—shadows of

---

1. For more on the oral literary of Mexican-descended peoples, see Américo Paredes's seminal study "*With His Pistol in His Hand*."

2. I am using the term *counterself* and its variants rather than the more standardized "implied author." *Counterself*, in my opinion, reflects more accurately the affinity the inscribed

the biographical authors who are unambiguously enmeshed in the project of writing and documenting their own lives and the lives of others through the very books we hold in our hand when we read texts like Oscar "Zeta" Acosta's *The Autobiography of a Brown Buffalo* and Gloria Anzaldúa's *Borderlands/La Frontera: The New Mestiza*. What is key here, however, is that while these texts purport to be examples of reportage, they are works of imagination based only in part on historical fact.

Within each of these texts, an imagined author is at work, communicating directly to an ideal audience. This reading situation creates high ambiguity: many readers often wish to conflate the biographical author with the fictional author who claims to be the person writing the text we read. Readers must hold a simultaneous distinction when reading these works, a distinction which on the one hand reminds us that the works are creative endeavors of fiction, while on the other hand they are nonfiction from the perspective of the inscribed author.[3] However, this distinction threatens to collapse, or maybe readers see the text as one or the other—but not as both simultaneously. Such a reading task rarely occurs when a heterodiegetic narrator is present. While it is possible to take a heterodiegetic narrator as a stand-in for the biological author, the ontological blurring that occurs in my case studies is noticeably absent. In Acosta's and Anzaldúa's texts, the fictionality of the narrator is often in doubt because the fictionality of the narrative is obscured.

At the heart of these texts is the compulsion to document experience and represent a newly formed state of consciousness or self-awareness. However, these texts are creative works, not sociological documents. Naturally, my argument foregrounds issues that surround communication to an audience, and specifically an audience that seems to live outside of the fictional author's sphere of experience—whether it be the experience of a Chicano in the years leading up to the Chicano movement of the late 1960s or the experience of a Tejana Chicana lesbian. Thus, when the biological author cedes the storytelling to a character within the narrative, albeit a counterself, the reader receives a re-creation of experience through the consciousness of the fictional author. Because each text announces itself as a document by a subjective (and fictional) author, issues related to unreliability, selectivity of narrated events, and the constructedness of the text all encroach upon and influence the reader's attempt to reconstruct the storyworld. The difficulty is that these two works

---

persona has with the biological author rather than with the persona suggested by the narrative text. The authorial counterself is a near-duplicate, obtrusive version of the biological author.

3. By *inscribed author*, I mean the protagonist who claims to have written the narrative, not the Boothian implied author.

are so like life writing that readers have treated them unproblematically for much of their publication history.

This chapter takes up these two case studies to examine how consciousness is constructed in Latino/a narratives during the politically charged 1970s and 1980s (i.e., the Chicano movement and Chicana Feminist movement). Not only is my interest in uncovering how Acosta and Anzaldúa depict consciousness within their narratives; I am also concerned with how these works challenge the reader and how these challenges may have influenced the development of Latino/a literature over four decades. This positions reading situations not only in terms of the author-text-reader relationship but also as reading the text within the context of history, as Jauss's horizon of expectation maintains (*Toward an Aesthetic*). In fact, one trend this chapter reveals is how certain texts were ill considered or misrepresented based on erroneous expectations of Latino/a literature in the early post–Chicano movement era. In a subsequent chapter, I show how more recent considerations of similarly styled works such as Sandra Cisneros's *Caramelo* and Junot Díaz's *The Brief Wondrous Life of Oscar Wao* seem to have found an audience willing to engage with it without the constraints of stereotypical expectations for what Latino/a literature ought to be, revealing the shifting horizon of expectation for Latino/a literature itself.

ACOSTA'S SEARCH FOR THE BROWN BUFFALO

Oscar "Zeta" Acosta remains an enigmatic figure in Latino/a letters. Despite the concerted recovery of Acosta's work by Frederick Luis Aldama, Ilan Stavans, Manuel Luis Martinez, Ramón Saldívar, and others, Acosta looms like a phantom of the Latino/a imagination—more myth than actual person. Due largely to his notorious disappearance in June of 1974 (presumably in Mexico), his two novels *The Autobiography of a Brown Buffalo* and *The Revolt of the Cockroach People* (along with a handful of short stories) now speak for Acosta in his absence. Perhaps this is a fitting legacy to the self-knighted "Chicano lawyer" who was both a brown Gargantua and a countercultural Beat figure with a license to practice law. His legacy in Latino/a letters is curious. For someone who was a participant in several of the key historical moments of the Chicano movement, with relationships with the movement's central figures—one of the few writers who unabashedly incorporated these landmark events in Chicano history into his storyworlds[4]—his books were largely dismissed

---

4. *The Revolt of the Cockroach People* centers on Acosta, aka Buffalo Zeta Brown, and the landmark "Trial of the St. Basil Twenty-One." Unlike the meditative tone of self-discovery that

by Anglo readers at the time of their publication, and perhaps mostly by the Chicano community itself. Little has changed in the intervening forty years.

For instance, in Manuel M. Martín-Rodríguez's 2003 study, *Life in Search of Readers*, Acosta does not garner a single passing reference despite the study's concern with the historical trajectory of Chicano/a literature and its interaction with readers. I am indebted to Martín-Rodríguez's study, for it lays out much of the history surrounding how Chicano/a literature has evolved a readership over time—thus providing insights invaluable to my study. My point is not to criticize unfairly Martín-Rodríguez for not addressing the gaping lacuna where Acosta ought to be. That he omits Acosta in his study of how Chicano/a authors and their writings have shaped their readership indicates the little impact Acosta's books had on contemporaneous and subsequent audiences. Acosta's troubled relationship with his readership (or lack thereof) is an intriguing incongruity I hope to bring to light in this chapter.

Stavans notes that Acosta wrote a novel when he was thirty-three "which no publisher accepted and only one or two acknowledged receiving" (*Bandido* 7), a manuscript that remains lost. Though he had much to write about, Acosta struggled to find an audience, even after his two irreverent, ideo-politically charged novels were published. Further, if one views *Autobiography* or *Revolt* as social documents of protest, ones that speak or "write back" to power, Acosta's books should have been runaway best sellers. In both novels, Acosta makes a move to unite Chicanos via his narratives. Further, there ought to have been a measure of pride within the Chicano community regarding Acosta's efforts, as there was with the exaltation of Rudolfo "Corky" Gonzales's epic poem *Yo Soy Joaquín*.[5] While Gonzales's poem was printed at a furious rate to keep up with a grassroots distribution and was performed widely in Luis Valdez's Teatro Campesino, Acosta's *Autobiography* languished, and his notoriety, according to Stavans, is nonexistent in both Mexico and the United States (*Bandido* 10–11). Acosta, Stavans posits, "opted for literature as a redeeming act, the written word as a way of knowledge and salvation" (11). Undaunted by publishing rejects and a failed political campaign for sheriff of Los Angeles County, Acosta was irreverent and defiant of the power structure that had taken so much from his people. As he states near the end of *Brown Buffalo*:

---

infuses *The Autobiography of a Brown Buffalo*, the political struggles of Chicanos dominates *Revolt*. Despite this, *Revolt* is arguably even more critically ignored than is *Autobiography*.

5. The *Norton Anthology of Latino Literature* claims that *Yo Soy Joaquín* "came to define the movement; Latino historians consider it a Chicano epic. In the 1970s, *I Am Joaquín* sold over 100,000 copies, becoming the first Chicano bestseller. While the book's importance was mainly political, it has also influenced some contemporary writers" (787).

> Ladies and gentlemen . . . my name is Oscar Acosta. My father is an Indian from the mountains of Durango. Although I cannot speak his language . . . you see, Spanish is the language of our conquerors. English is the language of our conquerors. . . . No one ever asked me or my brother if we wanted to be American citizens. We are all citizens by default. They stole our land and made us half-slaves. They destroyed our gods and made us bow down to a dead man who's been strung up for 2000 years. . . . Now what we need is, first to give ourselves a new name. We need a new identity. A name and a language all our own. . . . So I propose that we call ourselves . . . what's this you don't what me to attack our own religion? Well, all right. . . . I propose we call ourselves the Brown Buffalo people. . . . No, it's not an Indian name, for Christ sake . . . don't you get it? The buffalo, see? Yes, the animal that everyone slaughtered. Sure, both the cowboys and the Indians are out to get him . . . and, because we do have roots in our Mexican past, our Aztec ancestry, that's where we get the *brown* from. (198)

This passage, an imagined speech of Oscar's[6] call to political action and solidarity, is what might be called in political parlance *red meat*—rhetoric designed to fuel the motivations and subsequent actions of a political base. Further, it is the culmination of Oscar's meanderings within the narrative, one that gives him a purpose in life: "I merely want to do what is right," he states (198). On face value, Acosta's books seemed destined to be as widely distributed and read as Gonzales's poem among Chicanos, if no one else. Instead, *Autobiography* reached publishing purgatory quickly, falling out of print by the late 1970s.

With a motivated and mobile Chicano base, fueled by unfair labor practices, discrimination, and the injustice of serving their country through military action only to be treated as less than a citizen at home, the historical situation was primed to establish Acosta's works as utter triumphs to the Chicano spirit and imagination. In fact, because of its overtly political message and support of the Brown Power movement, *Autobiography* was arguably better positioned for success than another Chicano novel also published in 1972: Rudolfo Anaya's *Bless Me, Ultima*. However, the comparative reception of the two works is striking. Anaya's novel is unequivocally proclaimed as the Chicano masterpiece that proved harbinger to the so-called Chicano Renaissance. It has never been out of print, and as of 2015 *Bless Me* holds the distinction as perhaps the most widely taught Chicano work in high schools and universities across the United States.

---

6. Henceforth, I will designate the biological author as *Acosta*, and the fictional counter-self of the biological author as *Oscar*.

My intent here is neither to compare the inherent value of the two works nor to declare that one is superior or better suited to represent Chicano experience than the other. Rather, placing Anaya's novel in historical context alongside Acosta's helps us understand the challenges surrounding and raised by these works, specifically, *Autobiography*. Though history is often disputed depending on who recounts it, we can agree on several points regarding the year 1972. First, the year serves as a midway point for the Vietnam War, four years after the portentous Tet Offensive in 1968 and three years before the end of the war. The Watergate scandal and the massacre of Israeli athletes at the Summer Olympics in Munich also mark 1972 with turbulence on both a national and a global scale.[7] Historian Ramón A. Gutiérrez recalls the sociopolitical climate surrounding this year this way:

> Memory teaches the ethnic Mexican population in the United States that it has been in times of war that our lives, our liberty, and our property have been robbed as part of grand geopolitical power grabs. In these times our national identity has served as a communal tie of solidarity and opposition. At the end of the U.S.–Mexico War in 1848, Tejanos, Californios, and Nuevo Mexicanos united as Mexicanos to resist the capricious use of force that had despoiled them of their land, water, livelihood, and human dignity. During World War II, Mexicans marched into the fields of battle to prove their fealty to the United States as Americans. As citizen soldiers they expected that when they returned home, they too would enjoy the fullest benefits of equality. It was not to be. Despite the rhetoric of the American dream, which promised upward mobility, and despite the GI Bill, veterans were still relegated to segregated balconies at movie houses, still denied beds in white-owned hotels, still barred from eating in many restaurants or swimming in public pools during the heat of summer. Every day they were the victims of arbitrary state violence through police harassment and judicial neglect, if not contempt. (188)

Gutiérrez's recollection of 1972 is very much in the spirit of Oscar's call to action at the end of *Autobiography*: "When I have the one million Brown Buffalos on my side," he states, "I will present the demands for a new nation to both the U.S. Government and the United Nations . . . and then I'll split and

---

7. "Nineteen seventy-two. Dare we forget?" Ramón A. Gutiérrez asks. "Thirty years earlier, in 1942," he reflects, "Mexicans in the United States were still trying to prove their American identity, despite their citizenship. More than thirty years later, in 2007, Mexicans in the United States still struggle for their rights and dispute those who would declare us felons for having crossed the border when indeed the border has long ago crossed us" (189).

write the book" (198). Yet Acosta's book, despite its pursuit of a civil rights–inflected sense of self-worth, fell by the wayside among readers, while *Bless Me*, Anaya's bildungsroman that yearns conservatively to preserve *curandismo* and accumulate ancestral knowledge, rocketed to the top of Chicano/a letters—a position it has yet to relinquish.

For reasons that no scholar has yet attempted to discern, a ready-made audience comprising real individuals primed to engage with *Autobiography* failed to respond as Acosta's ideal audience did and instead turned to Anaya's folkloric coming-of-age story with zeal. Acosta's text targets a radical, like-minded audience, while Anaya's text invites an old-line readership that senses the slipping away of tradition and yearns to recoup it through nostalgic reminiscence.[8] This apparent disjunction in audience reception has less to do with the historical sociopolitical moment than it does with the narrative design of Acosta's novel, his representation of the inner workings of Oscar's mind, and, further, Oscar's representation of the minds of those with whom he interacts. The constellation of these minds accounts for Oscar's ascendance to the role of Brown Buffalo, or the identity of Buffalo Z. Brown.

FORMAL ISSUES IN *THE AUTOBIOGRAPHY OF A BROWN BUFFALO*

Autobiography is one of the first Latino/a narratives to break with a linear narrative structure. Unlike earlier examples of ethnic American autobiographies such as *The Autobiography of Malcolm X* by Malcolm X and Alex Haley; *Down These Mean Streets* by Piri Thomas; *A Wake in Ybor City* by José Yglesias; and *Barrio Boy* by Ernesto Galarza all of which feature an account of the protagonist's life from early childhood to young adult, *Autobiography* eschews linear temporality. If, as Frederick Luis Aldama notes, "To be 'recognized,' the racial and ethnic Other has had to convince his or her audience of the reality of his or her experience and, thus, adhere to narrating codes that do not call attention to the gap between mimesis and reality" (*Postethnic Narrative Criticism* 48), it is unsurprising that such autobiographies seek to chronicle the protagonist's life-as-experienced. This type of narrative has become a part of a larger

---

8. To be clear, I am not arguing that *Bless Me* and *Autobiography* seek the same readership. They clearly do not. What I am arguing is that the readership each text seeks was available in 1972, but for reasons that remain unknown, *Autobiography* essentially went unnoticed. Acosta's novel seems to be an example of the Zen koan: If a tree falls in the woods and no one is around, does it make a sound? In this case, if no readership notices *Autobiography*, will it be read? The evidence suggests that whatever sound *Autobiography* did make was slight at best.

tradition in Latino/a literature wherein the narrator chronicles the autobiographer's life in chronological order, from childhood to adulthood. Through the temporal instabilities presented in Acosta's text, *Autobiography* breaks from this established tradition, along with many other characteristics that distinguish it from other ethnic autobiographies, as Aldama has noted.

But I reiterate here that despite its title and use of the autobiographical narrative trope, *Autobiography* is a work of fiction. Aldama makes this point clear in *Postethnic* by distinguishing the biological Acosta from the character Acosta depicted within the storyworld and by identifying "Acosta's use of magicorealism to reform the genre of autobiography" (47). This subversion of the autobiographical genre and its conventions is a risk that Acosta takes, one whose potential payoff is based in the reader's ability to recognize the conventions of autobiography and to recognize that Acosta is manipulating these conventions to his own narrative ends. I will return to the implications of a reader's inability to recognize *Autobiography* as a work of fiction later. But first, I wish to lay out the salient formal features of Acosta's text.

Rather than begin his "autobiography" with his childhood as conventional autobiographies do, Oscar delays revealing this time in his life until the second paragraph of chapter 2: "Although I was born in El Paso, Texas, I am actually a small town kid" (71). Instead, he begins his narrative on July 1, 1967, gazing at his naked body in the mirror, establishing his body as a central image for the rest of his autobiography. The opening passage presents Oscar in a vulnerable position—not one of childhood but rather of adult self-doubt and depression. The result is an increased pathos and uncertainty.

At first it appears that Oscar is confiding in someone as he takes an inventory of his body: "I should lay off those Snicker bars, those liverwurst sandwiches with gobs of mayonnaise and those Goddamned caramel sundaes. But look, if I suck it in just a wee bit more, push that bellybutton up against the back; can you see what will surely come to pass if you but rid yourself of this extra flesh?" (11). The first part of the second sentence quoted here seems to invite the reader to match Oscar's gaze—to see what he sees. Yet, as the second part of the sentence reveals, Oscar is rebuking himself for his poor body image and how he has the power to change it if he motivates himself enough to do so. Already in this opening, Oscar signals multiple audiences. When he narrates in first person, his observations are directed to an unacknowledged narratee, as in the passage "Every morning of my life I have seen that brown belly from every angle. It has not changed that I can remember. I was always a fat kid" (11). Oscar is in traditional autobiographical mode here. But as I have already shown, there are moments when at least two separate audiences are acknowledged. The first of these is the reader of his autobiography, whom

Oscar often calls upon to consider certain actions or consequences in his own life. These readers are revealed in invitations such as "See that man with the insignificant eyes drawn back, lips thinned down tight?" (12). This question is not simply rhetorical: Oscar is addressing the ideal reader of his autobiography. There also come moments when Oscar addresses himself. When he says, "Just think of all the broads you'll get if you trim down to a comfortable 200" (11), he is talking to himself, becoming his own narratee.

Folk psychology ascribes mental defect to individuals who have a penchant for talking to themselves. Though I do not contend that Oscar suffers from mental illness, he knows of his own consciousness and activity of mind. Further, as *Autobiography* progresses, the reader discovers that Oscar is prone to imagining (or hallucinating) certain figures in his daily routine. There is a blurring of what he considers the real world and the world in his mind, often brought on by frequent alcohol and drug abuse. The consistent appearance of Oscar's "Jewish shrink," Dr. Serbin, as a hallucination, reinforces Oscar's mental instabilities, highlighting his struggle to find a normative center within his world. Not only is Oscar aware of his own mental functions; he also consistently attempts to find out what often prove to be the inscrutable minds of the people in his life.

In one poignant moment, Oscar recounts the powerful attraction he once had for a girl named Jane Addison in his elementary class. Jane is disturbed to find that Oscar has announced his feelings for her by carving her initials into the knuckles of his left hand. When he proudly displays his hand with the letters "J-A" scrawled into his flesh, Jane, unnerved, retreats into silence, rendering Oscar into invisibility. "She squinted, gave me a queer look and just shook her head over and over again as she walked away in a daze," he laments (90). Oscar is incapable of meeting people, and women especially, on their own terms. After describing Jane's response to his "tattoo," Oscar confesses, "Even at that age, I knew that women never tell you what they really think of you" (90). He is constantly frustrated by women who, perhaps out of embarrassment, are not up-front and honest with him. His formative experiences with women dictate much of his distrust of women in his later years, something that has caused many readers and critics to rail against this apparent misogyny or, at the least, Oscar's less-than-admirable attitude toward women.

For example, Marci L. Carrasquillo has highlighted Acosta's problematic attempt at self-actualization, stating that his "significant epiphany about the nature and complexity of identity does not lead Acosta to understand the gendered aspects of his 'choice'" (78). Here Carrasquillo cites Oscar's revelation that he is "a Chicano by ancestry and a Brown Buffalo by choice" (*Autobiography* 199). Carrasquillo contends that Acosta does not go far enough in constructing "the larger, radical identity project" (80) his protagonist works to achieve, that Acosta fails by not breaking from the grip of patriarchy both in Chicano culture and in white male America. While I concur with Carrasquillo in the male-as-master-of-his-own-destiny sentiment in *Autobiography*, I maintain that for at least several reasons this is not necessarily as severe a shortcoming as Carrasquillo would have it. First, if *Autobiography* is seen as a social document and historical artifact written by someone with immediate dealings with the Chicano and Brown Power movements, then Oscar's attitude toward women is historically accurate, albeit problematic. But *Autobiography* is not a social document; it is a work of fiction. This issue stresses Aldama's contention that Acosta uses a willful blend of realist and nonrealist narrative techniques by using "jumps in time and space, [...] distinguish[ing] between author and narrator who is 'designing' his past as a story that is governed by fictive, rather than factually based, mimetic codes" (*Postethnic* 50). When Carrasquillo notes that Acosta "does not mitigate the larger problem of gender in his narratives" (80), she foists a retrograde constraint on *Autobiography* that does not enlighten our understanding of Acosta's novel. Put another way, just because Acosta (or any other author) does not take his or her narrative in one predetermined direction or another does not affirm that the larger project (in this case, identity formation) is undermined; it does not uphold the notion that the project is fatally flawed. Instead of arriving at an appreciation of the novel that takes Oscar for the limited, flawed character he is, Carrasquillo concentrates on what he, and thereby the narrative, lacks. Acosta, who has demonstrated his ability to stretch beyond the bounds of realism even within a genre form (autobiography) that has a serious affinity to realism, could easily have recast Oscar as a valiant defender of the emergent rise of feminism in the Chicano community (a fact that feminist theorists would have trouble with in its own right (i.e., a male champion of feminism), especially with Gloria just around the figurative corner). But instead Acosta ironizes Oscar's experiences through moments of self-deprecation, depictions of hallucinatory experiences, and delusions of grandeur—for irony is the engine that drives *Autobiography*.

Carrasquillo's dissatisfaction with Acosta (i.e., that he did not go far enough to undermine entrenched patriarchy) speaks to my larger point about challenging reading situations. For readers with an affinity for feminist thinking, or even those who advocate for a gentler treatment in Acosta's text of the equality and respect that should be afforded to all peoples regardless of gender, race, ethnicity, and so on, Oscar is an inscribed author with suspect norms and values that ought to be denounced. Yet this characteristic (some would say flaw) is complicated by moments in the text when he becomes a sympathetic figure, as, for example, when he recalls his humiliation at the hands of Junior Ellis. The ideal audience recognizes Oscar's character imperfections, noticing that tongue is often squarely in cheek when Oscar narrates, a result of the narrative's saturation in irony. I aver that Acosta renders Oscar in exactly this ironic fashion to demonstrate the complexity of the self to begin with. One strength of *Autobiography* is its ability to allow the reader within the space of Oscar's ironic mind, troubled though it may be. The result is the ever-present ebb and flow of the potential for empathy for Oscar—there is the urge to help Oscar, even as we recoil from his attitudes and treatment of women and race.

When Aldama proclaims that reading *Autobiography* "re-form[s] its reader's expectations by providing a multidimensional self-narration that superimposes, combines, and critically amplifies traditionally segregated genres and repressive ideological structures" (*Postethnic* 59), he shows the response of an ideal readership—one that is willing and able to recognize the fictional, ironic nature of the narrative and the collision of conflicting emotions at work when one reads this difficult text—not a reader content with highlighting what Acosta might have done otherwise to satisfy a different, say, feminist readership. The challenge here is to have one type of actual reader, perhaps a feminist, willingly to step into Acosta's ideal audience without prior expectation. Not that the ideal audience is invested in the problematic norms and values that Oscar embraces. Instead, Oscar's imperfection reflects not only upon Latinos but also upon all of the United States. Rather than outlining the feminist limitations in Acosta's work, it is far more productive to posit why these omissions exist in the text to begin with. Ultimately, *Autobiography* is as limited as it is groundbreaking, and it challenges readers to recognize this.

ACOSTA'S CONSCIOUSNESS FORMATION THROUGH NARRATIVE

Acosta's books have been examined from a multitude of approaches: identity, political, counterculture, and so on. But what is striking is Acosta's (and, later, Anzaldúa's) desire to achieve a new consciousness through a singular force of will. I explore Anzaldúa's exploration of the New Mestiza consciousness at length in the second half of this chapter, but for now I will focus on *Autobiography*, for Oscar, too, longs to reach a higher state of understanding of both himself and his relation to his environment (i.e., the external). In addition, Oscar's proclamation of assuming this higher state of being, what he calls the *Brown Buffalo*, predates Anzaldúa's New Mestiza by at least a decade, though most likely it is closer to twenty years if we consider that Acosta's experiences in the 1960s played an integral part in his adoption of this worldview.[9] Oscar takes readers with him on a mental road trip as he escapes the constraints of the world that seek to hold him back, leading his reader to the Brown Buffalo promised land. This narrative decision makes the novel's open ending all the more impressive and, at the least, better understood. Oscar's is not a literal action that changes the world. Rather, the movement toward an articulated resistance to these hegemonic forces (e.g., capitalism, religion, an oppressive majority) is a manifestation of his mind expressed through narrative design. By experiencing his visions along with him throughout the text, the reader, too, is invited to enter Oscar's group and become a Brown Buffalo Person. Here again Oscar's attainment of an enlightened consciousness prefigures Anzaldúa's New Mestiza because it is something that arises from within and is maintained within the mind. Acosta's and Anzaldúa's argument is that the power of their internalized and newly adopted consciousness has the force of will to have a palpable effect on real-world structures of oppression and constraint. What is worth examination is how differently these two texts, so similar in their desire for a new consciousness, have been received by their actual audiences.

Much of ethnic literature and ethnic studies in the United States is concerned with the matter of consciousness.[10] Mostly, however, consciousness as it appears in ethnic studies is often synonymous with self-consciousness, a personal awareness of one's place in the world. As Latinos (and Chicanos in particular) occupied a marginalized space for most of the twentieth century, their hyperawareness of their position relative to the world, and especially the United States, always at the fore, consciousness was central to their ideological and political discourse. Interestingly, in that crucial year of 1972, the same year Acosta published *Autobiography*, George Rivera, Jr., published an article titled "Nosotros Venceremos: Chicano Consciousness and Change Strategies." An important move, according to Rivera, was that Anglo scholars on Mexican American life were being replaced by young Chicano scholars. "Things are as they should be," he wrote. "Chicanos are speaking for themselves" (57). Rivera expertly laid out the Chicano history in the United States and noted the concept of the Chicano consciousness by invoking none other than W. E. B. Du Bois, for whom the notion of consciousness was of prin-

---

9. I am indebted to Samuel Saldivar III for raising the possibility that the New Mestiza already had a precursor in the Brown Buffalo.

10. Perhaps no other scholarly work serves as the headwaters of this trend than W. E. B. Du Bois's highly influential text *The Souls of Black Folk*. Taking Du Bois's lead, ethnic writers and scholars have worked to frame their own existentialism and subjectivity in terms of consciousness.

cipal consequence. "Why is there no Mexican American W. E. B. Du Bois, Ralph Ellison, or James Baldwin?" Rivera wonders, as he answers his own rhetorical question: "Because Chicanos had been systematically deprived of higher education. However, limited but increasing opportunities in education are now giving rise to a Chicano consciousness that is being felt throughout the Southwest" (57). While Rivera never defines what he and others mean by *Chicano consciousness* (instead he posits strategies for changing the Chicano consciousness), based on context, inference, and the invocation of Du Bois, we can take him to be using *consciousness* in the same way Du Bois uses the term. In defining *double-consciousness* as it applies to African Americans, Du Bois states, "It is a peculiar sensation, this double-consciousness, this sense of always looking at one's self through the eyes of others" (11). Thus, Chicano consciousness can be understood as looking at one's (Chicano) self through the eyes of non-Chicanos.

It is imperative that the notion of a Chicano consciousness be made transparent and concrete, for all too often in ethnic studies, forms of minority consciousness become nebulous and abstract. Chicano consciousness is akin to an acute awareness of one's self as a Chicano/a. Such an understanding is fraught with the difficulty of defining what it means to be a Chicano/a, which foregrounds the pursuit of identity formation. Thus, when Rivera decries the lack of writers and thinkers like Du Bois, Ellison, and Baldwin in the Chicano/a community, it appears ironic in retrospect that one such writer and thinker for Chicanos was already in his midst. In Acosta, Rivera had a Chicano who was speaking for himself in pursuit of clarifying the somewhat vague notion of a Chicano consciousness.

Though the word *consciousness* never appears in *Autobiography* in the Du Boisian sense, Oscar's realization of his Chicano identity—what Juan Bruce-Novoa describes as "a new stage in Chicano literature, a new consciousness" (61) and what Frederick Luis Aldama alternately articulates as "*mestizo* worldview" (*Postethnic* 51) and "magical realist consciousness" (*Postethnic* xxx)—reaches its apex in the final chapter of *Autobiography*, with an invitation to the reader to experience what Oscar calls a "bad trip." In what is an effective metaphor for Oscar's mental frustration that results from placing himself within an identity category that makes sense to him, he explains: "There isn't much sense in trying to explain what a 'bad trip' is. You simply lose your marbles. You go crazy. There is no bottom, no top. The devil sits on your head and warns you of your commitment. You see for the first time what the bottomless pit is all about. And you hang on for dear life" (*Autobiography* 183). As Oscar has made his entire narrative precisely about explaining the bad trip that has been his life, he is highlighting the futility of his project. Throughout the book the reader has been mentally engaged with Oscar—sitting with him as he resists losing his virginity in a brothel for as long as he can, gazing with him as he describes his vomit-cum-art in what might be called a gastronomic ekphrasis, listening to the ubiquitous Procol Harum with him as he recounts the hallucinatory-styled lyrics of their song "A Whiter Shade of Pale." Oscar himself is reminiscent of the Emersonian Transparent Eyeball as *Autobiography* draws to a close: "I have no desire to be a politician. I don't want to lead anyone. I have no practical ego. I am not ambitious. I merely want to do what is right" (198). He believes he has achieved something akin to a Chicano consciousness.

With Acosta's book and his constructed, fictional counterself, the fictional mind he created challenged real minds of readers, both in the time near *Autobiography*'s publication in 1972 and as recently as 2010, if we consider Carrasquillo's critique of what she perceives to be a limitation or undermining of Acosta's book. Contemporaneous readers who longed for a Chicano voice to unite Chicanos and infuse the community with pride, as Rivera did, were not swayed by Acosta's narrative creation depicting his real-life struggles with achieving a sustainable identity, despite Oscar's self-aggrandizing statement that "once in every century there comes a man who is chosen to speak for his people. Moses, Mao and Martin are examples. Who's to say that I am not such a man? In this day and age the man for all seasons needs many voices. [. . .] Perhaps that is why I've been taught so many trades. Who will deny that I am unique?" (198). Few can deny that Oscar is unique, for it is this uniqueness that often affronts readers of *Autobiography*.

Acosta's manipulation of the autobiography genre succeeds when recognized as such. Readers, then and now, have often engaged with *Autobiography* along the same lines as they have other works of actual autobiography. The back cover of the 1989 Vintage edition of *Autobiography* prominently displays a quotation from a *Publishers Weekly* review that describes Acosta's book as "A Chicano *Manchild in the Promised Land*." In fact, *Autobiography* has more in common with Hunter S. Thompson's *Fear and Loathing in Las Vegas* than it does Claude Brown's *Manchild*. And this commonality rests at the level of narrative discourse, its use of biographical material worked upon by the imagination to yield a narrative marked by what Dorrit Cohn terms *signposts of fictionality*.[11] And the most glaring sign that Acosta's text is a work of fiction

---

11. In her influential article "Signposts of Fictionality: A Narratological Perspective," Cohn claims that it is the level of narrative discourse that demarcates history from fiction: "These exceptions to the onomastic distinction between narrator and author, no less than this distinction itself, prove the rule: homodiegetic fiction is determined by the presence of an imaginary speaker incarnated as a character within the fictional world. This 'embodied self,' as Stanzel

is that his book purports to be the autobiography of a Brown Buffalo rather than the autobiography of Acosta. The Brown Buffalo is a way for Oscar to situate himself within society—an effort to reunite with the Chicano people from whom he found himself estranged by his own making.

In reality, despite Oscar's narrative attempt at reunification with his people, except for a few luminaries such as Juan Bruce-Novoa, who was among the first to laud Acosta's efforts, Chicanos have disregarded Acosta's writings. Despite his passion for Chicanos and Chicano/a causes, Acosta could never find the readership he so desired. Stavans recounts two separate conversations he had with Sandra Cisneros and Rudolfo Anaya regarding Acosta's writings. What Stavans recounts is a painful indictment of the pervasive disregard for Acosta's narratives:

> [Cisneros] was washing her hair when I asked her about Zeta. "What am I going to tell you, Ilan? *Tu sabes,* I really have nothing to say. I have his books, sure. But I've never read them, not entirely. His writings never spoke to me. I never found anything to identify with in them." I inquired about Zeta's feminine fetishism. "I don't know," she replied. "That's an ongoing problem in Chicano letters. I guess I would only read him if I was in jail!" (*Bandido* 116)

That Cisneros, an ambassador for Chicana Feminism, would so casually disregard Acosta's writing as not having "anything to identify with in them," despite her admission of not having carefully read Acosta's texts, is stunning. Cisnero's remarks reflect in miniature the Chicano community's general reception to Acosta's work. But it is Anaya's comments to Stavans that best encapsulate Acosta's inability to find a zealous readership to align with his ideal audience. Stavans writes:

> Anaya, another classic Chicano writer, never met [Acosta]. "I read his work when it first came out," he writes in his correspondence, "and even taught it in my Chicano literature classes. The students like *The Revolt of the Cockroach People,* but had a harder time with his other book [*Autobiography*] even though it spoke to the problem of lost identity. Zeta put a different slant, a zing, to our literature, and the tragedy of his disappearance is that it cut short his development. He had a lot to share, and it was cut short." (*Bandido* 116)

---

calls it (1984: 90), is brought to life by a discourse that mimics the language of a real speaker telling of his past experiences. It is therefore easy to visualize the structure of a fictional autobiography as an imaginary discourse directly quoted by the author, implicitly preceded by an inquit-phrase" (794).

Unlike Cisneros, Anaya at least recognized that Acosta had "put a different slant" on Chicano/a literature. He intuited that Acosta was on a trajectory to continue his development as a writer and saw in his work something of merit. It seems these two writers, Anaya and Acosta, who published two different but equally important novels in 1972, recognized *Autobiography* as having something significant to say while failing to find the readership it so desperately sought.

BORDERLANDS/LA FRONTERA: THE NEW MESTIZA AND ITS CRITICS

The success and influence of Anzaldúa's 1987 book *Borderlands* cannot be overstated. Its minority-within-minority viewpoint was received as a watershed moment for women's studies and the rising Chicana Feminist movement. Anzaldúa interjected the traditionally conservative and male-dominated Chicano movement with the voice of the empowered and self-aware Chicana lesbian. The book was met with overwhelming praise, its metaphor of the borderland being its most transportable concept.[12] With its third printing in 2007, *Borderlands* has affected readers in ways not seen in academia. For instance, María Herrera Sobek, writing in a 2006 article in *PMLA*, speaks of Anzaldúa and her work with what can only be described as reverence, seeing her not only as a champion for the various liminal positions from which she spoke but also as someone with nearly martyr-like qualities:

> The price Anzaldúa paid for her political stance was dear. Her writing advocating a new morality and a new set of ethical standards for Chicanos/as extracted a heavy toll in feelings of guilt, betrayal, inadequacy, ostracism, rejection, and more. To take up arms against popular opinion, established morality, and tradition is not easy. To veer away from the traditional path of obedience, loyalty, purity, self-abnegation, and self-effacement the average Chicana is taught in her formative years is to unleash tornado-like forces of self-flagellation and bitter invectives from relatives, friends, and society. The mere attempt at writing—an act of self-disclosure—becomes a danger-

---

12. Anzaldúa's book helped give rise to borderland theory as a widespread approach to cultural and literary studies. But what is more, her notion of the borderland has, ironically, migrated from the highly localized and actual geographic border that separates Texas from Mexico to geographic borders from China to Poland and beyond. When adopted as a metaphor for all physical and metaphysical sites—a violent site where binaries and oppositions meet—Anzaldúa's work has proven to be both highly popular and surprisingly durable.

ous psychological and political undertaking. ("Gloria Anzaldúa: Place, Race, Language, and Sexuality in the Magic Valley" 269)

Here Herrera Sobek notes the liberating effects and the dangers of writing against power. She also conflates Anzaldúa's book with her life, seeing them as linked. Yet despite the dangers of Anzaldúa's "psychological and political undertaking," her work met with more acclaim than vitriol. If there were negative consequences that affected Anzaldúa because of *Borderlands*, one could scarcely recognize them based on how widely the book and its message have been embraced.

Herrera Sobek's acute veneration of Anzaldúa and her work ("We are grateful to the Magic Valley for giving magic words to Anzaldúa; magic words that continue to live and inspire us in her poetry and prose" (271) is not an exception but rather represents the majority assessment of *Borderlands* and its author. For example, María Lugones begins her interpretive essay of *Borderlands* by citing her personal investment in *Borderlands* and, seemingly, the book's investment in Lugones when she writes:

> *Borderlands* has been a very important text for me. I have found company in it. *Desde el primer momento pensé que éramos hermanas en pensamiento.*[13] I have carried Anzaldúa's insights and metaphors with me for several years in my daily ruminations and in my daily exercise of triple vision. I could say that I have lost perspective on this thought text in making it mine, or I could say that I have gained perspective in finding borderdwelling friendship in it. I find her thinking intertwined with my own. (31)

Reactions such as Herrera Sobek's and Lugones's have become a commonplace (or at least default position) whenever discussions of *Borderlands* arise. Readers often speak of *Borderlands* with conviction and readily admit the book's influence on their lives. This has created a challenging situation in its own right. It often proves difficult to critique or criticize something that is cherished and venerated by so many people because it is sometimes deemed as a personal challenge or an affront to the author. A male critic must often tread lightly when engaging with a feminist text, as Ramón Saldívar does in *Chicano Narrative* when he claims that "a self-conscious analysis of our own interpretive methods becomes even more important for the male critic as he tries to read texts by women authors" (173). Though male critics may take heed of Saldívar's recommendation, male critics must likewise be allowed to critique feminist texts on the texts' own terms. A text such as *Borderlands*

---

13. "From the first moment, I sensed that we were sisters in thought."

exists as an overt challenge to male patriarchy and dominant forms of discourse. It is understandable that Anzaldúa herself would welcome the criticism and that her text would be all the stronger for it.

However, readers have placed such high personal stakes on Anzaldúa's book that any harsh criticism of her writings is often met with a robust defense. Thus, when Aldama proclaimed in the introduction to his book *User's Guide* that texts whose "authors who rest heavily on clichés of identity—the inclined, 'authentic,' ancestral-rooted, borderland lesbian mestiza described in Anzaldúa's *Borderlands,* for instance—create Kleenex narratives: once we finish (if we finish), we find the nearest garbage can" (7), critics heavily invested in Anzaldúa and her work defended her vociferously. For example, Raphael Dalleo's review of Aldama's book takes specific exception to the notion that *Borderlands* is a "Kleenex narrative," calling it Aldama's "most mean-spirited comment of all" in which "Gloria Anzaldúa is mocked" (176). Dalleo cannot resist taking Aldama's bait and conflates Anzaldúa the person with the text of *Borderlands* itself. As a scholar of narrative, Aldama is more interested in the text itself than he is in identity positions of the text's author, as he states in his introduction to *User's Guide.* His criticism is with the text of *Borderlands* itself and those who make similar identity claims, and as I have said above, Aldama's deadpan critique of Anzaldúa's text is a rarity in discussions of *Borderlands.*

This state of criticism is understandable, as *Borderlands* itself is seen as giving voice to a collective identity of women who have been violated and silenced over centuries, if not throughout history. Leveling harsh criticisms at Anzaldúa's work might seem like a tacit attempt to silence Anzaldúa herself, echoing Ramón Saldívar's warning cited above. The response of *Borderlands* by readers and their staunch defenses of both the author and her work are at the heart of my examination. And, as narrative theory has convincingly shown, we can discern the difference between the text and the biographical author: stern criticism (fair or otherwise) of the text does not equate to condemning the actual person who created the text. However, some supporters of Anzaldúa's work often take such criticism as an *ad hominem* attack on Anzaldúa herself.

Anzaldúa, however, sets up exactly this relationship of contestation between herself, her text, and her critics. She unambiguously invites her would-be detractors to enter the fray—to dare to contradict her. Time and again she unifies the act of writing with the political, the inscribed text as a response to the silencing of women. The reason that her text exists in the first place, one would assume, reveals the historical marginalization of similar voices. She has broken through where others have not, her book seems to announce.

Two factors are at work here that must be identified before continuing with an examination of *Borderlands*. The first of these is the holistic approach to Anzaldúa's work that most critics take. By this I mean a focus on the larger, metaphorical ideas Anzaldúa puts forth that relegates the details to the background. Such examinations of *Borderlands* gloss over many challenging moments within the text, such as Anzaldúa's use of essentialist rhetoric to make her claims, as when she says, "White anthropologists claim that Indians have 'primitive' and therefore deficient minds, that we cannot think in the higher modes of consciousness—rationality" (37). The narrator views all "white anthropologists" as having an essentialist view of Indians, but her own views on white anthropologists are equally essentialist.

The second of these factors concerns a relationship with the text itself. As Deborah L. Madsen puts it:

> These [Chicana] writers subvert conventional forms of literary expression to make them express colored women's experiences. [. . .] Chicana writers insist that the reader work hard to understand the specialized racial or ethnic references included in the text, such as references to Mexican mythology and cross-cultural references. In important ways the subject of Chicana writing *is* the Chicana subject: feminine subjectivity in a Mexican American context is the primary subject matter of Chicana literature. This is a literature that embodies the quest for self-definition, and so voice is a matter of both form and content." (4–5)

If Chicana writing is the Chicana subject in some metonymic way, then criticism of one is criticism of the other, as Daello's review of Aldama's book suggests. However, if we agree that Chicana writing uses recognizable forms of narrative worldmaking, even if they are used unconventionally, then we should be able to explore how these narrative worlds are constructed as well by using the tools of narrative theory. Thus, despite Anzaldúa's claim to the contrary, a fractured narrative form does not equate to a Chicana *tejana* lesbian-feminist identity. Because the narrative form Anzaldúa uses is not inherent to any identity (i.e., anyone can use her hybrid literary form, albeit the response to such forms might differ because of context), a critical exploration of *Borderlands*'s form, such as the one I pursue here, is not a denunciation of Chicana identity. As much as some Chicana feminists would have it, I posit that identity cannot be reduced to a narrative form. Nor should it be. Again, the (mis)use of magical realism I referenced in my introduction suggests the problems that arise when identity and narrative form are linked. Anzaldúa uses an unconventional narrative form only in reaction to the conventional, dominant forms of discourse. Hypothetically speaking, if fractured narratives were conventional, Anzaldúa would have needed to use a linear narrative to write against the dominant discourse. My point is that while the same narrative form may have different consequences across different audiences, narrative form itself is not inherently linked to an identity, and vice versa.

Though many readers consider *Borderlands* to be a work of nonfiction while others see it as a theoretical/metaphysical work, I would like to consider it as a creative work, if not outright fiction. Just as Acosta's *Autobiography* reimagines autobiography as a creative manifestation of the quest for identity, Anzaldúa's *Borderlands* also uses autobiographical material to construct her particular storyworld. In fact, each book seeks an ideal audience but must often settle for a less-than-ideal reader. However, Acosta's book is much more novelistic in form, which results in a more clearly defined storyworld. Anzaldúa's book, in contrast, adopts a critical stance. So while both texts creatively use autobiographical elements, the two texts reach out to audiences in different ways.

In an interview with Ann E. Reuman, Anzaldúa describes her target audience as follows in response to the question, "Do you have particular audiences in mind when you write?"

> My most particular audience, I think, are women—are feminists, are lesbians, are Chicanas, are. . . . So that's my primary audience. But I also am looking to talking with some of the gentler, less masculinity-oriented guys. And just people who are opening their minds up, who are exploring things. My audience is always expanding. Some poems if they're entirely in Spanish, like in *Borderlands* where there are about eleven poems that I didn't translate, that I just left in Spanish—those have particular audiences: you know, Mexican and Chicano, Spanish-speakers, white people who can read Spanish. And the theoretical stuff that I talk about in the universities, that's more of a scholarly audience. (10)

Anzaldúa's account of her audience is altogether consistent with the form of her text, which, as she suggests, opens itself to specific readers while thwarting access to others without a *shibboleth*, a key of sorts that allows reconstruction of the storyworld inscribed in her text. Particularly fascinating is Anzaldúa's admission that her book is *not* intended for certain readers (i.e., heterosexual, "masculinity-oriented" males). It is an admission that Oscar Acosta would surely not have made for his own book, especially in light of what Carrasquillo describes as *Autobiography*'s revelry in patriarchy and machismo.[14] Despite Anzaldúa's contention that her book was not for all audiences, scholars still assert that the thing that makes it a challenging text allows a multitudinous readership. As Sheila Contreras states in *Blood Myth*:

> Whatever its unstated, unrecognized, and, indeed, even unconscious ideological and discursive debts, *Borderlands/La Frontera: The New Mestiza* presented its audiences with unfamiliar generic forms as it transgressed, merged, and shifted the borders of academic and popular speech, scholarly and creative presentations, the conventions of masculinity, femininity, and erotic or sexual orientation. [. . .] It remains one of the most popular texts to be read outside of a Chicana/o Studies curriculum. (114)

The popularity of *Borderlands* among its audience presents an interesting conundrum that is often not accounted for within scholarship—a conundrum that scholars have yet to examine. A commonsense evaluation of the situation raises the following question: How could a text that yielded such a challenging reading experience become so popular among readers? This goes against what usually happens in such situations. Readers who are frustrated too much by a text will rarely become that text's champion. The more specific knowledge required for complete storyworld reconstruction, the smaller the flesh-and-blood audience (one that most reflects the ideal audience) becomes. Yet instead of falling by the wayside as *Autobiography* did, *Borderlands* found a vast audience. Much of the positive and emotional response to Anzaldúa's work is rooted in *Borderlands*'s ability to move readers from its textual designs to an imagined space (or storyworld) where readers with certain identity characteristics heretofore marginalized—that is, the identity characteristics of the

---

14. There is an apparent double standard at work here. While a full exploration is outside the scope of my project, I think the differing receptions of Acosta's and Anzaldúa's works speak more to the identity-based approaches to which Aldama's scholarship provides significant perspective. In other words, because *Autobiography* features a figure who embraces hypermasculine ideology, the work is fatally flawed; because *Borderlands* embraces a feminist discourse, the work is radically empowering. The positioning of each text vis-à-vis identity power structures is often the platform on which critical inquiry of *Autobiography* and *Borderlands* occurs. Yet at the level of text and audience, each text necessitates similar cognitive functions and reading protocols; indeed they are strikingly similar. If we momentarily remove ideological valences readers bring with them to the text, one could say that *Autobiography* and *Borderlands* take correspondingly multifaceted approaches in narrative design that yield severe limitations on the reading experience and storyworld reconstruction. Readers, however, tend to bring personal ideology (among other things) with them as they read. This fact highlights the importance of investigating how the minds of flesh-and-blood readers engage with those fictional minds inscribed within a given text, especially texts whose protagonists claim to move toward a higher consciousness.

ideal audience—may cohabit this space of the mind, activating "dormant areas of consciousness" (*Borderlands* vi) wherein what Anzaldúa names "The New Mestiza."

THE NEW MESTIZA CONSCIOUSNESS

Despite its wide support, *Borderlands* remains a rough text. Anzaldúa herself lamented the rush to publication that impacted her book:

> Every time I read passages from *Borderlands* I see typos and spelling mistakes. My other concern [regarding publication] was that Chapter Six, on writing and art, was put together really fast. In fact, all seven chapters were written after the book had already gone into production and I was trying to write an introduction. [Aunt Lute Press was] already typesetting the poetry, and the introduction became the seven essays. And [Chapters] Five and Six, the one on language and the one on art and writing, were the last to go in, and they were the roughest of all. And especially Chapter Six I felt like I was still regurgitating and sitting on some of the ideas and I hadn't done enough revisions and I didn't have enough time to unravel the ideas fully. (Reuman 4)

Here Anzaldúa reveals that the formation of the most-cited aspect of *Borderlands*—the first seven chapters—was an afterthought, or at the least it was not part of her initial plan for the book. Although Anzaldúa notes her sensitivity to what she sees as the roughness of parts of her writing, the text itself gives a sense of her mind at work. Through less careful editing, Gloria's mind remains provocatively unfiltered and, arguably, more powerful. Infelicities in her prose heighten the sense of a real mind at work, just as Acosta's ironic prose does in *Autobiography*. Just as Oscar nods to his abilities as a writer time and again in *Autobiography*, Gloria, too, takes stock of the book she is writing:

> In looking at this book that I'm almost finished writing, I see a mosaic pattern (Aztec-like) emerging, a weaving pattern, thin here, thick there. I see a preoccupation with the deep structure, the underlying structure, with the gesso underpainting that is red earth, black earth. I can see the deep structure, the scaffolding. If I can get the bone structure right, then putting flesh on it proceeds without too many hitches. (66)

In her musing, she echoes Oscar's ekphrastic evaluation of his vomit art in *Autobiography*: "The designs of curdled milk and scrambled eggs with ketchup are a sight, a work of genius. I ponder the fluid patterns of my rejections and consider the potential for art. Dali could do something with this, I'm sure" (25). Though Anzaldúa's is an earnest attempt at self-reflection, and Acosta's bemusement is in keeping with his self-critical yet irreverent tone, both are enraptured by the creative processes of their work as readers glimpse the workings of their minds, and the sense we are receiving their thoughts unfiltered speaks to the convictions of their journey and beliefs.

Gloria's observation of the deep structure of her book is an invitation for the reader to do likewise. Beth Berila posits that *Borderlands*'s

> experimental form and politics challenge readers to make meaning in ways that reveal the constant *work* that goes into constructing national identities. [. . .] Calling attention to people's participation in this process—whether that participation is about contesting or upholding dominant narratives—Anzaldúa highlights the costs of validating dominant national narratives in ways that do violence to other narratives, and urges readers to hold multiple, contestatory accounts simultaneously. (121–22)

Berila's announcement of *Borderlands*'s form as a willful challenge to the reader is neither groundbreaking nor novel; Anzaldúa herself identifies this as one of her central motivations for her writing style: "Let the reader beware—I here and now issue a *caveat perusor*: s/he must do the work of piecing this text together. . . . As the perspective and focus shift, as the topics shift, the listener is forced to connect the dots, to connect the fragments" (*Making Face/Haciendo Caras* xvii–xviii). Anzaldúa alludes to the oft-cited characteristic used to describe *Borderlands*: its fragmented quality. Yet this quality of her narrative is hardly as radical a process as Anzaldúa and proponents of her work would have it. One thing that allows the reader to make sense of the world inscribed in the text, any text, is the reader's ability (or inability) to take the textual cues provided by the author to reconstruct it. So while Anzaldúa highlights political valences to defamiliarizing and entrenched notions of nation, patriarchy, sexuality, and so on, the narrative structure she uses can hardly be said to be radical at all.

The key here is that Anzaldúa's narrative is radical within the context of writing by women of color. Not only are fractured narratives a hallmark of modernism and postmodernism across the board, but we can also note defamiliarized reading strategies inculcated by texts going as far back as 1759 with the publication of the first installment of Laurence Sterne's *The Life and Opinions of Tristram Shandy, Gentleman*. Berila and others conflate the text as a challenge to the reader with the text as a "radical form" (123), but here the two terms must be disambiguated. A text may present a significant challenge to its reader while eschewing recalcitrant, experimental narrative form.

Richard Rodriguez's *Hunger,* told as a series of journalistic essays, is a case in point. Rodriguez's challenge to his audience lies not in his narrative design but rather in his attitude toward such controversial policies as Affirmative Action and bilingual education. Formally innovative texts may not be considered radical in a political sense. *Borderlands* uses an unconventional narrative structure while it engages in overtly political issues, but its form itself, its *narrative* form, is not radical.

The title of the seven collective chapters of *Borderlands* is "Atravesando Fronteras/Crossing Borders." Yet the borders have occurred only in Gloria's mind, experienced vicariously within the mind of the willing reader. Thus, the scaffolding to which Gloria refers has been established first within her own mind, supported by her arrangement of the prose and poetry in her book. This is a crucial aspect of reading Anzaldúa's book that should not be missed, for the notion of identity and identity formation is inextricably linked to the concept of crossing borders. The site of differentiation between the self and other may be viewed as a border, and these sites are acutely involved in the process of identity formation.

Patrick Colm Hogan articulates how identity formation operates in terms of what he labels "practical identity" and "categorial identity." Practical identity, according to Hogan, "comprises what we do or can do. It is the total of our capacities, propensities, interests, routines—most important, those that bear on our interactions with others" or "more technically, [. . .] the complex of representations and procedural competences that enable [. . .] thought and action" (*Understanding* 8, 26–27). Hogan cites the ability to speak a language as an exemplar of practical identity. Categorial identity "is our inclusion of ourselves in particular sets of people, our location of ourselves in terms of in-group/out-group divisions" (8). In other words, categorial identity manifests when one locates him- or herself within a social group (29).

Hogan's typology helps us understand *Borderlands* as it operates at the reading (cognitive) level. More so than Acosta's, Anzaldúa's project appropriates the powerful metaphor of the border and underscores both its functionality and its historical influence on marginalized people generally, and herself specifically. Ingrained in her exploration of the border, necessarily, are the process and the consequences of identity formation, manifested in a blending of language, history, and consciousness. Above all, the willing reader is invited to journey with Gloria via her thought processes, reflections, and descriptions of emotion and philosophical musings. While the geographic location of the borderland is the most prominent and concrete image in *Borderlands,* Gloria renders it as an imaginative and transportable space of the mind. As there are invariably readers who belong to some marginal group (as Hogan's account of both practical and categorial identities suggests), there is an openness to Anzaldúa's work that is not found in *Autobiography*, at least not to the same degree. It is easier for readers to identify with Anzaldúa's target audience than it is with Acosta's. Though Oscar sometimes invokes empathy even as he repulses and as he advocates for a like-minded collective of "Brown Buffalo people," his concept of identity is less transportable (among social groups) than is Gloria's. Therefore, despite the surface recalcitrance of Gloria's text, its use of a near-universal metaphor (the border) for a way of rethinking identity and (re)claiming power is not surprising, but rhetorically effective.[15]

I attribute the wide adoption and utility of *Borderlands* not so much in its narrative form but rather in its heavy reliance on and articulation of metaphor. As noted above, Gloria opens the book with an examination of her use of the border:

> The actual physical borderland that I'm dealing with in this book is the Texas-U.S. Southwest/Mexican border. The psychological borderlands, the sexual borderlands and the spiritual borderlands are not particular to the Southwest. In fact, the Borderlands are physically present wherever two or more cultures edge each other, where people of different races occupy the same territory, where under, lower, middle and upper classes touch, where the space between two individuals shrinks with intimacy. (Preface, n. pag.)

Again I note the universal scope of the borderland metaphor as articulated by Gloria herself. As she broadly defines it and in light of Hogan's concept of categorial identity, where identity has to do with group memberships rather than traits or abilities, this metaphor is readily adopted and becomes relevant to nearly anyone who reads *Borderlands*. Despite Anzaldúa's identification of her ideal audience with categorial identities of woman—Chicana and, in a broader sense, lesbian—so long as a reader can claim membership in a marginalized group that rests on the liminal side of a division (or border), that reader can inhabit the larger consciousness to which Gloria consistently alludes.

Further, the border as metaphor itself is powerful. Hogan's exploration of metaphors, as they apply to the self in terms of the nation, shows how certain metaphors can "cultivate a sense of belonging to the nation and its culture" and further that metaphors are "crucial, both conceptually and emotionally"

---

15. Here it is important to disentangle concepts of universality from notions of essentialism. Despite rhetoric to the contrary, there are identifiable universals that apply to all of humanity. As borders of all types exist in the world (otherwise, everything would be a conglomerate of undifferentiated stuff), the border as a metaphor works well in imagining the demarcation point between two distinct units or properties. For more on the concept of universals and their usefulness for literary study, see Hogan, "Literary Universals."

(*Understanding* 10–11). Put another way, certain metaphors provide something akin to a scaffold upon which people attach thoughts and emotions. With the driving metaphor of the borderland, Gloria invites readers to engage with her thought processes, traversing border after border—borders of geography, borders of time, borders of history—as she steadily builds the architecture of her storyworld, resulting in the New Mestiza consciousness. Though rarely discussed in this fashion, the New Mestiza consciousness can be adopted by anyone who assumes a categorial identity that occupies a marginalized position in society. As unlikely as it sounds, the New Mestiza consciousness could theoretically be espoused by heterosexual males given the right social conditions—namely, so long as the heterosexual males are in an underprivileged and potentially oppressed position. Because of the wide and readily accessible adoption of this way of thinking, the reading process whereby the reader's mind can assume Gloria's mind makes such a position possible. However, ideological structures would most likely make such identity formations problematic because heterosexual males are less oppressed than other groups in U.S. society. In fact, they are often the oppressors.

MINDING THE NEW MESTIZA

Though section two, "Un Agitado Viento/Ehécatl, The Wind," is the most overtly traditional part of *Borderlands,* with its usage of several recognizable formal attributes of poetry, scholars devote most of their attention to section one. Based on essays, reviews, and interviews, it is hardly controversial to call section one the most popular section of *Borderlands.* What is surprising about this is Anzaldúa's own admission that the first seven chapters should introduce, at the time before publication, what she felt to be the more substantive aspect of her work, the section containing the poetry. One wonders what motivated this serendipitous turn of events for Anzaldúa. Anzaldúa's coeditor of *This Bridge Called My Back,* Cherríe Moraga, had already published her own multiform text, *Loving in the War Years,* in 1983. Yet while the model and the inspiration for this hybrid form were readily available to Anzaldúa, her text differs from Moraga's in several key aspects.

First, *Borderlands* readily incorporates works by others, resulting in a pastiche-like structure to the chapters. Second, there is a shifting perspective that lends *Borderlands* a sense of motion and mobility. This is mostly accomplished by the narrating presence that recedes and approaches at its own will. Third, there is an acute relationship to history. The narrator often adopts historical discourse as she works to expose certain relevant moments within history, moments that serve the larger design of the narrative. Fourth, though *Loving* contains what are clear works of creative verse, the prose never presents itself as anything other than nonfiction. If we set aside Moraga's poetry and consider only her prose in *Loving,* there would be no real controversy in calling it creative nonfiction—it does not claim to be historically accurate, while it is clearly rooted in Moraga's experiences. Anzaldúa's prose makes the leap from creative nonfiction to the nether category of philosophical musing.

It is instructive here to attend to the narrating presence in *Borderlands.* Before going very far in this investigation, we already have a significant question that requires answering: Is the narrating presence consistent throughout the text? The answer seems to be yes, particularly in light of Gloria's self-reflexive consideration of her project in chapter 6, "*Tlilli, Tlapalli*: The Path of the Red and Black Ink." Thus, as the unifying consciousness of the text, we can trace her movement of thought throughout the work as Gloria herself becomes a metaphor that directly interacts with the dominant metaphor of the border: the bridge. We may think of this image as a narrative bridge, facilitating the reader in moving from poem to prose, epoch to epoch.[16] Anzaldúa's own consideration of "the 'I' who writes, the 'I' who is in the text, the 'I' who reads what is in the text and reflects on it and even puts that reflection into the text" in *Borderlands* ("Coming" 5) is particularly telling in its admission of the distinction between the various selves of Anzaldúa. Unlike Oscar in *Autobiography,* who is essentially the same narrating consciousness throughout (though one who adapts to narrating conventions such as recounting an experience versus narrating the present moment), there is more than one Gloria. There is the arranger of the text, inserting a quote here, a poem there. There are speakers within the poetry whom the reader can take as Gloria, but this conclusion is arrived at merely because it is inserted between prose that Gloria narrates. We can note several distinct permutations of Gloria's self, of Anzaldúa's counterself.

Though accounting for the various guises and functions of the "Gloria" inscribed and implied within the text may seem an unnecessary complication, it is necessary if we are to understand how readers engage with the text at a cognitive level. Such an analysis may help make clear the emotional connection many readers have for *Borderlands.* There is more at work in Anzaldúa's text than powerful metaphors—though her metaphors are highly transport-

---

16. Of course, one cannot help connecting the metaphor of the bridge with the title of Moraga and Anzaldúa's feminist collection, *This Bridge Called My Back*—a title stemming from another metaphor that highlights the woman as a structure that is trod upon to allow movement and mobility of the oppressor. Thus, one might say Anzaldúa reappropriates the image of the bridge in *Borderlands.*

able and applicable. To be sure, so many differing voices within a single text will create a different reading experience than reading a narrative with a stable narrator. So how do so many vantage points suggest an ideal readership and also potentially affect willing readers?

First, David Herman reminds us that though "narrative can be seen as a prototype for all perspective-taking, version-making activities," it is important to remember that "stories not only facilitate but also formally encode ways of seeing. [. . .] Thus, to say that an event or object or participant is focalized in a certain manner is to say that it is perspectivally indexed, structured so that it has to be interpreted as refracted through a specific viewpoint and anchored in a particular set of contextual coordinates" (*Story Logic* 302). One of the salient features of Anzaldúa's text is its penchant for shifting focalization. This issue complicates the structure of *Borderlands,* for not only do we have a variety of guises under which the narrator operates; we have a variety of narrators who focalize their narrative through other consciousnesses and often move back and forth between them, sometimes from paragraph to paragraph. Even beyond the different narrators and narrating states, the shifting focalization imbues the relatively short book with the sense of an expansive canvas of space-time. As Anzaldúa's project is to provide for a new way of engaging with and understanding the world—her New Mestiza consciousness—she uses a multiplicity of refractory perspectives and vantage points throughout history to this mindscape for the reader. While scholars have given abundant critical attention to Anzaldúa's recuperation of pre-Colombian myths as the primary vehicles that allow her argument for the New Mestiza to carry so much weight, I contend that the shifting narrating consciousness and varying focalization also embody a bridge to the realm of consciousness she titles the "New Consciousness." A closer look at how each narrative consciousness operates in *Borderlands* reveals the strategies that Anzaldúa uses to break away from traditional forms of life writing.

In the early sections where history is narrated, there is already the presence of code-switching from the multiple languages Gloria uses (Standard English, Standard Spanish, Chicano Spanish, Slang English) throughout the book. Thus, even in what readers recognize as written history (via prototypes of authoritative historical discourses found in history textbooks), the narrator is already shaping the reader's prior knowledge of the history of Chicanos, if not creating it altogether. For instance, the narrator opens the first prose section of chapter 1, "The Homeland Aztlán/El otro México," with a metaphor of her own creation, one that will serve as the building block of her overarching metaphor embedded within the book's title: "The U.S.-Mexico border *es una herida abierta*[17] where the Third World grates against the first [World] and bleeds. And before a scab forms it hemorrhages again, the lifeblood of two worlds merging to form a third country—a border culture" (3). Here the narrator establishes the current state of the border noting the irony of how something as verifiable as a geographic line or border, one that can be easily mapped out with the most basic of tools, creates the "vague and undetermined place" (3) that we call a *borderland*. She further provides a limited representation of the residents of this geographic space, individuals she calls *los atravesados*,[18] whom she describes as "the squint-eyed, the perverse, the queer, the troublesome, the mongrel, the mulatto, the half-breed, the half dead; those who cross over, pass over, or go through the confines of the 'normal'" (3). The narrator's explication of the borderlands vis-à-vis *los atravesados* is crucial to her entire project and helps us understand the orientation of her mind.

Based on her knowledge and experience of the borderland, it is a site of social outcasts. However, a more comprehensive examination reveals that the residents of the borderlands are not the homogeneous outsiders the narrator describes. The actual United States-Mexican border is populated with individuals who do not fall into Gloria's categorization of the "prohibited and forbidden" (3). In addition, she stereotypes all "gringos in the U.S. Southwest" as people who see "the inhabitants of the borderlands [as] transgressors, aliens—whether they possess documents or not, whether they're Chicanos, Indians or Blacks. Do not enter, trespassers will be raped, maimed, strangled, gassed, shot" (3). As we read this, we are confronted not only with the challenge of not simply interpreting what is being said (the narrator uses straightforward language; this lends such gravity to the statement in the first place) but also with understanding this situation from the narrator's vantage point. From a factual point of view, the narrator cannot possibly be correct. Surely there are some "gringos" in the U.S. Southwest who do not view residents of the borderlands[19] as transgressors or aliens; finding even one undercuts the power of the narrator's accusation. If readers take the narration as factually accurate,

---

17. "is an open wound."
18. Literally, "those who have crossed over."
19. It should be noted that although Anzaldúa often refers to the "U.S.-Mexican border" in *Borderlands,* it is more accurate to say she means the Mexico-Texas border. I insist on this clarification because many other Chicano/a writings address issues of the Mexico-Arizona border, the Mexico-New Mexico border, and the Mexico-California border. Each of these has its own dynamic, and conflating them into a homogeneous area is inaccurate. In fact, issues that impact one Texas city on the border, such as El Paso, may not necessarily be of concern in another Texas city such as Brownsville. But because Anzaldúa often seeks the transcendent metaphor with wide appeal, her homogenization of the border is not surprising.

as one might when reading nonfiction, then Anzaldúa has problematized her project before it has even started.

Yet if we recognize that we are reading the mind of an individual who has occupied a liminal space in society (on many levels), then we understand more accurately the import of the narrator's words. This same narrative voice appears later in the chapter, stating, "The Gringo, locked into the fiction of white superiority, seized complete political power, stripping Indians and Mexicans of their land while their feet were still rooted in it" (7). By using the same essentialist rhetoric often used by oppressors regarding the oppressed, Anzaldúa creates a challenging reading situation. It ought to be uncomfortable to read, and, for many, it is. What makes it even more of a challenge is that the narrator is invested in (one could say biased toward) the Chicana position. Again, this rhetoric does not pose a problem if it emanates from what appears to be a subjective position such as a homodiegetic-intradiegetic narrator, because it would then appear relative and particular to the viewpoint of one individual. However, these statements that purport to depict certain actions, attitudes, and thought processes of a group she has homogenized (i.e., gringos) appear within authoritative statements that sound very much like the very essentialist thinking Anzaldúa would rail against as applied to those who share her categorial identities (e.g., Chicana, feminist, lesbian, Tejana). How would we read uncontextualized statements that essentialized the actions of "the feminist" and "the Chicana"?

There are several ways we can account for this narrator's attitude. One might say that, in fact, what Anzaldúa is doing here is akin to Audre Lorde's metaphor of using the master's tools to dismantle his house.[20] Anzaldúa, using her satirical historian narrator, highlights the dangers of this form of rhetoric. It is difficult to disentangle whether these moments in the narration are ironic, especially if we read it from a nonfictional perspective. If we see these moments as being narrated by a fictional narrator, the challenge in reading is mediated. We see the device come to the fore and recognize that Anzaldúa has conjured a fictional counterself, a narrator with the same powers of historical authority (and essentialism) that we find in some historical or sociological accounts of Chicanos/as. The fictionality of the narrator gives us a clue of how the reader is to take what are otherwise troubling statements about "gringos"

---

20. In her essay "The Master's Tools Will Never Dismantle the Master's House" from chapter 1 of *Sister Outsider*, Lorde vehemently upholds that when women of color stay within the structures developed by privilege and patriarchy as a means of educating "male ignorance," they unwittingly use the "old and primary tool of all oppressors to keep the oppressed occupied with the master's concerns" (113). By comparison, Anzaldúa uses the same sorts of rhetorical strategies used by the hegemony she excoriates in order to make her point.

in the U.S. Southwest. To be sure, this narrator does not revel in these essentialist statements; they are deployed sporadically and with deliberate care. Often they are used to illuminate certain experiences common to particular categorial identity groups. Yet a thorough examination of the text reveals a narrator who has a penchant for discussing "the Chicana," "the Negro," "the Gringo," "the Catholic," "the white," "the queer," and so forth. It is enthralling how *Borderlands*, hailed as a triumph against hegemony, a breathtaking show of defiance and resistance to patriarchy, so readily deploys problematic rhetoric and thinking in service of *undoing* oppressive stances.

Near the end of chapter 1, the narrator moves into a third-person plural position with the statement "We have a tradition of migration, a tradition of long walks. Today we are witnessing *la migración de los pueblos mexicanos*, the return odyssey to the historical/mythological Aztlán" (11). Here the narrator aligns herself with Chicanos with a pronominal shift to a collective identity. This shift is a key moment in *Borderlands*, for it aligns the narrative consciousness with a collective consciousness of a specific categorial identity group. It is the opposite of what occurs in *Autobiography*: Oscar waits until the close of the narrative until he mentions his call for the greater collective consciousness he calls the "Brown Buffalo people," while Gloria incorporates the struggles of Chicanos with her own sense of self. Unlike that in *Autobiography*, the narration in *Borderlands* moves from a large, collective categorial identity group (i.e., Mexican Americans) to a more exclusive group (i.e., Chicanas) until the key identity group is hyperexclusive (i.e., Chicana feminist lesbian). It should be noted that the more restricted the identity group with which the narrator affiliates herself, the more metaphysical the narration becomes as the narrator reaches for a realization of the New Mestiza. By chapter 7, "*La conciencia de la mestiza*/Towards a New Consciousness," Anzaldúa has finally reached not only the subtitle of her book but also the target audience that she mentions in her interview with *MELUS* (Reuman 9–10). Again invoking the we-narrator, Gloria unifies her ideal readership in light of her project—a project that has been unambiguous from the beginning, despite its unconventional form:

> We are the people who leap in the dark, we are the people on the knees of the gods. In our very flesh, Revolution works out the clash of cultures. It makes us crazy constantly, but if the center holds, we've made some kind of evolutionary step forward. *Nuestra alma el trabajo*, the opus, the great alchemical work; spiritual *mestizaje*, a "morphogenesis," an inevitable unfolding. We have become the quickening serpent movement. (*Borderlands* 81)

In 1990, Ramón Saldívar concluded his book *Chicano Narrative* by holding up Anzaldúa's *Borderlands* as a high-water mark for Chicano/a narrative. Without a sustained and critical engagement of Anzaldúa's text, Saldívar nonetheless heralds *Borderlands* as a paragon of excellence in Latino/a letters. Regarding the opening of *Borderlands* and the image of the border as an "open wound," he writes:

> With their special ties to the borderlines demarcating the differential structures of contemporary American life, Chicano narrative texts might well serve as the patterns of that dialogical model of a new American literary history. [. . .] What it means to construct a life in the liminal chronotopes defined by the cognitive mappings imposed on the subject by the imaginary political lines drawn between Mexico and the United States is the substance of [Anzaldúa's] autobiography. [. . .] We might well thus extend Anzaldúa's guiding figure of the border as the *primary metaphor* of the particularly dialectical subject position articulated by each of the texts that we have discussed. The trajectories of the lives of these subjects take them across borderlines precisely into the prohibited and forbidden zones that contain the residue of the unnatural boundaries forged by the unfulfilled potentialities of contemporary American culture. (218, emphasis mine)

Anzaldúa herself states the guiding principle of her book in chapter 6, "*Tlilli, Tlapalli*: The Path of the Red and Black Ink": "[The Aztecs] believed that through metaphor and symbol, by means of poetry and truth, communication with the Divine could be attained" (69). Seen in this light, *Borderlands*'s successful reception with audiences has much to do with the metaphorical transportability upon which Anzaldúa relies so heavily, one that often mediates many of the overt challenges in reading the text. Ultimately, the New Mestiza consciousness, like Anzaldúa's own professed ideal readership, is highly exclusive. It is exclusive of heterosexual males (White, Chicano, or otherwise) and binary oppositions. This exclusivity ought to have created a challenge within readers' minds, particularly when Gloria explains that "*La mestiza* constantly has to shift out of habitual formations; from convergent thinking, analytical reasoning that tends to use rationality to move toward a single goal (a Western mode), to divergent thinking,[21] characterized by movement away from set pat-

---

21. "In part, I derive my definitions for 'convergent' and 'divergent' thinking from Rothenberg, 12–13" (Anzaldúa 97). Anzaldúa here references Albert Rothenberg's *The Creative Process in Art, Science, and Other Fields,* and specifically Arthur Koestler's work on "bisociative thinking," which essentially describes the process of combining the rational with the irrational during the creative process.

terns and goals and toward a more whole perspective, *one that includes rather than excludes*" (79, emphasis in original). Thus, Anzaldúa is deliberately willful in the text as a means of modeling how the New Mestiza operates—one that reaches out as it pushes away, disarmingly inviting and abruptly recalcitrant at the same moment.

In closing, I return to the respective audiences that took up *Autobiography* and *Borderlands* after their publication. Anzaldúa produces a defiant, stentorian voice that ostensibly emanates from a liminal position within society: the socially, culturally disenfranchised peoples who have suffered from patriarchy, colonialism, racism, and sexism. Her book, despite using an unconventional structure, unambiguously denotes the audience it seeks. *Borderlands* is an example of a text with a challenging structure that ultimately doesn't challenge its audience via its structure; rather, it is a book whose thematic content challenged ideas and assumptions of power. Acosta, on the other hand, was writing for an audience that did not yet exist. In a personal interview (4/17/2012), I posed a straightforward question regarding *Autobiography* to Ilan Stavans: "Who is Acosta's audience?" Stavans replied, "Who *is* Acosta's audience?" Stavans's question to me suggests the audacity of *Autobiography* as well as the difficulty in discerning what type of audience Acosta had in mind. Acosta's text is mocking, self-hating, existential, vitriolic—and yet hopeful. But it came at a time when his narrative playfulness seemed frivolous in light of the very real political struggles of Chicanos in the United States in the late 1960s and early 1970s. For her part, Anzaldúa envisions the borderlands as an open wound, noting that actual people had been and were currently being brutalized because of their identities. Conversely, Acosta continually finds new ways in his text to open the wound even further. In the end, Acosta's and Anzaldúa's texts undoubtedly frustrate, disturb, and confound readers to varying degrees and results. As we will see in the next chapter, the use of Spanish in the United States is among the most pressing in Latino/a culture.

CHAPTER 2

Translingual Minds, Narrative Encounters

Reading Challenges in Piri Thomas's *Down These Mean Streets* and Giannina Braschi's *Yo-Yo Boing!*

IN THE PREVIOUS chapter I examined how Oscar "Zeta" Acosta and Gloria Anzaldúa use carefully designed fictions that pose as life narratives to work toward the expression of a Chicano/Chicana consciousness. One strategy used by both Acosta and Anzaldúa to expand readers' understanding of Chicano/a literary production and use of narrative form is to use several languages and dialects within their respective narratives, an approach that has been termed *code-switching*, which John J. Gumperz defines as "the juxtaposition within the same speech exchange of passages of speech belonging to two different grammatical systems or sub-systems" (59). This chapter presents two works that also use a code-switching strategy: Piri Thomas's *Down These Mean Streets* and Giannina Braschi's *Yo-Yo Boing!* Published over thirty years apart, these two works, in working to shape their storyworlds, make language a salient feature of their narratives. To different degrees, they use language and code-switching as the primary means to challenge the reader. Thomas infuses his narrative with sporadic Puerto Rican Spanish and English slang, while Braschi writes full sections of her narrative in either Spanish or English. And because language is inextricably bound to identity, the authors' use of language and code-switching at once enables the reader to apprehend characters more completely (as in Thomas) and puts more distance between the characters and reader (as in Braschi). In short, this interaction of minds and understandings of identity at the site of the storyworld has the potential to complicate notions of identity within the minds of the audience.

Of course, the bilingualism[1] of Latino/a writers is ever at the forefront of examinations of their writings. Beyond matters of phenotypology, differences in language tend to signify cultural and ethnic positioning in the United States. Language is undeniably a political issue in the United States, one that is often deployed in attempts in nation-defining. The English language is overwhelmingly the dominant language in the United States, despite the fact that a large concentration of citizens is descended from peoples whose primary language was something other than English. Thus, the history of immigration reveals a transition of language often occurring in families who immigrate to the United States, typically resulting in a loss of the mother tongue in favor of English. The loss of one's ancestral language is a common by-product of assimilatory processes in the United States. Examining how the English and Spanish languages (as well as their variants) are combined in different ways in the two selected novels, this chapter extrapolates from case studies to consider how these languages are inextricably linked to issues of race, class, and culture in Latino/a literature.

Beyond political implications of language acquisition and loss, the generation of Latinos that tends to grow up with other-than-English-speaking parents is composed of individuals who develop the ability to code-switch between English and Spanish. The difficulties of this experience have been explored by Gloria Anzaldúa, Richard Rodriguez, Gustavo Pérez Firmat, among others, who often show what they see as the deleterious effects of the two languages as they abrade one another. Further, these writers' experiences arise from their respective historical and geographical situations. Anzaldúa and Rodriguez speak of growing up during the 1960s in Texas and California, respectively. Conversely, Pérez Firmat was born in Cuba in 1949 before immigrating to the United States in 1960. The experiences as Latinos in the United States for these authors highlight the complexity of being Latino/a, as well as the complexities of language usage in the United States. Their experiences emphasize how Latino/a experience in the United States is not homogeneous, and I include them here briefly as a reminder that although my case studies

---

1. There is a difference between bilingualism and code-switching, both in how narratives are constructed and in what is required to decode the narrative. One of the major differences is that code-switching can often be understood from the context even if the reader or listener is unfamiliar with the second language. Bilingualism, however, suggests that equal mastery of two languages is in evidence. Another way of viewing the difference between code-switching and bilingualism is that code-switching is an aspect of bilingualism. See Lesley Milroy and Pieter Muysken's edited collection of essays *One Speaker, Two Languages*.

are texts written through the lens of the Puerto Rican experience, they are not representative of all Latino/a experience in the United States.

THREE LATINO/A PERSPECTIVES ON BILINGUALISM

For instance, Anzaldúa recounts the oppressive restrictions of speaking Spanish in public schools, an act that often resulted in corporal punishment and humiliation at the hands of schoolteachers and administrators. In chapter 5 of *Borderlands,* titled "How to Tame a Wild Tongue," Anzaldúa writes, "I remember being caught speaking Spanish at recess—that was good for three licks on the knuckles with a sharp ruler. I remember being sent to the corner of the classroom for 'talking back' to the Anglo teacher when all I was trying to do was tell her how to pronounce my name. If you want to be American, speak 'American.' If you don't like it, go back to Mexico where you belong" (53). Such moments help reveal the formative experiences that Anzaldúa ruminates upon in her book, and indeed her text is often seen as a declaration of linguistic freedom. Anzaldúa's own mother, "mortified that [Gloria] spoke English like a Mexican" (54), viewed speaking English very differently than her daughter did: "'I want you to speak English. *Pa' hallar buen trabajo tienes que saber hablar en ingles bien. Qué vale toda tu educación si todavía hablas ingles con un* 'accent'" (54).² Anzaldúa sees her desire to use language freely as inherent to the First Amendment to the U.S. Constitution and accuses Anglos of figuratively ripping away the tongues of Spanish-speaking Chicanos. "Wild tongues can't be tamed," she laments, "they can only be cut out" (54). Forcing individuals to cease the use of one language in favor of another is thus tantamount to dismemberment and silencing for Anzaldúa.

Yet Anzaldúa's anecdote of her mother's rebuke illustrates the issue of language as viewed and practiced at home, though it is something about which Anzaldúa does go into detail about in her text, despite her evident disdain for her mother's alignment (albeit for different reasons) with the Anglo purveyors of linguistic discipline at school. Her mother sees speaking English flawlessly as a measure of success, a skill set that will enable her daughter to find an excellent job (which most likely means one that is less reliant on physical toil and labor). Further, speaking English well enough for communication is not good enough. For her mother, it must be spoken without an accent. Her view, in hindsight, is naive and ill informed, though well meant, even as it reflects the specificity of sociohistorical context for Latinos, especially across genera-

---

2. "To find good work, you have to know how to speak English well. What good is all of your education if you still speak English with an accent."

tions. Anzaldúa's mother perhaps does not realize that there are a variety of accents that flavor American English. Nor does she intuit the other factors (such as xenophobia and racism) that work to keep Chicanos from gaining higher social and economic status.[3]

On another side of this issue of language is the essayist and cultural critic Richard Rodriguez. Five years before the publication of *Borderlands*, Rodriguez published *The Hunger of Memory* to both acclaim and criticism. Rodriguez, a Chicano born of working-class Mexican immigrants, raised as a Catholic in Sacramento, California, believes that bilingual education is a destructive force on those who speak Spanish at home and English in school. Rodriguez's troubled relationship with language began when he initiated his education and culminated in his position as an essayist who has railed against Affirmative Action and bilingual education. He sees the two languages as mutually incompatible: Spanish is the language of the family, of intimacy, of privacy, while English is the language of the public sphere. As a result, Rodriguez has been the target of sustained criticism for his conservative views on language and the Chicano/a experience.[4]

Central to Rodriguez's views on language is his advocacy of a sort of dualism between the two languages, that there are, in fact, two spheres for which one language or the other must be readily deployed: Spanish as the language of the family; English as a public language. Essentially, Rodriguez is more concerned with issues of privacy and publicness than with advocating for one language over the other. He is very much in support of keeping the family discourse away from educational contexts, and this belief in linguistic dualism has been the defining feature of Rodriguez's contribution to Latino/a and American letters.

Rodriguez makes very clear assertions regarding Latinos and their use of both English and Spanish: "I worry these days that Latinos in California speak neither Spanish nor English very well," he states in an interview with Scott London. "They are in a kind of linguistic limbo between the two," he

---

3. One cannot help sympathizing with Anzaldúa's mother. In *Borderlands* Gloria renders her not only as naive but as dangerously oblivious to the patriarchal and homophobic structures that Gloria identifies within Chicano culture. However, as is the case with many parents, Anzaldúa's mother sees the value of education and linguistic sophistication as a key to her daughter's future success. Ironically, despite the apparent angst toward her mother, Anzaldúa's contribution to feminist theory and ethnic studies proves the validity of her mother's attitude about English. Though there is a frequent code-switching in *Borderlands*, the text is predominantly written in English and has contributed the most to English-language scholarship.

4. As with the case of Anzaldúa, Rodriguez places himself in the untenable position of critiquing a system that has enabled him to criticize it. Yet he acknowledges this fact when he opens *Hunger* by invoking Shakespeare's most infamous native: "I have taken Caliban's advice. I have stolen their books. I will have some run of this isle" (2).

states. "They don't really have a language, and are, in some deep sense, homeless" ("Crossing Borders"). Rodriguez has the unyielding conviction that the two languages must never be allowed to mix, which in reality is an untenable position to adopt, especially when one considers the growing number of Latinos in the United States. In order to fully participate in the United States, one must be able to handle English fluently by reading, writing, and conversing in English. Without this fluidity of participating in English discourse, Spanish-only speakers limit their ability to interact with large swaths of society at a socioeconomic level.

One of the defining traits of language is that it is transmuted over time and space. What we call Standard English today bears little resemblance to the tongue of the Anglo-Saxons who recounted the epic of *Beowulf*. The fact is that languages are shaped by the interactions of cultures. However, the transformation of language often occurs at a geologic rate, as it is shaped over the course of great stretches of time and as a result of conquests. Thus, Rodriguez's fantasy of a dual-track bilingualism can never be achieved in a nation where languages crash one upon the other with little regard for essayists or novelists, much less in a society that now has the technological means through social media such as Facebook and Twitter to integrate private and public discourses.

Ostensibly, Rodriguez's lament at the lackluster uses of language among Latinos (in one language or the other or both) does not acknowledge the possibilities of code-switching as a viable and valid means of expression. Indeed, his description of "a kind of linguistic limbo between the two" could readily be applied to a person's blending of Spanish and English to produce speech heavily reliant upon the technique of code-switching.[5] He does not conceive of (or at the very least he disdains entertaining the possibility of) hybridized discourse resulting from the process of code-switching—a process that may someday yield a true bilingualism where Spanish and English are used together, equally. Instead, he views the blending of these two languages as a metaphor for homelessness, for not having a linguistic tether to a heritage or legacy.[6] Indeed, Rodriguez's own path through the process of language

---

5. Despite the apparent arbitrary nature of which words appear in English and which appear in Spanish, research by Joshua Fishman, John J. Gumperz, Jan-Petter Blom, Peter Auer, and others suggests that code-switching is a highly technical (though often innate or instinctive) skill that often depends on connotations and nuance which accompany one word that may not apply to its corresponding translation. This fact has a significant bearing on narrative worldmaking and storyworld reconstruction.

6. Tacit in his position on language is the hard truth that speaking English—and speaking it well—has very real consequences from a socioeconomic perspective. As English is dominant in the United States, an inability to fully participate in English discourse limits one's potential.

acquisition is as atypical as his educational career.[7] His Spanish, lost to him at the insistence of his parents who mandated that he speak English to them at home, reminiscent of Anzaldúa's mother's admonition to her daughter to speak without an accent, remains elusive until Rodriguez returns to it as an adult. Yet the Spanish he acquires, much like the English he masters, is the Spanish language of academia and professionalism, not the *caló* spoken in the streets of his native California. Thus, because Rodriguez intuited Spanish and English as residing in separate domains, he never allowed the possibility that the two languages might be blended to yield something distinct from either one taken alone. Where Anzaldúa sees a model for empowerment, Rodriguez identifies a severe limitation.

Gustavo Pérez Firmat provides yet another perspective on the issue of English/Spanish usage. In his significant work *Life on the Hyphen*, Pérez Firmat examines the plausibility of those immigrants who left their nation of birth as a child—what he calls a "one and a half generation"—to live "within the hyphen." For Pérez Firmat it is possible to participate in both English- and Spanish-language contexts in the United States with ease. But, as I noted earlier, not all Latino/a experiences are homogeneous. Cuba's political relationship with the United States has had a profound impact on Cuban Americans, specifically because of the ability of Cubans to become U.S. citizens more easily than, say, Mexicans.[8] Further, the experiences of Pérez Firmat, as a light-skinned Cuban American, are distinctly different from those of an Afro Latino such as Piri Thomas. Thus, I wish to emphasize that Pérez Firmat's experiences, along with those of Anzaldúa and Rodriguez, demonstrate the complexity of using Spanish *and* English, and how that complexity is made manifest through the disparate Latino/a experiences shaped by a variety of sociohistorical and geopolitical contexts.

Perhaps the most illustrative example is to consider how these three Latino/a authors recount their grade school experiences in the United States: Anzaldúa was literally punished for speaking Spanish at school (*Borderlands* 53); Rodriguez was silent in class because he felt that English was not his to use, until the Catholic nuns who were his teachers visited his home and urged

---

But the ability to master English and then have the power to choose when to deploy a second language such as Spanish is an empowering move that Rodriguez does not acknowledge.

7. That is to say, Chicanos with the talent and ability to perform successfully throughout their college careers only to turn down a professorship at Yale University are rare.

8. The Cuban Adjustment Act of 1966 enabled Cubans who fled to the United States to be allowed one year of residency during which time the process of achieving legal U.S. citizenship would be expedited. Though it has been slightly revised (since 1995 a Cuban must now actually make it to U.S. soil), this U.S. policy has clearly had a significant impact on how Cuban Americans view issues of immigration, citizenship, and language.

Richard's parents to speak English at home (*Hunger* 18–20); Pérez Firmat had taken an English class while still in Cuba, so that his first experience in a U.S. classroom was not "the typical experience that many immigrants have of walking into an American classroom and not understanding anything" (Montagne). Hence these authors' relationships with English and Spanish are widely divergent.

THE CONSTRAINTS ON USING TWO LANGUAGES IN NARRATIVE

Related to these issues of language is also the materialistic reality that publishers work to enhance rather than hinder sales of their books. This last fact, especially during the middle of the twentieth century, has resulted in Latino/a authors who were highly aware, and perhaps even self-conscious, of their use of Spanish.[9] Some of the early novels of what has come to be known as the Latino Renaissance, such as Villarreal's *Pocho* and John Rechy's *City of Night*,[10] use only the slightest amount of Spanish.[11] Yet as Latino/a literature progressed through the twentieth century and into the twenty-first century, Latino/a authors continued to press the boundaries for the use of Spanish and a heightened level of code-switching in the creation of their storyworld. As a consequence, readers required access to Spanish signifiers in order to fully reconstruct the inscribed storyworld. In short, a shift in obligation from the author to the reader has steadily occurred throughout the development of Latino/a literature. That is to say, where authors were once obliged by audiences and publishers to exercise narrative restraint, authors are more and more leaving it to readers to do the work of going outside of the text to gather the information needed to reconstruct storyworlds.

---

9. One readily notes this discomfort of using Spanish when reading José Antonio Villarreal's 1959 *Pocho.* One of the striking features of this novel is Villarreal's decision not only to translate conversation and dialogue within the narrative that takes place in Spanish within the storyworld, but also to render these moments into translations of literal English. The result is an odd, markedly stilted English that gives the impression that the novel's characters are speaking in antiquated idioms.

10. While *City* was viewed as a major work of LGBTQ literature, it did not significantly engage in issues of Latinidad. Rechy was not truly considered a writer of Latino/a literature until he wrote *The Miraculous Day of Amalia Gomez* in 1991.

11. Though Latino/a literature is written predominantly in English, there are early examples of Latinos writing mostly, if not entirely, in Spanish. Some examples are Aristeo Brito's *El diablo en Texas* (1976), Miguel Mendez's *Peregrinos de Aztlan* (1974), and Rolando Hinojosa-Smith's *Klail City Death Trip* series (1973–2006).

Alfred Arteaga, in his essay "An Other Language," carefully measures the dimensions of the tension between Spanish and English in Chicano/a poetics, identifying the source of that tension in what he calls a "border discourse" (11). By doing so, Arteaga urges that the very real border that exists between two nations provides a source of political and economic struggle—one that takes precedence above all other critical lenses when considering Chicano/a poetry. While Arteaga locates his essay in Chicano/a poetry, because he extrapolates his investigation from the nexus of Spanish and English textual features of poetry, I can only assume Arteaga would insist on the same distinctions when it comes to Chicano/a prose narratives. Undoubtedly, the conflicts generated in the sociopolitical realm, particularly when it comes to matters of language (i.e., the discussion of making English the official language of the United States), are often echoed within the whole of Latino/a literature. Arteaga writes:

> In poem and in daily speech, English and Spanish bestow different levels of authority on text and speaker. The relative imbalance in authority grows daily in the present era in increasing legislative suppression of languages other than English. English carries with it the status of authorization by the hegemony. It is the language of Anglo America and of linguistic Anglo Americans, whether or not they be ethnic Anglos. Further, it is the language of the greatest military and economic power in the world. Spanish is a language of Latin Americans, south of the border and north. Across the border, Spanish is a Third World language; here it is the language of the poor. (12)

The prescience of Arteaga's words, originally written in 1994, rings true into the second decade of the twenty-first century, as issues related to the uses of Spanish within U.S. society become more salient as the Latino/a demographic grows. There is little debate that the friction between these two languages and among their regional dialects is inherently political.

However, the interplay between Spanish and English, especially within Latino/a literature, is not nearly as neat as Arteaga maintains. That said, when Arteaga states, "The authoritative discourse is, after all, a prescribed monologue structured to inhibit dialogue with the natives. Who would read these lines I now write, if they were written in caló?" (16), he brings up an excellent point. If we were to outline briefly the factors we must consider in attempting to answer Arteaga's question, we would have to take note of the authorial decision to write in English and not caló; we would consider the publisher's aim of reaching the largest buying audience possible; we would need to acknowledge audience expectation; and so on. Arteaga implies that for him to reach the reading audience he seeks, he is constrained to write in the colonizer's language. Thus, Arteaga and other like-minded scholars view code-switching as an act of resistance or defiance, even at the risk of not being widely read, if read at all.

Momentarily setting aside the claim that code-switching is an act of resistance, I note that other scholars such as Steve Kellman see code-switching as an "urge towards verisimilitude" (*Switching Languages* xv) where writers such as Sandra Cisneros are, in fact, emulating a particular linguistic world, a world, as Rodriguez would agree, that is situated within the Latino/a family dynamic. For example, Kellman sees the code-switching found in Rolando Hinojosa-Smith's writings as "echoing actual speech, not patenting a new language" (xvii). Kellman's take is not inconsistent with Arteaga's.

Yet here we may address the central concern of this chapter, which is the function of code-switching and bilingualism as it affects both narrative worldmaking as well as the reader's reconstruction of the storyworld. I take it as a given that an author has mastery of the storyworld that he or she creates, though they are not in control of the meanings that can be ascribed to their texts.[12] However, rather than see an author's use of code-switching as an act of resistance, I also see it as an invitation for the reader to take up the challenge of rearticulating the storyworld from the blueprint provided by the author. While I recognize the writing of certain narratives and poetry as highly political acts, it is not a given that those printed texts have any political clout without a measurable readership. Further, though I agree that an author may write a narrative (or any document) as a sign of protest or resistance, the text itself cannot "resist."[13] Instead, what must be considered is the successful engagement with the author's storyworld as manifest in a stable mental model on the part of the reader. In question, then, are those identifiable attributes of a narrative that work to thwart readers' efforts by the use of certain enstranging[14] devices such as code-switching, self-translation, and so on.

---

12. This is not an absolute by any measure. Authors are ultimately urged to revise, redact, and otherwise adjust their narratives at the behest of their publishers. However, even if authors are compelled to alter their manuscripts before publication, the adjustments made are ones that they create—thus, my contention that authors are masters of their storyworlds.

13. The idea of a resisting text is found throughout postcolonial and ethnic-as-Other scholarship. On its face, this idea purports to empower the text, its subject, and its author. However, a truly resisting text is one that is hard to imagine. The power of any text lies in its engagement with its readership. A text may resist an ideology or hegemony only via those individuals who are prompted to collective action. In short, the resisting text is an imagined text. For an excellent exploration of the ability of ethnic literature to resist, see Patrick L. Hamilton's *Of Space and Mind Cognitive Mappings of Contemporary Chicano/a Fiction* (2011).

14. Viktor Shklovsky's notion of *ostranienie* is often translated as "defamiliarization" or "estrangement." However, Benjamin Sher's more recent translation of this word is "enstrange-

Further examination of the phenomenon of code-switching reveals the process and its product to be a complex issue. For many Latinos bilingual in Spanish and English, certain thoughts, ideas, and concepts may carry more nuance and complexity in one language than the other. As creators of narrative worlds, Latino/a authors have more materials (i.e., words) and devices (i.e., how to employ Spanish words at the level of narrative form) upon which to draw when deciding how best to inscribe the storyworld via the narrative blueprint. The availability of a larger lexicon does not necessitate or yield a higher (or lower) quality of narrative product any more than a painter with twice the available hues will produce a greater number of masterpieces than one who has only a few colors on the artist's palette. However, the freedoms and constraints surrounding the usage of a code-switching technique of narrative have a direct effect on storyworld design and audience reception.

READING RESISTANCE IN PIRI THOMAS'S *DOWN THESE MEAN STREETS*

Piri Thomas's *Down These Mean Streets* (hereafter *Streets*) works to challenge its audience on many levels, one of which is the level of racial politics in the United States. In a 1996 interview in the *Massachusetts Review,* Thomas recounted to Ilan Stavans ("Race and Mercy" 54) the first time he took a bus trip to the American South as a young man. The quotidian ride proceeded without incident until he reached the Mason-Dixon Line, whereupon another driver relieved the bus driver in something akin to a shift change. This new driver promptly ordered "all colored to the back." Aghast, Thomas watched as all of the African American passengers did as the driver ordered. Thomas, however, refused to relinquish his seat near the front, saying to the driver, "Look, I'm puertorriqueño." Incensed at Thomas's insolence, the bus driver menaced him and said, "I don't care what kind of nigger you are" (351). Eventually, Thomas acquiesced, urged by a friend to move to the back of the bus.

Thomas's anecdote, which appears in a slightly different form in *Streets*, is instructive for conceiving of how race intersects with nationalism and Latinidad in the United States. He narrativizes the pervasive and rampant racism of the pre–Civil Rights Act of 1964 in the American South, while displaying his own struggles to achieve self-identify as an Afro Latino. In addition, it is useful to examine the impetus for Thomas's anecdote: Ilan Stavans (Thomas's interviewer) provocatively stated, "Race is an issue ubiquitous in your [Thom-

ment," which seems to be a better fit for this concept of dehabituating things that have become so commonplace that they go unnoticed (xviii).

as's] work. In fact, very few Latino writers today are brave enough to discuss it in such plain, uninhibited ways as you do" (350). In effect, Stavans boldly equated an unflinching engagement with race in Latino/a fictional discourse with the bravery of challenging hegemony so unequivocally.

Yet Stavans's assumption is problematic: just because a Latino/a writer does not engage overtly with a given thematic element (i.e., race) within his or her narrative does not mean that such a writer is not "brave enough" to do so. On the other hand, Stavans is unfortunately correct in noting the lack of frank, direct engagement with issues of race or, as I claim, pertinent challenges to reader expectation and ideology, in the narratives of many U.S. Latino writers. But what Stavans and others recognize as "brave" or "bold" within Thomas's narrative is his use of language and dialect, which are bound to his struggles to come to terms with his own problems with self-identification.

Indeed, the historical context here is important in understanding my argument. When Thomas published his hard-hitting autobiography *Streets*, it put Afro Latino experiences in America on raw display for the world's consumption. Thomas's book relentlessly portrays an American trapped in the sulcus of identity, tantalizingly, frustratingly, a part of any number of groups without ever gaining full acceptance by any of them. Released less than three years after the Civil Rights Act of 1964, *Streets* was poised to serve as a clarion call for Afro Latinos, an ever-growing section of the American population. Instead, Thomas's account of his life was, has been, and continues to be one of the most banned books in American literature. As Dawn B. Sova notes, *Streets* was first challenged in 1971 by the Community School Board 1250 in Queens, New York. Thomas himself appeared during the trial, not in defense of the book's depiction of his life but rather for the right "of the truth to be said" (116). Leaving aside matters of truth for the moment, Thomas's book was banned for its narrative discourse—its manner of depicting the events of his life via the language used to give texture to that experience and the world.

Nearly five years later, in 1976, *Streets* "was among nine books that school board members in Island Trees Union Free School District No. 26 in New York identified as being 'objectionable.' After a review committee examined the books, *Streets* was placed on a restricted list because it was judged by the committee to be 'pornographic and filthy'" (117). It took a ruling by the United States Supreme Court to remove the ban on Thomas's book. Problematically or not, Thomas's book was assuredly a part of a larger movement toward recognition—Afro Latinos such as Arthur Schomburg had already initiated momentum in bringing attention to the cultural relevance and artistic endeavors of this segment of the population to which he himself belonged. Thus, the literary significance of Afro Latinidad, which promised to be a bonfire incited by *Streets*, proved to be a sputtering flame.

One contributing factor in the book's reception may have been that Thomas's experiences were so far from prior, widely available, representations of Latinos. Though the Nuyorican movement was already making its mark on American letters by 1967, *Streets*, in seeking to explore the sociopolitical, racial, and linguistic interstices in which Piri[15] continually finds himself, used several key attributes of U.S. Latino prose narrative—namely, code-switching and Afro Latinidad. So not only did Thomas challenge racial struggles based on his experiences in a pre–Civil Rights Act; he challenged the very notion of how one defines a Latino/a. These challenges are made palpable through his use of language and dialect.

Streets is notable for being one of the first Latino/a narratives that extensively integrated Spanish into what is basically an English text. As Eugene V. Mohr explains:

> Despite obvious limitations in style and structure and in the range of experiences described, Thomas's were the first books by a Nuyorican to gain a national reading. And Thomas, because of the insistent moral commentary which runs through his work, remains the most serious and interesting spokesman for second-generation Puerto Ricans in New York, even for those who deplore the image he projects and the willingness of readers and reviewers to accept that image as an accurate generalized description of "what it's like" in El Barrio. (61)

So, while *Streets* reached a national audience, it presented readers with significant challenges of language and content. When first published, *Streets* provided a glossary that explained "all Spanish and slang terms in the text" (ix). This glossary has become inextricably linked to the novel itself, even appearing in the thirtieth-anniversary edition published in 1997. Further, this glossary is a paratextual element insisted upon by the publisher, not Thomas.

I initiate my analysis of Thomas's text by jumping to the end, for the glossary can indicate how Spanish is used to create the storyworld blueprint. To begin with, the glossary is two pages long (339–40) and glosses 135 words and phrases for the convenience of the reader. More specifically, eight of the glossed terms are not derived from the Spanish language but rather are Eng-

---

15. As has become standard in scholarship where the biological author and protagonist are similarly identified, I will refer to the author as Thomas and the protagonist as Piri. Also see chapter 1.

lish colloquialisms such as *bread* (money), *fuzz* (cops), *stud* (any hip male), and *turf* (home street). The glossary of *Streets* betrays the publisher's concern that buying audiences will be thwarted by the languages and dialectal variants Thomas uses. This publishing decision also reveals a very material concern that publishers have when imagining audiences who will purchase works of Latino/a literature. While the glossary is clearly an attempt at making storyworld reconstruction less taxing for the reader, the intrusion of a glossary within the covers of Thomas's book nullifies a significant challenge his text presents to readers. Therefore, one way of looking at how *Streets* challenges readers is to locate the publisher's effort to alleviate those challenges in the first place. We then might consider how the text functions without the glossary, as Thomas originally intended.

I move now from the glossary at the end of *Streets* to the beginning of the text and the prologue. Thomas's initial use of Spanish appears on the first page of the prologue when he uses the word *mundo* or "world" (ix). Next to the word *mundo* appears an asterisk with a footnote at the bottom of the page that says "All Spanish and slang terms in the text are explained in the glossary that begins on page 332" (ix). With this footnote, the monolingual English reader is immediately set at ease; all Spanish that appears in the text has been stripped of its ability to destabilize the reader. While I will examine how paratexts function within a Latino/a work of literature in greater detail in chapter 4, I must mention here that the presence of the glossary as a reference work within Thomas's book undermines the narrative world Thomas creates, as well as subordinating Thomas all the while. Unlike the paratextual material that appears in Junot Díaz's *The Brief Wondrous Life of Oscar Wao* and Sandra Cisneros's *Caramelo*—paratexts created by their respective authors that serve as a structural ingredient of the storyworld—the footnote and glossary in *Streets* were created by someone other than Thomas. And, since the glossary serves as reference material for the reader, that is to say, because it functions as an authority that hovers above Thomas's text, there is the sense that Thomas's text requires a corrective, that it is unable to stand on its own.

The insertion of reference materials within a text, of course, is an important feature of scholarly editions intended for use by students seeking to make sense of difficult material within a work of literature—such as the Norton Critical Editions. Though a scholarly edition's defining and contextualizing of materials is expected because the scholarly apparatus (e.g., footnotes) is presented as an authority, such apparatuses rarely take up the straightforward issue of translation. In other words, scholarly editions work to enrich a student's understanding of issues that may be missed by the student due to a lack of historical context, for example. The glossary in *Streets*, however, is insultingly didactic, for it robs Thomas of the import of his words as well as denying readers the opportunity to learn new words by attending to how they are used in context.

Another way of looking at the presence of the glossary in *Streets* is to understand its superfluous nature. For example, the use of the word *mundo* cited above becomes intelligible when read in its context: "This is a bright *mundo*, my streets, my *barrio de noche*, / With its thousand lights, hundreds of millions of colors / Mingling with noises, swinging street sounds of cars and curses, / Sounds of joys and sobs that make music. / If anyone listens real close, he can hear its heart beat—" (ix). *Mundo* is the noun that is further described and enriched by the phrases "my streets" and "my *barrio de noche*." Even a reader who does not know that *mundo* translates as "world" can understand, by the context in which the word appears, that Piri is speaking of his immediate environs and surroundings—the space he inhabits and the rich texture created by the "noises," "sounds," and "heart beat" that partially form his mundo.

Further, the prologue is itself both an announcement to the reader and an invitation into Thomas's world. The prologue opens in direct address: "YEE-AH!! Wanna know how many times I've stood on a rooftop and yelled out to anybody: / 'Hey, World—here I am. Hallo, World—this is Piri. That's me. / I wanna tell ya I'm here—you bunch of mother-jumpers— / I'm here, and I want recognition, whatever that mudder-fuckin word means'" (ix). In this opening, Thomas establishes that Piri has longed to reach out to an audience, even a faceless audience in the dark Harlem night—that he yearns to make his presence known by explaining that "this is Piri," even though it takes him the entire length of the narrative to come close to understanding who he is. Three times he vehemently states that he is "here," an emphatic declaration that puts his resiliency and capacity for survival on full display. His opening salvo is a direct challenge to those who have heretofore ignored him or his story, calling them "mother-jumpers." Piri's demands are frank and indicate what lies ahead in the rest of the book: "I want recognition." Finally, he expresses his frustration with his inability to satisfactorily define what the word *recognition* means. The opening to the prologue, then, establishes issues of character formation vis-à-vis his world as well as the difficulty of understanding what is meant when certain words are used. Because this is the overriding impetus for *Streets*, the glossary diminishes the dynamic of the author-text-reader relationship, as it removes one of the prominent linguistic challenges Thomas presents to the reader.

CODE-SWITCHING IN *DOWN THESE MEAN STREETS*

But if the glossary were not an original part of the authorial blueprint in *Streets*, a consideration of the text sans the publisher's insertion of reference material could help us see the sorts of challenges Thomas intended audiences to encounter and negotiate. Indeed, *Streets* is a linear narrative that takes Piri from pre-adolescence to adulthood with only intermittent analepses and prolepses. This adherence to linearity and chronology removes any sort of complexities that may arise from deviations from chronological telling. Instead, challenges to readers manifest in the form of thematic content and the use of language. Yet what is clear is that Thomas is not using language as a means of confounding the reader for purely aesthetic reasons, as we will see later in this chapter in Giannina Braschi's *Yo-Yo Boing!* For instance, Thomas has designed his storyworld with a monolingual English reader in mind, for with the exception of 127 different words and phrases in Spanish, the 300-plus-page book is predominantly written in English.[16] While the very thought of using a lexicon of just over one hundred Spanish words was perceived as challenging enough for the publisher to insert a glossary, Thomas's technique of suffusing his narrative with Spanish actually nurtures the reader and, by degrees, makes the need for a glossary mostly superfluous.

For example, Piri often expresses himself in Spanish only to immediately translate what he just said into English. Early on in *Streets* Piri is roaming the streets after being struck by his father for making too much noise. He soon happens upon two junkies in his building who are about to shoot themselves up with heroin. When Piri makes the decision to leave the area, he startles the junkies: "I got up, and the scraping of my shoes started a panic. The two junkies jumped up and made it. They thought I was *la hara*—a cop. Their running feet down the stairs made me feel sorry for them. But, Jesus, I was hong-ree" (5). Piri immediately translates his use of *la hara,* an indication that while he wants to be faithful to certain lexical markers and signifiers he is comfortable in uttering, he also wants his narrative to be understood by an English speaker.

It is helpful to note the context of this first example of self-translation in *Streets*. Besides his quest for understanding his identity and place within both his family and society, Piri's interaction with the various languages and dialects is the hallmark of his ability to express himself. Further, Piri continually misreads situations, forcing himself to account for them in the best way he can. In this case, Piri misunderstands two situations involving adults, which

---

16. The majority of works of Latino/a literature are unequivocally targeted at an English-speaking audience.

is only natural for the twelve-year-old boy he is at the time. First, he cannot understand why his father has reacted so violently upon being awakened. Piri cannot make himself understood to his father, and so he is frustrated in his inability to express himself—a theme that arises numerous times within the narrative: "He didn't give me a chance. Even before the first burning slap of his belt awakened tears of pain, I was still trying to get words out that would make everything all right again" (4). Piri operates under the assumption that if only he could use certain words to communicate what he is feeling, his life would then be devoid of hardship and emotional duress. Accordingly, so much of Piri's bildung is centered on learning the uses and abuses of language. This brief but powerful scene establishes the larger issues that play out in *Streets*. Piri constantly finds himself in situations of heightened emotionality, which dampens his ability to communicate, resulting in a dynamic relationship between language and emotion.

When Piri decides to return home lest his mother worry, he encounters the two heroin junkies beneath the stairwell of his apartment complex. He misunderstands one of the junkies who says to the other, "*Coño*, man, cook this shit up" (5). While the junkie is referencing the preparation of heroin, Piri interprets the word *cook* literally: "My mouth began to water. I wondered what they were going to cook," he says (5). So the inability to express himself to his father, as well as his misunderstanding of what the two junkies were doing, both precede his self-translation of the noun *la hara*. Here one of the dominant themes of Thomas's text—the struggle to understand and the need to be understood—manifests in how Piri uses Spanish throughout the text.

In particular, Piri's use of Spanish is often aligned with his tender relationship with his mother. Of all the members of Piri's family, his mother is the one who unambiguously uses Spanish throughout the text. In fact, Piri's mother code-switches consistently in her reported speech, and her speech most resembles Piri's own use of language. Though Marta Sánchez and others have examined how issues of masculinity and machismo are depicted in Thomas's text, there is reverence to the powers of the maternal figures in Piri's life. He often expresses his notions of salvation and recuperation in terms of his relationship to his mother and his idealistic romance with Trina, the girl he betroths himself to midway through *Streets*. In fact, Piri's language shifts when he speaks to these two women and when he reports dialogue or conversations with them.

An early scene reveals Piri's maternal connection to Spanish. One morning after Piri's father loses his job with the WPA, Piri's mother keeps him home from school. "*Hijo*, today you no go to school. I want you to go to the Home Relief Office and help me explain about your father losing his job with the WPA," she tells him (41). In effect, Piri's mother requires his facility with both English and Spanish. This fact reveals much about the Thomas family's material reality and how language factors into the very economics of the household and the ability of the caregivers to provide basic sustenance to the children. The scene that depicts Piri's efforts at translation is a masterful depiction of how power is located within language.

"It seemed that every mother had brought a kid to interpret for her," (42) Piri remarks when he observes how many families have come to apply for assistance at Home Relief. As he and his mother await their turn, Piri cannot help attending to the various snatches of conversation he hears. He identifies a man named Mr. King as the "most understanding investigator" (42), to whom so many women are pleading their cases in turn. At one point, Mr. King remarks to one woman of her husband's tirades, "He says things like that because he's just overwrought" (42). Piri's mind dwells on the word "overwrought": "It sounded like a word you'd use when somebody had split his wig" (43). Piri's instincts as to what overwrought means are not far from the mark; the woman's husband is clearly under mental duress, and Piri's precocity shows his penchant for linguistic autodidacticism.

Often in this remarkable scene, Piri listens to the various mothers reduced to begging, and it both tires him and triggers memories of all of the times he himself has been to the Home Relief Office. He is brought out of his reverie when it is his turn to interpret and translate for his mother. Of the investigator's questions, Piri states, "I broke down all his words into Spanish for Momma, all the time thinking about the stiff, cardboard Home Relief checks and how they brought life to many" (44). What remains implicit in Piri's remark is that his bilingualism is what gives his mother the ability to plead her case to the investigator at all. Further, Piri fulfills several functions as narrator in this scene. Not only does he twice report his mother's dialogue in its original Spanish, but he also manages to complete the dual task of translating his mother's words to the investigator while simultaneously translating for his audience. This is an example of James Phelan's theory of disclosure functions that follow a dual track wherein the narrator conveys one message to the narratee while the implied author uses the narrator to convey a message to the audience and, specifically, what he describes as "redundant telling, necessary disclosure" (12). Yet it is slightly different in the scene where Piri speaks to the Home Relief investigator, for his redundant telling is inextricably linked to his act of translation. In this case, Piri's translation of his mother's words comprises a salient aspect of the scene that allows us to examine the constraints on Thomas's uses of Spanish throughout the text.

It is easy to see that Piri's translation of his mother's words to his interlocutor is a device that allows a monolingual English reader to understand what Piri's mother says when she states: "*Déle que tu padre perdió su trabajo, porque el boss le tenía antipatía,*" and later, "*Piri, déle sábanas, frizas, un matre, zapatos para los nene, abrigos y unos pantalones para ti*" (44–45).[17] When Piri then translates his mother's statements into English for the investigator, the monolingual English reader is then aligned with the investigator as Piri speaks to both at the same moment; both are awaiting Piri's translation. The result is that, in such moments when Piri must translate or interpret Spanish into English within his storyworld, it is because he is *compelled* to do so. In this scene with his mother and the investigator, Piri acts as the intermediary between two entities who, in other contexts, wield greater power than he does. Yet here, Piri is in the middle of the power dynamic: he is still subordinate to the investigator while having at least as much authority as his mother, if not more.

To press this point further, this scene is illuminating in how it depicts the issue of translation, and especially how it treats the subject of audience. We can identify at least three receivers of Piri's translation of his mother's words: the investigator, the narratee, and the ideal readership. Piri assumes the investigator to be a monolingual English speaker, and so he accordingly translates his mother's first statement with a clear, unadulterated rendering of her Spanish into English. But immediately the investigator replies, "I gathered that, son." And more specifically, he clarifies for Piri, "My Spanish is not that great, but I catch a little here and there" (44). In this moment, Thomas puts on full display how linguistic assumptions are often tethered to phenotype. Piri cannot grasp the potentiality that the investigator can mostly understand what Piri's mother is saying. For him, the investigator is associated not only with English but with a specific kind of English: "[the investigator] started to read a stack of papers that had all our personal life put down in good English for all to dig" (45). Piri's recognition that his family's life story has been rendered into government legalese is, in miniature, not unlike the effort Piri takes in telling his own life story to his audience. But rather than the supposed authoritative account found in the investigator's stack of papers, Piri assumes the authority to narrate his own story in the manner of English that best suits his purpose of the telling. Moreover, Piri is best positioned to narrate when he has the ability to code-switch when it suits his storytelling purposes.

---

17. "Tell him that your father lost his job because the boss didn't like him.... Piri, tell him [we need] sheets, blankets, a mattress, shoes for the kids, coats and some pants for you."

UNNECESSARY TRANSLATIONS

Still, the matter of unnecessary self-translation bears further examination. For example, at the end of chapter 5, Piri recounts how much more enjoyable it is to go to the market with his father than his mother: "Poppa discounted the vendors' friendly '*Cómo estas?*' He said that 'How are you?' were the first Spanish words the vendors learned so they could win the people's confidence and gyp them in their own language. I wondered if Poppa didn't like Jews the way I didn't like Italians" (46). Piri's translation of "*Cómo estas?*" is redundant both to himself and to bilingual readers. Unlike the scene when Piri translates his mother's words to another character, Piri translates his father's words to his narratee, who apparently can understand other moments of Piri's narrative that are given in untranslated Spanish but cannot do so here. This moment in Piri's narrative forces us to scrutinize and understand why Piri translates his father's words, words that must be offered in Spanish because they are bound to Piri's reflection of the wisdom given to him by his father.

As "*Cómo estas?*" are literally the first words the market vendors learn, it is understandable why Piri reports the exact words his father has marked as a ploy by the vendors—Spanish words suited for a specific rhetorical occasion. Yet the second sentence reveals the awkwardness of superfluous translation that arises outside of the storyworld. One question that may help get at the underlying impetus for this moment of translation is to ask for whom Piri translates his father's words. When Piri says "He said that 'How are you?' were the first Spanish words," his translation has caused him to be inaccurate. Clearly "How are you?" is not in Spanish within Piri's narrative. If Thomas were striving for verisimilitude, as Kellman observes of many bilingual writers (*Switching*), Piri would repeat the Spanish words uttered by the vendors, the words his father was quick to point out with disdain as a confidence-gaining trick; for it is not that the vendors say "How are you?" in the effort to complete a sales transaction, but rather the vendors blithely mimic a standard greeting in Spanish: "*Cómo estas?*" The vendors' disingenuous use of a customer's native tongue gives them a certain duplicity and falseness as far as Piri's father, and therefore Piri, are concerned. And yet Piri falsely translates the Spanish greeting in his own narrative. Why is this?

As Pérez Firmat says, "Of all the varieties of translation, perhaps none is more faithless than self-translation. Although the technical challenges are the same, it adds a dimension of personal and creative reassessment missing from second-party translations. The author who translates his or her own work knows it too well, rather than well enough" (*Tongue Ties* 105). Pérez Firmat's contention with self-translation is the endeavor of translating one's own writing completely into another, as in an author who writes a novel in Spanish and then translates the same novel into English—a writer such as Rolando Hinojosa-Smith. What level of disdain, then, would Pérez Firmat have for a writer who checks his own use of Spanish by needlessly supplanting it with an English translation? Again, Pérez Firmat's experiences as a light-skinned Cuban émigré informs his take on the use of language, which is rooted in specific historical contexts.

This moment of self-translation in *Streets* is indicative of the historical context of the book's publication (1967), the publisher's insistence that the text not alienate monolingual English readers, and the imposition that a monolingual English audience places on a bilingual author. In addition, Thomas's book cannot, as Giannina Braschi's *Yo-Yo Boing!* does, challenge the monolingual English reader to the point that at least half of the narrative is in untranslated, unglossed Spanish. Thomas's book, banned for its frank depictions of sex, racism, and drug use, works hard to naturalize its use of Spanish for the English reader. Especially in the first half of the novel, language looms large in the narrative progression. In chapter 10 Piri discusses moving to Long Island from Harlem—the first time in his life that he has been away from home:

> This Long Island was a foreign country. It looked so pretty and clean but it spoke a language you couldn't dig. The paddy boys talked about things you couldn't dig, or maybe better, they couldn't dig you. Yeah, that was it; they didn't dig your smooth talk, and you always felt like on the rim of belonging. No matter how much you busted your hump trying to be one of them, you'd never belong, they wouldn't let you. Maybe they couldn't. Maybe they didn't belong themselves. (*Streets* 88)

Piri's simile that describes his feeling "like on the rim of belonging" is an apt characterization of the bilingual Latino/a writer in the early contemporary period of Latino/a literature in the United States. Indeed, as Pérez Firmat observes:

> Given the number and size of the Spanish-speaking communities of the United States, it is perhaps surprising that what has come to be known as "Latino literature," the imaginative writing by and about Hispanics in this country, exists almost entirely in English. As the monolingual expression of a largely bilingual population, Latino literature detaches culture from language, celebrating the former even as it silences the latter. Even the English of Latino writers, with some exceptions, bears little resemblance to the hybrid sounds and rhythms of the barrios where many of them grew up.

What happened to the García girls has also happened to the writers: They have lost their accents. (*Tongue Ties* 137)

No matter how hard he tries, Piri can't "dig" the language spoken outside of his home. Thus, it is easy to assert that Latino writers have lost their accent, as Pérez Firmat claims.

On the other hand, *Streets,* despite its penchant for removing linguistic obstacles from its monolingual English readers, maintains a recognizable devotion to its Spanish accent, its mother tongue. We can see the tension that arises in the narration, especially when Piri recounts his mother's speech, for it is his mother that is the predominant Spanish speaker (other than Piri) in the book. The end of chapter 10 is perhaps the most prominent example of this tension. Piri is frustrated at how his phenotypically dark skin makes him "some nigger" in the eyes of strangers who cannot keep from making racist comments within Piri's earshot—comments exacerbated because Piri is with Betty, a White girl. When Piri makes his decision to return to Harlem, he tells his mother, "I can't get along with anything, no matter what I do. Nothing falls right. I don't like Long Island and *los blancos,* and this world full of shits. I can't put my hand on it, but there is something wrong with all of us—Pops, José, James, Sis, me, and the whole world. Moms, I think the only ones got the right to be happy is dead" (90–91). Though she disagrees with his decision, Piri's mother acquiesces to his resolve, saying, "Take care of yourself. *Que Dios te bendiga y te guarde.* God bless you and protect you" (91). It is a tender moment that will affect Piri for the remainder of the narrative.

Yet if we are to understand his mother's dialogue, she gives him a blessing in Spanish and then redundantly gives him the exact blessing in English. Clearly, Piri is bilingual and does not need to hear his mother's blessing translated for him. Rather, the translation is, again, for the benefit of the reader. Now, it may be that Piri's mother is redundant in her speech and that she continually translates her own Spanish into English for the benefit of her son, but this is highly unlikely. Remember that Piri's mother cannot effectively communicate in English to begin with, as demonstrated in the scene with the Home Relief investigator. Thus, we have a clash between disclosure functions and narrator functions, as described by Phelan.

When Thomas (as implied author) provides an English translation of the blessing spoken in Spanish, we see it as a device that benefits the monolingual English reader and aids in storyworld reconstruction. Even without the help of the glossary as a reference, Thomas renders this moment as lucidly as possible. However, when considering Piri as narrator, this device of self-translation compromises his reliability as a narrator, even if it is in the service of a lucid narrative. In essence, Piri puts words in his mother's mouth—English words at that. This is a significant compromise at the level of narrative design, one that illuminates how issues of audience and storyworld reconstruction supersede mimetic functions in a code-switching text. In other words, the reader's ability to make sense of the text overrides Piri's act of reporting exactly what his mother said without having to translate it.

Interestingly, Phelan contends that readers have an instinctive impulse to "preserve the mimetic" (*Living* 2). In this case, an interpretation that desires to preserve the mimetic would suggest that Piri's mother wished to make herself completely understood to her son by emphatically stating her blessing in the two languages spoken in their home. Phelan gives the example from Robert Browning's dramatic monologue "My Last Duchess," in which the Duke redundantly makes a statement already known to himself and his addressee, the envoy. When the Duke proclaims "The Count *your master's* known munificence," Phelan sees an example of an "uncharacteristically gratuitous" reiteration that is seemingly superfluous (2). Similarly, Piri's mother's translation of her Spanish blessing to her son is equally superfluous. Like the Duke in Browning's poem, the blessing is redundant as far as Piri is concerned. Thus, the unnecessary translation of Piri's mother's blessing is for the reader's benefit, reminding us that Thomas has a monolingual English reader in mind.

In early examples of Latino/a literature, such as *Streets*, adherence to the mimetic is a salient feature only insofar as it does not override the needs of a monolingual English reader. That is to say, if a Latino/a author from this time period in U.S. history (i.e., 1967) wished to create a storyworld that truly reflected his bilingual experience, limits to the level of bilingualism in their narratives would be manifest and imposed externally—by editors, publishing houses, and readers. The further such authors pushed the use of Spanish in their mostly English texts, the more concessions (e.g., self-translation) and devices (i.e., glossaries) would need to be adopted to ameliorate the distancing effects of a bilingual blueprint for their storyworld.

The rather shocking result of this sort of a priori constraint is that, to a large degree, and because of necessary self-translations to accommodate a monolingual English reader, Latino/a narratives that purport to be autobiographical and drawn from the author's experience are necessarily a fictionalized account. In the case of *Streets*, it is evident from the text that Piri's mother cannot converse comfortably in English, yet her direct discourse is often rendered in English. This is a fascinating point that raises questions of fictionality. In other words, if Piri reports that his mother said words that she actually did not say, can this be considered Dorrit Cohn's "signpost of fictionality"? If so, this move to fictionalize certain elements of autobiographical material leads to at least one provocative conclusion: Latino/a authors are compelled at times, if not often, to conjure moments of fiction within their narrative blueprints, not because it suits the design of their projected storyworlds but because audiences and publishers demand it. As Pérez Firmat reminds us, "Perhaps more than other types of serious writing, Latino literature caters to the limitations of its audience, which expects that the author and her stand-ins will act as cultural tour guides. [. . .] Like other ethnic writing, Latino literature is bound to a pedagogical imperative that requires it not only to distract, entertain, elevate, but also to teach" (*Tongue Ties* 140). While I agree with Pérez Firmat, I would also add that in rendering some of the narrative in Spanish, the publishers and audiences have been challenged to accept this issue of narrative design—even if publishers still have the power to insert a glossary between the covers of a book like *Streets*. Thomas's text opens a space for the code-switching Latino/a writers who would follow him and whose level of bilingual mastery would arguably culminate in Giannina Braschi's *Yo-Yo Boing!*

In the end, Piri challenges the reader by attempting to design an unfiltered narrative that moves to express his life experiences in ways that are true to his lived experience, experiences that are generally not shared by his readership. However, that Thomas is compelled to acquiesce to moments of superfluous self-translation and a specifically targeted glossary speaks of the publisher's conception of what might be viewed as too onerous a challenge for the book's readership. That Thomas's frank depictions of drug use, violence, and sex ended up being more of a challenge to readers' sensibilities, as opposed to his use of Spanish, underscores how Thomas's publisher treats the Spanish language as a foreign aspect of Piri's experience rather than trusting the readership to acknowledge this ingredient of Piri's narrative. Rather than allow readers to accept Thomas's challenges presented to them by his narrative, the publisher's intrusion signals the historical context of how otherness was handled in the late 1960s.

BILINGUALISM IN GIANNINA BRASCHI'S *YO-YO BOING!*

If *Streets* was an opening salvo for a code-switching aesthetic in Latino/a literature that initially proposed a challenging reading situation for monolingual English readers, *Yo-Yo Boing!* (hereafter *Yo-Yo*) is an unabashed assault on readers, thanks in large part to fact that Giannina Braschi is writing in the 1990s rather than the late 1960s, as was Thomas. Braschi's text presents many challenges in storyworld reconstruction. Initial reviewers lauded Braschi's virtuoso performance and the deft manner in which she works with both

English and Spanish. Indeed, unlike the majority of Latino/a narratives in the United States that are predominately written in English with only sparse usage of Spanish, *Yo-Yo* goes to great lengths to use both languages, and some have identified a third language in Braschi's text: Spanglish.

Some guiding questions will help orient my analysis of Braschi's novel. First, under what assumptions of audience does Braschi design the storyworld blueprint? Second, what authorial decisions present significant challenges in storyworld reconstruction? Indeed, these two questions are undoubtedly related, as Braschi's notion of an ideal readership allows her the freedom to select devices within the purview of that ideal audience. On the other hand, any given reader unequipped with the decoding and reading abilities of Braschi's ideal audience will experience difficult, if not insuperable, impediments when working to co-construct a mental model of Braschi's storyworld. Although the most prominent difficulty readers will encounter when reading *Yo-Yo* is likely to be its use of language, the structure of the narrative discourse itself presents further challenges in reading the text. In effect, Braschi unites two sets of reading challenges for her audience to negotiate. In fact, *Yo-Yo* is arguably the most challenging Latino/a novel ever written for a monolingual English audience.

The subject of translation has been a significant issue in this chapter, and here the topic of translation as a challenge to the reader truly comes to the fore. In considering a novel such as *Yo-Yo* at the level of language barriers, we might also speak of the translator as a kind of ideal audience. That is to say, in order to even begin to attempt to face the challenges embedded within the narrative discourse of the novel, the reader needs a basic level of mastery of both English and Spanish. Of course a monolingual English reader will find his or her own inability to read Spanish to be a serious impediment to reading the short stories of, say, Jorge Luis Borges in the original Spanish. But even someone who can read Spanish fluently will invariably be presented with certain challenges in reconstructing Borges's labyrinthine storyworlds. Thus, there is the challenge of language comprehension, as well as the challenge of decoding the narrative discourse so that a representative mental model might be constructed. For his or her part, the translator can help alleviate the problem of storyworld reconstruction at the level of language. Thus, what a translator has to say about translating a work can tell us much about the challenges of language.

Tess O'Dwyer, the translator of *Yo-Yo* into English, has spoken of the seemingly implausible difficulty of translating a novel that is already, in essence, half translated:

> After translating Giannina Braschi's collected poetry into English, I figured her new bilingual novel *Yo-Yo Boing!* would be a piece of cake. After all, *Empire of Dreams* is poetry and *Yo-Yo Boing!* is fiction. Shouldn't prose be easier? And, wouldn't it stand to reason that a bilingual book would take half the time to translate since the author already did half the job? I thought so, but it didn't take long to change my mind. (34)

O'Dwyer, herself confident in translating the source language Spanish into the target language English, was apparently put off by Braschi's bilingual novel. Yet O'Dwyer's comment regarding the novel's audience, written while she was in the midst of her translation project, is particularly illuminating: "The ideal audience for *Yo-Yo Boing!* is obviously a savvy bilingual reader who can enjoy the novel hot off the shelf 'as is.' Others will have to wait until I can figure out how to translate all the code-switching bilingual dialogues, without losing all their humor and gusto" (35). Here we have a professional translator who admits to her own difficulties while working with a code-switching text, a somewhat stunning statement.

YO-YO BOING! AND ITS CRITICAL RECEPTION

The critical reception and scholarly examinations of *Yo-Yo* are at once laudatory and hesitant. It is clear that Braschi's text causes critics discomfort when they speak of it. An anonymous reviewer in *Publishers Weekly* called the novel "a literary liberation and a frustrating challenge" (49). For the reviewer, the source of frustration is not merely the predominance of Spanish within the text but also the narrative discourse:

> Dispensing with a traditional story line, the work takes the form of an exuberant discussion involving an indeterminate number of speakers. Confusingly, these interlocutors are indicated only by a dash, not by name, while they yo-yo between languages and from subject to subject: writers, films, sex, childhood, family and, ultimately, Puerto Rican artistic expression in New York City. (49)

Even this reviewer betrays the expectation readers have for a "traditional story line" with clearly delineated characters, and because Braschi owns every aspect of her storyworld blueprint due to her equal mastery and fluency in Spanish and English, the reviewer sees this as an aesthetic affront to his or her effort in reading. In conclusion, the reviewer states, "Braschi's mélange of prose and poetry, English and Spanish, is admirable for its energy, its experimental format and its insistence on a Spanglish as a literary language, but those very qualities will render it of interest only to the most literary-minded of bilingualists" (49). This is a clear instance of damning with faint praise by a reviewer whose prior expectations of Latino/a narrative (to say nothing of narrative in general) could only have yielded a lukewarm response.

By contrast, David William Foster's review of *Yo-Yo* engages with Braschi's project on its own terms rather than seeking to make it fit certain expectations of what a novel (Latino/a or otherwise) ought to be. Foster's review reflects his expertise in matters of Latin American and U.S. Latino/a literary and cultural production:

> Code switching is a discourse modality usually associated with Chicano writing. However, one of the most notable characteristics of Braschi's novel is the agile and productive use of an interlingua poised between English and Spanish. [. . .] Her novel is a superb exploration of the lived experiences of urban life for Hispanics, in this case New York City, and her principal interest is in representing how individuals move in and out of different cultural coordinates, including one so crucial as language. (202)

Foster, who, like Braschi, can move from Spanish to English with ease, is able to see beyond the in-your-face presentation of a language other than English. Whereas so many postcolonial critics from Homi Bhabha to Guyatri Spivak have articulated a theory of resistance to hegemony at the level of discourse, seeing the introduction of languages other than English as a means of challenging ideopolitical structures, Foster's review does not concentrate on this supposed function of language. Instead of seeing Spanish as a means of undermining English-language hegemony, Foster considers Braschi's text as reflecting Spanish- and English-speaking worlds as coeval, even in the heart of New York City at the cusp of the twenty-first century—what he identifies as an "interlingua" and "a synergetic fusion" (203). Rather than see Spanish infusion in an English text as resistant or disruptive, Foster sees Braschi's equal use and treatment of *both* languages as something new, as an "interlingua."

However, José Torres-Padilla, in his essay "When Hybridity Doesn't Resist," takes issue with Braschi's decision to foreground the aesthetic of her novel. Torres-Padilla states, "By not taking a firm stance of resistance against imperialism and hegemony, by actually obscuring this power relationship behind an argument over aesthetics, Braschi's novel in fact supports the continuing colonial status of Puerto Rico and undermines any desire for self-determination that might effect real change" (292). While in other parts of this book I've noted issues of authorial constraint that originate from publishers, producers, and audiences, Torres-Padilla's essay is an example of the a priori critical pressure from scholars that is often applied to ethnic writers. For Torres-Padilla, Braschi's project fails to press the issue that he sees as the central concern of Puerto Rican writers—the island's relationship with the United States. In other words, according to Torres-Padilla, Braschi's novel is so concerned with aesthetics (both in content and at the level of form) that the text loses is potential to impact the material reality of Puerto Ricans as well as the consequences of colonialism that still affect Puerto Rico today—as if that were the sole reason for Braschi to write her novel.

Unfortunately, this is the same sort of criticism that was leveled at both critics and producers of literature since the time of the Russian Formalists and perhaps to Plato, and even more recently with Latin American Boom authors. The Russian Formalists such as Viktor Shklovsky and Boris Tomashevsky desired to delve deeply into observable phenomena within a text. While their work continues to resonate within literary criticism, opponents of their method averred that the Russian Formalists were unconcerned with issues that lay outside of the text. This is true, but their specialization should not be considered a failure. Similarly, the Latin American Boom authors such as Carlos Fuentes, Alejo Carpentier, Julio Cortázar, and Gabriel García Márquez, while praised for their exploration of narrative form, were nevertheless criticized for being too concerned with the formal design of their narratives. Torres-Padilla's take on *Yo-Yo* echoes these attacks on literature that engages with social, ideopolitical struggles in a different way.

Narratives that introduce nonhegemonic languages amidst hegemonic ones are seen as resistant. Interestingly, however, Torres-Padilla's argument is that *Yo-Yo* "intentionally merges various registers in the two languages but not in any way that could be typified as resistant or oppositional" (293). Using Homi Bhabha's articulation of what resistance means in terms of language and language within a text vis-à-vis hybridity (161–62), even Torres-Padilla is critical of Bhabha's flimsy explanation of how hybridity can have a material consequence on our reality and not simply in academic conversations:

> Bhabha has been taken to task for this position, which seems to neglect questions of power that go beyond the abstract or the discursive. I mention it here, however, because even this rather feeble resistance eludes Braschi's text. *Yo-Yo Boing!* certainly does not present any outright political opposition to the United States and its power as a colonizer over Puerto Rico. The hybridity in the text consists of an overlaying and interweaving of varying

registers in both languages, a consistent deft dialogic playing of one language with and against the other. (294)

So, even by Bhabha's standards, Torres-Padilla sees Braschi's text as a failure at the level of resistance.

AUTHORIAL CONTROL OF THE NARRATIVE BLUEPRINT

This brings me to a somewhat obvious question: Why should it be in Giannina Braschi's agenda to create a narrative world that is strategically designed to resist hegemony in ways that fit with other people's expectations? There should be no mandate that any author identified as a member of a marginalized group must write one type of novel, poem, play, film, and so on. In fact, this is the very issue at the heart of this book—the notion that a Latino/a author *is compelled*, a priori, to create works of literature that do a specific kind of political and ideological work within society. Now, I recognize that certain works of literature may have the power to mobilize individuals toward a collective action, and certainly authors may take this view in creating their narrative worlds. But this surely is not the only thing so-called multicultural literatures can do.

The moment we begin to impose a kind of essentialist agenda on our creators of literature, we immediately restrict and constrain what authors may or may not do. And by constraining them, we limit the possibility for narrative expansion of form and genre. Torres-Padilla rails against the overt aestheticism in *Yo-Yo*, claiming it to be "rife with bourgeois fetishes, frivolous talk about material things and a cloying concern with name-dropping" (299). He cannot conceive of the possibility that Braschi can make masterful use of bilingualism and hybridity while not blatantly furthering a particular political agenda. What's more, he cannot acknowledge that Braschi's novel can still pursue ideological and political agendas even with its concern with matters of aesthetics.

Here we can turn back to the claim that undergirds this book, that is, my claim that Latino/a authors are able to design, create, and publish texts that are blueprints for all manner of storyworlds. It is also worthwhile here to remember the historical context in which Piri Thomas and Giannina Braschi, both Puerto Rican, are writing. In addition, the life experiences of both of these writers tell us much about their approach to writing. Thomas, having garnered much of his education through his experiences on the streets as well as in prison, writes a bildungsroman in much the same pattern. Because he experienced racism, exploitative violence, drug use, and prison in particular ways, his narrative similarly exposes the socioeconomic factors that worked to bring his experiences to fruition in the first place. Though there is artistry and craft in Thomas's narrative, the fact that his "based on actual events" narrative and his lived experience are very nearly superimposed contrasts greatly with Braschi's narrative methods.

As her bionote states in *The Norton Anthology of Latino Literature*, Braschi was "born into the upper class in Puerto Rico [...]. Before she went to college, she had become the youngest female tennis champion in the history of Puerto Rico. She studied comparative literature in Madrid, Rome, and Paris, and the experimental and cosmopolitan nature of her creative writing partly reflects these European intellectual influences" (1971). Barring differences in innate talent and ability, the accident of Thomas's and Braschi's births allowed each of them to have vastly different life experiences that significantly influenced not only how they learned the craft of writing (Braschi in Madrid; Thomas in Sing Sing Prison) but also how they self-identified as Latinos. Add to this each author's respective relationship with English and Spanish, and we begin to see how a more than thirty-year gap between *Streets* and *Yo-Yo* tells us much about Latino/a authorial concerns and constraints when designing narrative worlds for a reading audience in the United States. Consider, for example, Thomas's notable but halting use of Spanish, together with the ex post facto glossary appended to it by his publisher. Conversely, Braschi wields her multilingualism with confidence and defiance.

There is no glossary in *Yo-Yo Boing!* to aid a monolingual reader, and that is an important fact that is not to be missed. While nearly every Latino/a work of literature is targeted at a monolingual reader, Braschi's ideal audience is clearly bilingual. And when I say bilingual, I do not mean a monolingual English reader who can recognize Spanish words in context such as *tortilla* or *policía*. I mean a reader who can read entire chapters of literary Spanish as easily as literary English. Braschi's equal treatment and use of both English and Spanish is, in part, what Torres-Padilla finds so disconcerting. The Spanish within *Yo-Yo Boing!* does not merely appear as a method of destabilizing English; the Spanish is as predominant as the English within her novel. Unlike Torres-Padilla, who sees this as a failed experiment of hybridity, I see Braschi's novel as a successful manifestation of how challenging a Latino/a work of literature can be—not only at the level of language but at the level of narrative discourse as well. In short, Braschi's use of bilingualism in *Yo-Yo* is a vital aspect of the narrative blueprint, even more so than any other code-switching novel written by a Latino/a.

BRASCHI AND BILINGUALISM

As Braschi describes in "Pelos en la lengua":

> El bilingüismo es una estética bound to double business. O, 'tis most sweet when in one line two crafts directly meet. To be and not to be. Habla con la boca llena and from both sides of its mouth. Está con Dios y con el Diablo. Con el punto y con la coma. Es un purgatorio, un signo grammatical intermedio, entre heaven and earth, un semicolon entre la independencia y la estadidad, un estado libre asociado, un mamarracho multicultural. (1977)[18]

Bilingualism, for Braschi, is this wonderful nether region balanced between two poles. But for Braschi, a master of both Spanish and English, bilingualism is the crux of a fulcrum, a sight of tremendous potential energy.

Another way of thinking of bilingualism as it relates to narrative worldmaking is simply by asking this question: Is the mental model that is created by a truly bilingual text somehow different if the same storyworld were blueprinted using one language? I believe that the answer is yes, and much of my answer owes a great debt to Richard Rodriguez, who, as I noted at the opening of this chapter, resolutely insists that Spanish and English in the United States must not be allowed to traipse over one another. Spanish, the language of the home and hearth, as it were, cannot coexist with the English language of legal and government discourse. I do not agree with Rodriguez's vehement position that the two must be kept apart, but I wholeheartedly agree that the two languages, as manifest in the United States, are situated within two separate worlds of discourse. Only recently have we been able to turn on the television to see a presidential debate moderated by the respected bilingual journalist Jorge Ramos. Latinos often experience Spanish only among family and friends, while English delivered in the coveted "Broadcaster English" dominates the airwaves. Braschi envisions and puts into practice an aesthetic in which the two languages are equal partners in the dance of narrative worldmaking.

Yo-Yo draws much of its energy from this separation of the two languages in the United States by juxtaposing them with equal enthusiasm. Unlike Bra-

---

18. "Bilingualism is an aesthetic bound to double business. O' tis most sweet when in one line two crafts directly meet. To be and not to be. It speaks with its mouth full and from the sides of its mouth. It is with God and the Devil. With the period and with the comma. It is a purgatory, an intermediate grammatical sign, between heaven and earth, a semicolon between independence and statehood, a state of free association, multicultural bullshit."

schi's earlier poetry, *Yo-Yo* is an amalgam of forms, voices, language, and subject. The novel is divided into three chapters: (1) Close-Up, (2) Blow-Up, and (3) Black-Out, as well as an epilogue; the first and last parts are written entirely in Spanish, while the lengthy middle part moves with ease between the two languages. An examination of each part will elucidate how Braschi's brand of bilingualism helps structure the architecture of her storyworld rather than merely supplement or enrich what is essentially an English-based narrative blueprint, as most examples of Latino/a literature are apt to exemplify. For example, not only is the opening chapter written entirely in Spanish, but it is also essentially one long paragraph told by an authorial narrator and focalized through a woman in her bathroom. There is a surreal quality to the narration, as the opening passage establishes:

> Comienza por ponerse en cuatro patas, gatea como una niña, pero es un animal con trompa feroz, un elefante. Y poco a poco, se le va desencajando el cuello, y poco a poco, le crece el cuello, una pulgada, luego dos pulgadas, luego cinco pulgadas, hasta que su cabeza se aleja tanto y tanto del suelo, casi diría que toca el techo de la casa donde habita, casi diría que da golpes contra el techo, ya no cabe su cabeza en esta casa, ha crecido tanto y tanto. Y de repente descubre que lo que ha crecido no es su cabeza sino su cuello. Es, entonces, definitivamente, una jirafa. (3)[19]

The unnamed woman, doing what women usually do in bathrooms in the morning, undergoes spectacular transformations through the use of metaphor. The novel opens with the woman on all fours, imagining herself as an elephant, growing beyond the limits of the room not unlike Lewis Carroll's Alice, until at last she realizes that she has become a giraffe. This scene, however, is not an example of magical realism, where we might expect a woman who transforms into an elephant and then a giraffe while completing her morning toilette. Instead, the narrator provides a window into the woman's mind, and we see her as she imagines herself. The opening chapter is an indication of the sorts of fictional minds we encounter as we progress through the novel. In this text, the ordinary and commonplace are consistently renewed in the manner described by Viktor Shklovsky as *ostranenie* (xviii–xix).

---

19. "She begins by getting on all fours, crawling like a little girl, but she is an animal with a fierce trunk, an elephant. And bit by bit, her neck becomes unhinged, and bit by bit, her neck grows, an inch, then two inches, then five inches, until little by little her head moves away from the floor, she could almost say that it touches the ceiling of her home, she could almost say that it hits against the ceiling, now her head no longer fits in this house, it's grown so. And suddenly she learns that what has grown was not her head but rather her neck. She is, then, definitely, a giraffe."

In fact, Julia Carroll describes the opening chapter as Braschi's fashioning of "a womb-like space in which the narrator's private acts of autoeroticism leave her feeling 'tranquila y feliz' and also confident about going public" (98). Though I agree that the opening chapter can be seen as a moment of emergence for the protagonist with its language of growth and renewal, I disagree that this initial section of the novel is told via interior monologue, as Carroll maintains (94). Interior monologue reveals the thoughts of a character as though unfiltered by a narrator, as though readers have bypassed the narrator in order to peer into the character's mind. The example *par excellence* is James Joyce's final chapter of *Ulysses*, where we get Molly Bloom's unmediated thoughts as she lies in bed:

> Yes because he never did a thing like that before as ask to get his breakfast in bed with a couple of eggs since the City Arms hotel when he used to be pretending to be laid up with a sick voice doing his highness to make himself interesting for that old faggot Mrs Riordan that he thought he had a great leg of and she never left us a farthing for all for masses for herself and her soul greatest miser ever was actually afraid to lay out 4d for her methylated spirit telling me all her ailments [. . .]. (608)

In this example of interior monologue, readers are swept up in Molly's musings, placed in the midst of her thoughts.

What we have in the opening chapter of *Yo-Yo* is significantly different, I contend. Someone is reporting the thoughts and experiences of the woman in the bathroom. If Carroll is to be believed, we are reading the woman's interior monologue as she views herself in the third person. The Spanish verbs unambiguously denote that a woman is being spoken of and not that a woman is speaking of herself. While it is plausible that the woman is speaking of herself in third person, Occam's Razor disfavors this possibility.

This may seem like a relatively minor narratological quibble, but I believe the distinction tells us something about the narrative blueprint Braschi creates. In Latino/a literature, character narrators dominate. Following in a close second are third-person limited narrators. Less frequent in Latino/a literature are narrators who focalize through a specific character and, moreover, report the mental activity of characters in an unbiased, unfiltered way. Braschi's use of this technique is a crucial development in the Latino/a literary tradition. Character narrators (as well as autobiographers/memoirists) consistently narrate from a subjective position. They are continually fighting the battle of reliability. As I posited in chapter 1, Oscar Acosta's veneer of verifiable autobiography is suddenly exposed when his narrative is held to the light of historical record. Character narration is complicated by its being, as Phelan claims, "an art of indirection" (7). To make matters worse, character narrators and life writers of so-called minority fiction can oftentimes be seen as representatives for the whole of the group they represent, as if somehow their narrativized experiences authenticate the experiences of millions of people.

On the other hand, third-person limited narrators purport to relate events as they occur within the storyworld. These narrators are limited because they are emotionally and personally removed from the characters within the story. Even when the third-person narrators are seemingly omniscient, the narrator appears to dip into the characters' minds only rarely, as in this example from Julia Alvarez's *How the García Girls Lost Their Accents*:

> Yolanda gazes at the cake. Below her blazes the route she has worked out on the map for herself, north of the city through the mountains to the coast. As the singing draws to a close, the cousins urge her to make a wish. She leans forward and shuts her eyes. There is so much she wants, it is hard to single out one wish. There have been too many stops on the road of the last twenty-nine years since her family left this island behind. She and her sisters have led such turbulent lives—so many husbands, homes, jobs, wrong turns among them. But look at her cousins, women with households and authority in their voices. Let this turn out to be my home, Yolanda wishes. She pictures the maids in their quiet, mysterious cluster at the end of the patio, Altagracia with her hands in her lap. (11)

Here the narrator moves closer to her thoughts, until at last the narrator reports Yolanda's direct thoughts: "Let this turn out to be my home." And soon the narrator has withdrawn once more to reporting events in the larger storyworld.

Such use of third-person narration is quite common in Latino/a literature. Thus, when we consider the opening of *Yo-Yo*, we see a narrator who maintains distinction from the consciousness of the woman in the bathroom while simultaneously acting as a conduit that allows the interaction of minds among author, narrator, character, and reader. The effect is that what we get is not the constructed words of the character but rather an account of events that provides partial, intermittent access to her conscious experiences. By maintaining distance with Spanish grammatical constructions that indicate "she," the nearly invisible narrator lends the authority of a third-person narrator to the woman's existential musings. The consequence of this mode of narration raises the issue of authentication explored by Lubomír Doležel. In "Truth and Authenticity in Narrative," Doležel describes the authentication function as "a necessary, maybe a central, concept of the theory of fictional existence in narrative worlds. What exists in a narrative world is determined by the authentication function. The authentic motifs and only these motifs represent *narrative facts*, the elementary constituents of narrative worlds" (12). As it pertains to the opening of *Yo-Yo*, the authentication function is unambiguously in question, for the reader cannot discern what to take as authentic in the storyworld. Doležel's proposed "three-value authentication function" sheds light on the opening of Braschi's novel:

> In this theoretical framework, it is possible to say that the narrator constructs a narrative world by introducing a set of narrative motifs, but he fails to authenticate it since his authentication authority is undermined. We are presented with fictional worlds whose existence is ambiguous, problematic, indefinite. These worlds are neither authentic, nor non-authentic, but create an indeterminate space between fictional existence and fictional non-existence. (23)

In the opening chapter of *Yo-Yo*, we have a narrator who lacks authentication authority. Doležel himself sees instances of narrators without authentication authority as "a very important factor in many modern narratives" (22), and I would make a similar claim for the importance of such a narrator in the development of Latino/a literature.

Further, Braschi's decision to render this scene in Spanish rather than English has a profound difference in maintaining the distinction between focalized character and third-person narrator. Simply put, were this scene written in English, the replacement of the pronouns "she/her" with "I/me" can easily accommodate a shift from first- to third-person narration. Conversely, in Spanish one can indicate another woman in ways that do not overtly invoke the Spanish pronoun for "her," *ella*. Because every verb must be conjugated to indicate another person, in this case a female, the text must undergo significant changes to indicate interior monologue. In the case of *Yo-Yo*'s opening chapter, the Spanish works to maintain the authority of the narrator while foregrounding the presence of the narrator despite the fact that we are reading the thoughts of the woman in the bathroom. Because the presence of the narrator is more pronounced in Spanish than it is in English, the authentication function is further compromised, as Doležel's work suggests. In other words, the narrator is reporting not the woman's physical transformation but rather the woman's thoughts as she explores her self and her environment. The result is an ambiguous storyworld that destabilizes the reader.

The third chapter bookends the first chapter by exploring other permutations of the character-narrator dyad. Chapter 3, titled "Black-Out," is divided into two parts: "Perro Realengo" and "Sardina en Lata." "Perro Realengo," or "Stray Dog," is narrated in the first person present by an unidentified person. Yet by this point in the narrative, it is safe to assume that each of the major protagonists of each chapter and section is a fictional version of Giannina Braschi. She begins this first section of chapter 3 on the move and with a sense of the unilateral movement that informs her art:

> Camino con botas, boteando el piso, golpeándolo, y mientras más rápido voy, más pierdo de perspectiva, porque dejo atrás, y nunca viro la cabeza para ver lo que dejé detrás. Digo que voy para el sur—y voy para el Sur—ya estoy llegando a mi destino. Pero mi afán, que triunfa sobre mi destino, me induce a darle otra vuelta a la manzana del norte, a llegar por el oeste, a admirar la punta infinita de la orilla de las aguas, a quedarme embelesada contemplando un maniquí, y los zapatos que lleva puestos—a desear ser yo misma el maniquí—a ver que el viento hace que vuelen periódicos—a ver un ratón entrar en un acueducto. (231)[20]

Importantly, the "I" in this section notes how she loses perspective the faster she moves, and that she never looks back to see what she has left in her wake. It is truly a bold statement of aesthetic creation, one that moves without having the past serve as a sort of constraint on the art of the present and the future.

In "Sardina en Lata," or "Canned Sardines," the narrative employs second-person narration in which the narrator directly addresses her narratee regarding the subject of following your own will or following the will of another, what she terms *el boss*. The metaphor of the can of sardines directly points to the issue of being defined and constrained, and it too can be seen as a statement of artistic conviction:

> Es tan fácil decir: no lo voy a hacer, que estás desempleada—todo lo que se desemplea se desenvuelve—se quita el envolvimiento que no te deja desenvolverte. Si te deprimen, te bajan, te están oprimiendo en una lata de sar-

---

20. "I walk in boots, putting boots to ground, beating it, and the faster I go, the more I lose perspective because I'm leaving behind, and I never turn my head in order to see what I've left behind. I say I'm going south—and I'm going south—I'm already arriving at my destination. But my quest that triumphs over my destiny, makes me do another turn to the apple of the north, in order to arrive from the west, to admire the infinite point of the edge of the waters, to stay enraptured, contemplating a mannequin and the shoes it wears—I wish I could be that mannequin—to see what the wind that blows newspapers does—to see a mouse enter into a sewer."

dina—mi pregunta es la siguiente: por qué te dejaste empaquetar en una lata de sardina—si tú no eres una sardina—y tu boss—y las otras sardinas que sí son sardinas—no se dan cuenta que tú no eres una sardina. De tanto estar condicionada a ser sardina, te crees que para existir tienes que estar ensardinada en lata—y oprimida por las otras sardinas que casi son tú misma—porque se te pegan tanto—rinde más quién más trabaja en menos tiempo, quién bajo la presión del enlatamiento y la compresión se comprime más en la lata, posee mayor talento para ser comprimido, mientras más te comprimen más tú te dejas comprimir—y mayor la tensión entre las ratas enlatadas en sardinas, que pican y muerden de feas, saladas y frías—más muertas que vivas. (242)[21]

What she calls the can of sardines can also be seen as the neat box into which Latino/a literature is often placed, much like the one or two bookshelves at the large chain bookstores that keep books segregated from one another. From the perspective of those Latino/a writers who feel constrained by those who would box them in, Braschi's narrator urges the listener to resist it as she has. As she states, "Why did you allow yourself to be packed into a sardine tin—if you are not a sardine?" With the first and third chapters, *Yo-Yo* opens with a woman whose consciousness and self-image is metamorphosing into something than cannot be contained, and it closes with the image of a woman moving forward while urging others to resist categorization and constraints. These chapters literally frame the middle chapter, titled "Blow-Up."

This lengthy second chapter is a *tour de force,* not only because of its linguistic sophistication but also because of the cognitive demands it presents the reader. There are long passages in Spanish, in English, and in code-switching Spanglish. Adding to the difficulty is the use (or non-use) of a narrator in this chapter. While the narrator is clearly present in the first chapter, there is a definitive lack of narrator in "Blow-Up." In its structure, it somewhat resembles Philip Roth's *Deception,* a narrative that dispenses with an overt narrator and allows the development and movement between characters and their

---

21. "It's so easy to say: I'm not going to do it, that you're unemployed—everything that is unemployed is easygoing—it removes the surrounding that doesn't allow you to relax. If they bring you down, put you down, pressing you into a sardine tin—my question is the following: why did you allow yourself to be packed into a sardine tin—if you are not a sardine—and your boss—and the other sardines that truly are sardines—they don't realize that you are not a sardine. Because you've been conditioned to be a sardine, you believe that in order to exist you must be sardined in a tin—and pressed with the other sardines that are almost you—because they stick to you so—the one who does more work in less time gets more, the one beneath the pressure of being canned tends to get canned, having more talent to be compressed, while they compress you the more you allow yourself to be compressed—and so the tension rises among the canned sardine rats that prick and bite from ugliness, salted and cold—more dead than alive."

dialogue to provide the impetus to the narrative progression. "Blow-Up" also owes a large debt to Manuel Puig's *Kiss of the Spider Woman*, the celebrated novel that features two nameless prisoners talking to one another in their cell with no narrator to mediate the characters' interior emotional and mental states. In each of these examples, readers are unable to rely on a narrator to orchestrate the narrative. The result is that readers must take the words of the characters and use them to fill in salient aspects of the narrative that may go unmentioned. The characters speak to one another, ostensibly without the awareness that readers are reading their words, jumping from story to memory to dream and so forth without any cues to the reader.

One more aspect of "Blow-Up" must be introduced before I begin a more detailed exploration of this weighty chapter of *Yo-Yo*. One cannot help noticing Braschi's use and appropriation of the title "Blow-Up," which is also the exact title of a translation of Julio Cortazár's short story "Las babas del diablo." Cortazár's story famously grapples with issues of how a story ought to be told, which seems to be of even more importance than the story itself. The story opens:

> It'll never be known how this has to be told, in the first person or in the second, using the third person plural or continually inventing modes that will serve nothing. If one might say: I will see the moon rose, or: we hurt me at the back of my eyes, and especially: you the blond woman was the clouds that race before my you're his our yours their faces. What the hell. (114)

Braschi's use of Cortazár's story as an intertext helps contextualize the middle chapter of her novel, for it is very much about how the narrative is to be told, as well as narratives in general. The protagonist, what appears to be a counterself of Braschi, constantly refers to her writing struggles. Indeed, Braschi seems to be playing with the notion of "continually inventing modes" in this section of her novel.

The middle section is structured as multiple vignettes that occur over a span of time and in multiple locations. Without the centering presence of a narrator, markers of time and space rarely surface in the narrative. In addition, while the competing dialogues provide the materials for characterization, readers are left wondering more obvious aspects of identity, such as name; familial ties; racial, ethnic, and national markers; and spatializing devices within the narrative. Things often taken for granted in a narrative are now conspicuously absent. Again, I take this to be another instance of Shklovsky's call to make the stone feel stony. The enstranging structure of this narrative presents the audience with frustrating challenges in reconstructing the storyworld. For example, the chapter opens in medias res with two people engaged in a quickly escalating argument:

—Abrela tú.
—¿Por qué yo? Tú tienes las keys. Yo te las entregué a ti. Además, I left mine adentro.
—¿Por qué las dejaste adentro?
—Porque I knew you had yours.
—¿Por qué dependes de mí?
—Just open it, and make it fast. Y lo peor de todo es cuando te levantas por las mañanas y te vas de la casa y dejas la puerta abierta. Y todo el dinero ahí, desperdigado encima de una gaveta en la cocina, al lado de la entrada. Y ni te das cuenta que me pones en peligro. Yo duermo hasta las diez. Y entonces me levanto y me visto rápidamente y cuando voy a abrir la puerta me doy cuenta que está abierta. Es un descuido de tu parte. Dejar la puerta abierta. Alguien puede entrar y robarme y violarme. Y tú tan Pancho, Sancho, ni te importa.
—Claro que me importa. Eso sí fue un descuido." (21)[22]

The argument is over the opening of the locked door to the apartment. The man has a set of keys, but he cannot understand why he must use the keys if the woman (presumably his paramour) can open the door for him. It is the sort of heated conversation typical of frustrated lovers, but it is significant that the chapter opens with a discussion concerning locks and keys. If we take this to be a metaphor for the larger project of writing and reading *Yo-Yo*, we might see the narrative as a locked door. Along the same lines, if the woman is a stand-in for Braschi herself (as it appears she is), then she is frustrated that she must open the door to let someone in who has the keys readily available. This metaphor can be read as a preemptive strike at criticisms such as that of Torres-Padilla, who criticizes Braschi for her overinvestment in formal and aesthetic issues. Why should she open the door if she has already provided the key?

22. "—You open it. / —Why me? You have the keys. I gave them to you. Moreover, I left mine inside. / —Why did you leave them inside? / —Because I knew you had yours. / —Why do you depend on me? / —Just open it, and make it fast. And worst of all is when you get up mornings and you leave the house with the door open. And all the money there, lying on the kitchen drawer near the entrance. And you don't even realize that you put me in danger. I sleep until ten. And then I get up and dress quickly, and when I go to open the door I notice that it's open. It's neglect on your part. Leaving the door open. Someone could come in and rob and violate me. And you, so willy-nilly, don't even care. / —Of course I care. That truly was an oversight."

Braschi is aware of her audience, just as her protagonist is aware of matters of narrative structure. "I read so much," the woman complains. "I'm bored to death by Ibsen. Do I act upon the reading. Act upon the character. What fills my brain?" (87). Further, she places herself within the context of other ethnic writers, saying:

> —Those were the puritan fanatics that England rejected. The harmless ones stayed home. We said, go fanatics, go to the wilderness of monkeys. And look at the mess they created. You call that Multiculturalism. They obliviated the Indians. And they continue to do so in the name of Big Mac. Eighty, ninety languages a day. Poof. Gone. Look at Toni Morrison, Maxine Hong Kingston, and Amy Tan—writing about their lost culture—long dead. No wonder the bloody Americans celebrate them—because now they are no longer black or Chinese, they're all GAP. Fifty years ago this was unheard of. American soccer players on the Brazilian team. French players on the British team. They sell themselves to the highest bidder. Is that diversity? No, now all the teams are the same! (135)

Indeed, Morrison, Kingston, and Tan do write about their lost culture, to the plaudits of critics and audiences. Yet the protagonist accuses these writers of no longer being a part of their "lost culture" but rather another part of the capitalist machine that drives the U.S. and world economies. It is a worldview critical of exploitation and capitalism that innocently passes as diversification. Braschi's project supports this worldview, as it refuses to pursue a reclamation project of something lost through either colonization or assimilation. Despite her protagonist's misgivings regarding the creative process (she struggles with both a lack of self-confidence as well as writer's block), Braschi owns the tools and devices of her trade. Whereas Latino/a authors have consistently acquiesced to audiences or to publishers' prescriptions concerning who their audiences are and should be, Braschi considers her audiences' needs and limitations as secondary to her own as a creator of poetry and narrative. This very issue comes up in one of the discussions in "Blow-Up":

> —Who have you read?
> —I don't read any of them.
> —It shows. You must realize you're limiting your audience by writing in both languages. To know a language is to know a culture. You neither respect one nor the other.
> —If I respected languages like you do, I wouldn't write at all. El muro de Berlín fue derribado. Why can't I do the same. Desde la torre de Babel, las lenguas han sido siempre una forma de divorciarnos del resto de la humanidad.

Poetry must find ways of breaking distance. I'm not reducing my audience. On the contrary, I'm going to have a bigger audience with the common markets—in Europe—in America. And besides, all languages are dialects that are made to break new grounds. I feel like Dante, Petrarca and Boccaccio, and I even feel like Garcilaso forging a new language. Saludo al nuevo siglo, el siglo del nuevo lenguaje de América, y le digo adiós a la retórica separatista y a los atavismos. (162–63)[23]

Braschi's fictional counterself understands the importance of book-buying audiences and markets, as does Braschi herself. That is to say, while she may acknowledge the difficulties her bilingualism may present to audiences, audiences will nevertheless adapt to these challenges or rather will make the effort to align with the ideal audience.

Throughout "Blow-Up," Braschi weaves a storyworld that is multilayered, intertextual, and cross-cultural, much like the New York City of the late twentieth century in which her story is set. Her novel is not located near the United States-Mexico border of Anzaldúa's imagination or the demarcated neighborhood of Spanish Harlem where Piri Thomas received so many life lessons. Rather, it is a highbrow work of Latino/a literature that situates itself amongst other examples of high art across nations, cultures, history, and language. The ideal readership in the case of *Yo-Yo Boing!* is capable of moving fluidly throughout the various challenges of the text, but those actual readers who are able to align themselves with the ideal reader become a smaller group as the various challenges presented by a text are piled higher and higher.

It is fitting, then, that the epilogue of Braschi's novel depicts what looks like a scene from a script or drama wherein a character named Giannina meets Hamlet and Zarathustra at a crossroads. Hamlet and Zarathustra are each carrying a dead body when they are joined by Giannina, who declares that she is going to bury the twentieth century. It is a stunning moment of self-reflexivity and self-evaluation of just how far Giannina has come. If we read Giannina as a Latino/a artist at the brink of a new century, looking to the

---

23. —Who have you read? / —I don't read any of them. / —It shows. You must realize you're limiting your audience by writing in both languages. To know a language is to know a culture. You neither respect one nor the other. / —If I respected languages like you do, I wouldn't write at all. The Berlin wall was demolished. Why can't I do the same? Ever since the Tower of Babel, languages have always served as a way of divorcing ourselves from the rest of humanity. Poetry must find ways of breaking distance. I'm not reducing my audience. On the contrary, I'm going to have a bigger audience with the common markets—in Europe—in America. And besides, all languages are dialects that are made to break new grounds. I feel like Dante, Petrarca and Boccaccio, and I even feel like Garcilaso forging a new language. Greetings to the new century, the century of the new language of America, and I say farewell to separatist rhetoric and atavisms.

past while considering the important issues of aesthetics and representation, it is clear that in burying the twentieth century, Braschi, through her fictional self Giannina, has moved beyond the limitations of identity-bound aesthetics—of the atavisms of Latino/a literature. By seeing the potential of audience to expand Latino/a literary form rather than constrain it, Braschi has set a new standard for how code-switching, bilingualism, and narrative discourse can be used to open up new avenues of expression not only in Latino/a literature but in other literatures of the United States as well.

To be sure, Piri Thomas and Giannina Braschi arose out of vastly different cultural, educational, and historical contexts. Their use of English and Spanish in their works is indicative of publishing constraints when it comes to the degree of bilingualism and code-switching in the works they market. Thomas is very careful in his use of code-switching, always with the understanding that his audience is uninitiated in the social and cultural experiences that have shaped his worldview and means of expression. Therefore, Thomas is continually working to balance his unique sense of self with his desire to reveal his narrative in the language and codes that best articulate his vision. Braschi, meanwhile, has very little constraints on the linguistic choices that help shape her storyworld. Her equal prowess with both English and Spanish becomes a crucial aspect of her novel, and her narrative design suggests that she anticipates readers who can easily decode both languages in order to co-construct the storyworld. Nevertheless, even though Braschi writes with the benefit of more than three decades of social change and altered expectations for Latino/a writers, her novel still results in a much smaller audience than Thomas's novel. But the key result here is that Braschi is empowered to write the type of narrative of her imagination, irrespective of sales figures and best-seller status. She has shown how Latino/a authors can design narrative blueprints with which only a small audience may contend. Braschi places her faith in her writing with the understanding that an audience will find it.

In the following chapter, I investigate how the comics form of storytelling has allowed authors such as Gilbert Hernandez to trust in their ability to design storyworlds that make fewer and fewer concessions to audiences.

CHAPTER 3

In Graphic Detail

Challenges of Memory and Serialization in the Storyworlds of Gilbert Hernandez

IF LATINO/A AUTHORS have had a trying time reaching a larger audience, the same might be said of those who write and illustrate comics. Thanks in large part to its pulp form and storylines that delved into fantastical worlds of their authors' imaginations, comics have been viewed, until the 1990s, with little regard as a literary genre.[1] Indeed, the dominance of superhero comics and the younger target audience of comics have helped give fodder to those who would cast this type of narrative as juvenile and not worthy of rigorous inquiry—something that comics artists and comics scholars have been resisting for decades. As Rocco Versaci makes clear:

> This misapprehension persists today. One of the clearest recent examples comes in rhetoric surrounding the August 2006 release of Sid Jacobson and Ernie Colon's *The 9/11 Report: A Graphic Adaptation*. This comic book adaptation of *The 9/11 Commission Report* (2004)—a book that details the events leading up to and including the attacks on September 11, 2001—was pro-

---

1. Perhaps the key text for the reconsideration of comics as a significant literary genre came in 1991 with Art Spiegelman's *Maus: A Survivor's Tale*, which won the Pulitzer Prize. In terms of critical scholarship, comics artists initiated the rise in comics critical scholarship with Scott McCloud's *Understanding Comics* and Will Eisner's *Comics and Sequential Art*. Other path-breaking studies in comics are Les Daniels's *Comix: A History of Comic Books in America* (1971), Thomas M. Inge's *Comics as Culture* (1990), and Coulton Waugh's *The Comics* (1947, reprinted in 1991).

filed in the *Washington Post* by Bravetta Hassell, who asks at one point, "can a topic as massive and sobering as Sept. 11 be dealt with effectively in the pages of a comic book?" (D1). The assumption here is that the weight of the topic is simply too much for the medium to bear. In response to her question, one reader—a pilot for a major airline—writes that he is "outraged by the attempt to depict the horrific events of Sept. 11 in a comic book format" and that "while shielding children from the details of this horrific tragedy is appropriate, telling the rest of society about it in a comic book isn't" [Villani A14]. The fact that the letter-writer has only seen the book through the limited scope of Hassell's article (and has probably not picked up a comic book in the last twenty years) is largely beside the point. What is important to note here is the assumption he makes that comic books are a juvenile medium that can only trivialize serious matters. (8–9)

Works of scholarship like Versaci's and others continue to make compelling arguments for the consideration of comics as a sophisticated, literary mode of storytelling. Embedded within this endeavor is the quest for respect, which is all well and good. However, one of the strengths of the comics medium is that because of the younger audiences for which comics have traditionally been marketed, there are fewer restraints on the possibilities of what comics can be. This younger audience, according to Bradford W. Wright, can be seen in how comic strips and comic books are marketed:

> Whereas comic strips are a syndicated feature in newspapers sold to a mass and mostly adult audience, comic books are created, distributed, and sold on their own merits to a paying and overwhelmingly young audience. [. . .] The content and themes explored in comic books have diverged drastically from those of comic strips. [. . .] They have explored virtually every genre of popular entertainment, including adventure, horror, mystery, crime, romance, the western, and humor. (xiii–xiv)

With such diverse options for storytelling in the comics medium, authors, including Latino/a authors, seemingly had the freedom to tell stories that were limited only by the bounds of their imaginations.

As Frederick Luis Aldama reflects in the opening of his introduction to *Multicultural Comics*, "All walks of life are on display in today's alternative and mainstream comic book worlds. [. . .] With author-artists at the helm like Los Bros. Hernandez, [Wilfred] Santiago, [Robert] Kirkman, and [Judd] Winick, to name a few, we see a multiplicity of shades, colors, and sexual orientations expressed in comic book storyworlds" (1). Notably, the relative openness of the comics narrative form has given comics authors the power to shape their storyworlds with little of the publishing constraints often experienced by ethnically identified authors who write novels and nonfiction. Given the freedom to create a wide array of storyworlds, such authors have reveled in exploring the possibilities of graphic storytelling. Regarding this result, Aldama writes:

> This isn't too surprising, given that author-artists of color have the capacity to imagine and feel outside of themselves. While categories used by academics and the media like Latino, Asian American, or African American, and so on, might be useful at first to make these author-artists' work visible, at the end of the day, they want not only to have their work judged by the standard of the great comic book author-artists, but also not to have their talent and imagination squeezed into only one identity-politics box. (2)

So, while comics have generally lacked the distinction of other literary forms, authors of multicultural comics have had the chance to write beyond expectations that are identity based. This is not to say that comics do not often fall back to those deeply ingrained stereotypes that pervade popular culture; large comics publishers such as DC Comics and Marvel Comics have reveled in one-dimensional caricatures of Latinos, as Aldama has demonstrated in *Your Brain on Latino Comics*. However, thanks in large measure to the boom in alternative comics, authors have continually pushed the boundaries of innovation and experimentation in graphic narrative: "Latino author-artists have radically extended the alternative-comic-book storytelling mode in various ways while they detail the everyday firmly located within a larger society and world. Finally, working within the alternative tradition doesn't preclude the use of more conventional modes of storytelling, such as melodrama or noir" (66).

Though identity-based expectations are relatively diminished, publishers still placed such constraints on Latino/a comics artists such as Frank Espinosa, author of *Rocketo*, who tells Aldama in *Your Brain*:

> Years ago, before *Rocketo*, when I was trying to break into children's books, I went to a couple of publishers with this idea for a line of children's books based on a little African American girl who has all these fantastic adventures. They didn't want it. They said, "No, no, no. This kid doesn't look like an African American character." And I said, "What are you talking about" And they said, "Well her father is an airplane pilot. And her mother is a graphic designer." And I said, "Yeah?" And they were like, "No, no. You want to write it so the people can relate to this. How about if her mother lives in

the ghetto." So I responded, "Have you ever lived in the ghetto? Because if you lived on 145th Street, that's the last place you want to think about when you're there."

Some assume that because we're Hispanics, and because we're African American, that's all we can write about. I took a trip to the bookstore when I was doing research for my children's books, and I was amazed to see that almost all books with African American children were colored in sepia tones. We are some of the brightest, most colorful people, and we've been reduced to sepia tones.

We as Hispanics, as African Americans, as any minority, can write the new *Lord of the Rings,* the new *Star Wars,* the new Harry Potters, but if all we do is just talk about one experience in our lives, we will remain trapped. (164–65)

Espinosa's experience is an example of the types of publisher-based constraints with which Latino/a authors must often contend, even in a medium as demonstratively diverse as comics. Yet it is the ever-expanding storyworlds of Gilbert Hernandez that continually challenge readers at the level of both form and content to reveal the diverse directions Latino/a comics may take.

THE COMICS OF GILBERT HERNANDEZ

In the previous two chapters, I examined specific works of Latino/a literature as a means of exploring both the cognitive challenges of representing consciousness and bilingualism in text-only narrative. In this chapter I turn to one of the most significant and voluminous works of contemporary comics: *Love and Rockets* by Los Bros Hernandez. A collaborative team known as Los Bros—Gilbert, Jaime, and Mario Hernandez—have steadily worked to create a Yoknapawtawpha-like storyworld with a dizzying array of characters, each with his own, oftentimes recondite, history that cumulatively enrich Gilbert's Palomar and Jaime's Hoppers 13. One of the factors in this continual unfolding of the *Love and Rockets* storyworld is the sheer span of time in which Los Bros have been publishing their comics: over thirty years and counting. Characters have died, gained weight, grown old, and expanded the bounds of the alternative comics form and the storyworlds they help give shape. Specifically, reading the comics of Gilbert Hernandez places audiences in a position of tracking time (in the form of character developments and narrative events) as well as mapping and revising models of the ever-expanding and -shifting storyworld space. What might these reading challenges tell us about how Latino/a comics engage audiences and their reading practices?

In his sometimes overlapping storyworlds that comprise the Love and Rockets series, Gilbert Hernandez has created such an intricate network of relationships among the characters and locations that the result is nothing less than a cognitively challenging graphic narrative that immediately presents readers with significant interpretive obstacles, no matter from where they enter the storyworld. Although it is relatively easy to enter into *Love and Rockets*, with each episode being readable on its own, each episode is nonetheless highly intratextual, or connected with other installments in the series. The result is that to reconstruct the storyworld according to its overarching blueprint, readers are necessarily compelled to read (or perhaps reread) more episodes of *Love and Rockets*.

To make matters more challenging for readers, with few exceptions, the installments of *Love and Rockets* are not truly serialized—or at least they are not presented chronologically. Instead, each installment of *Love and Rockets* may occur at any moment within the storyworld chronology or may focus on any one of its plethora of characters. To add to the difficulty of narrative comprehension, Jaime has revealed that he and his brothers worked independently, so that any given issue of *Love and Rockets* does not necessarily have a designed holistic cohesion. Compound this free-flowing design to the span of time between publication of installments, and the result is that there are at least two types of readers: those who read the installments as published over the years and those who are able to read *Love and Rockets* in its entirety as reprinted in one tome.

Memory is a crucial interpretive aspect for narrative comprehension. In understanding how memory works, psychologists view memory as a storage system that encompasses both short-term storage (or working memory) and long-term storage. This two-part model for memory storage has become commonplace in cognitive science and neuroscience. Both short- and long-term memory are engaged in the reading process. With regard to reading, the long-term memory system is crucial for creating and comprehending narrative. As Geoffrey R. Loftus and Elizabeth F. Loftus state in *Human Memory*, "Without long-term store there would be nothing: no books, no television, no learning, no communication—for it is our ability to recall the past that allows us to interact with our environment in a dynamic way" (56). In order to parse the story and hold its components in critical understanding so that the story makes sense in its fullest and most expansive sense, we need our working memory and especially our long-term memory function.

Research by Jeffrey M. Zacks and his colleagues has led them to develop a model termed *Event Segmentation Theory,* or EST, which "proposes that working memory representations of events exist because they improve perception and prediction." In other words, certain events (viewed as segmented units of perception) lead us to predict subsequent events. Further, Zacks points out that "events presented in narrative texts are segmented in much the same way as events presented in videos" and that event segmentation, if as important a factor in working memory as neuroscience suggests, "should affect how information is encoded into long term memory" (n. pag.). Not only does memory have an obvious impact on how audiences can comprehend narrative; EST may help us understand why certain narratives, based on where their event boundaries lie, may present more difficulties in reading comprehension than others. Time (both in the storyworld and in the reader's world), as represented in an audience's engagement with the event boundaries within the narrative, becomes a salient issue in reading *Love and Rockets*. Consequently, time has a significant bearing on the ideal readership and its ability to use memory in order to reconstruct a fractured storyworld as the fragments of narrative are collated over time.

In addition, various spaces are engaged when one is reading the comics of Los Bros. From the actual panel configuration on the page, to the spaces within the storyworld, to the cognitive modeling or mapping of space in the reader's mind, the spatialization of comics becomes something the reader must manage when engaging with *Love and Rockets*. Gilbert Hernandez manipulates time and space in ways that enrich their comics, ways that thwart simplistic notions that reading comics is mere child's play. Indeed, the ideal readership is not one composed of children, one-time readers, or even notoriously loyal comics readers of the past. The ideal readership for *Love and Rockets,* rather, has a much more prodigious memory, suggesting an audience that must be significantly more engaged with the storyworld at a cognitive level.

This cognitive requirement, as it were, has revealed itself in the actual audience's frustration at the narrative design of *Love and Rockets*. Hernandez's experimentation with the comics form has, at times, pushed even loyal audiences of many years to take to websites and blogs in order to complain about how it was becoming more and more difficult to read the comics. Such reader discontent came to its height with Gilbert Hernandez's *Poison River,* causing notable consternation from Hernandez himself. He has continually pushed his readership to expect a challenging experience when reading his comics, and Hernandez's efforts are reflected in other Latino comics that have taken up the call to create complex graphic narratives, such as Wilfred Santiago's *In My Darkest Hour* (2004).

In this chapter I wish to concentrate on the cognitive mechanisms that enable narrative comprehension, especially as they pertain to graphic storytelling. While the explorations of my previous chapters centered on fictional minds and bilingualism, the present chapter provides me the opportunity to trace how narrative design motivates not only observable reading protocols such as rereading but also mental operations such as the ability to access particular areas of memory that play out during reading. Arguably, the ideal readership has at the ready everything that is necessary to comprehend a narrative and reconstruct the storyworld in the manner indicated by the narrative blueprint. Another way of thinking of this issue is to imagine that the ideal readership may have something like eidetic memory, with the ability to recall even the most minor details and events within a narrative. In reality, several operations are ongoing in the complex process of memory storage. For example, working memory functions by segmenting and chunking discrete units, filling in gaps, determining what is most relevant to comprehension, and recognizing recursive features. All of this allows encoding in short-term storage and facilitates long-term storage.

NARRATIVE AND MEMORY FUNCTION

Certainly, there exist in the world individuals who are endowed with prodigious recall. One is reminded of Jorge Luis Borges's Ireneo Funes, who was "able to reconstruct every dream, every daydream he had ever had. Two or three times he had reconstructed an entire day; he had never once erred or faltered, but each reconstruction had itself taken an entire day" (135). Funes, whose capacity for memory was prodigious, is a victim of his own lack of delimiting functions of imagination. He recalls every detail, but he is unable to see his world and experience as a gestalt. Funes reminds us that to imagine is to select out and to exercise counterfactual thinking to ignore (or forget) differences, to generalize, to abstract, and so on. Of course, Funes is Borges's fictional creation. But, as is his tendency, Borges again proves to be a lens of human perception and cognition. And in this case, he shows us the faculty of memory gone awry, not because it cannot store memories but because it stores them all too well.

Most people, however, are not like Funes. For those whose memory function might be called typical, successful comprehension of narratives is largely dependent on their ability to recall and make use of details encountered in earlier portions of the narrative. But that is not all. As neuroscience and cognitive science has shown, there are different types of memory storage and retrieval systems. These systems of memory are engaged in different degrees depending on the type of narrative being read. Short stories, particularly those that can be read in one sitting, may draw heavily upon working memory in order to establish a mental model of the narrative while also drawing upon long-term memories in order to provide other enriching aspects of storyworld reconstruction, such as historical context, allusions, or comparisons to the reader's own lived experience. On the other hand, consider how memory operations might be different when one is reading a lengthy novel that must be read over the course of several days, perhaps weeks, with significant gaps of time between reading sessions. And there are also those types of narratives that are serialized or that appear in installments (regular or otherwise) over the course of years. In short, different forms of narrative engage reader memory systems in different ways—ways that in turn impact how successfully readers can create mental models of the narrative.

Scholars of literary narrative have begun to explore somewhat the issue of memory insofar as it relates to reliability, especially in the study of autobiography and nonfiction. When discrepancies arise between the factual record and the autobiographical narrative, the point of debate centers on matters of reliability and memory. When the autobiographer's memory is seemingly inadequate and discrepancies arise between the textual and extratextual world, audiences must account for this incongruity in some fashion, with the shadow of unreliability now looming over the narrative as a result. As Dan Shen and Dejin Xu have clarified in their essay "Intratextuality, Extratextuality, Intertextuality," readers at times grant some leeway in the creative rendering of fact.

In fictional narrative, this same distinction is also manifest. Narrators who evince clear duplicity are deemed unreliable, and scholars have labored to parse out when unreliable equals untrustworthiness and when it equals a deficient memory. For instance, William Faulkner's *The Sound and the Fury* employs two narrators who can easily carry the label of unreliable, but Benjy and Quentin Compson are unreliable for different reasons. The two chapters narrated by these Compson brothers reveal their cognitive processes, including their ability to wrangle with their own respective memories. Though much has been written of Faulkner's use of the stream-of-consciousness technique as well as the representation of consciousness of two antipodal minds (Benjy is cognitively impaired; Quentin is extremely intelligent), their engagement with memory, and specifically certain memories of their sister, Caddie, provides a major impetus for the narrative progression, or what Phelan would call a "global instability." According to Phelan, instabilities arise between various narrative relationships such as between characters, or between authorial and readerly constructs, that "provide the main track of the progression and must be resolved for a narrative to attain completeness" (*Experiencing* 16). *The Sound and the Fury* derives much of its power from these global instabilities as they relate to cognitive processes of both character and reader.

What has not been sufficiently explored in literary studies is how different kinds of narrative blueprints can place different demands on readers' memories. For example, what sorts of challenges on a reader's memory can a narrative present? In turn, how do readers manage such impositions of memory? These are questions that have begun to be investigated by researchers of neuroscience and the cognitive sciences. Such experiments have illuminated how reading comprehension of individuals with mental cognitive impairment (MCI) and Alzheimer's disease deviates from those of control groups. Many of these important investigations of how cognitive deficiencies impact narrative reconstruction when compared to control subjects have yielded important insights into how higher brain function interacts with narrative, which tells researchers something about how individuals with MCI may struggle with such activities as reading an important letter or understanding the directions on a prescription bottle. However, the narratives that are used in these cognitive studies are generally uncomplicated, with few difficulties presented to the control group. What then might more complex narratives reveal about cognition and the human brain?

Indeed, I assert that *Love and Rockets* is a complex and challenging work of narrative fiction. Though I acknowledge that the thematic material found in *Love and Rockets* may provide certain challenges to reader sensibility, morality, and taste, at time provoking outrage from audiences, these sorts of challenges lie within the purview of this chapter only insofar as the indelibility of certain images is a manifestation of memory function. Indeed, we can stomach more when the depiction is close to the dream-state, such as when the violence is rendered in animation in Quentin Tarantino's film *Kill Bill, Vol. 1* (2003). So, while events within the storyworld such as rape, murder, and suicide, as well as visual renderings of eroticized women, full frontal nudity and so on, may disturb certain audiences, it is the persistence of these visual icons within reader memory that interests me here.

READING AND COGNITION

It does not take experiments in cognition and neuroscience to confirm that we rely heavily upon our brain's capacity for encoding, storing, and retrieving memories of our experiences. Our brain is not modular but rather reticular—a series of concentrations of neural activity, such as Broca's area for language function. However, conclusions derived from cognitive research have helped us better understand how the complex memory system operates, yielding an explanatory model that has delineated different types of memory: long-term and working memory; episodic, semantic, and procedural memories; and so on. Our capacity for memory is what enables our interaction with narrative. Indeed, our system for establishing expectations is motivated by memories of prior experience. Thus, when we prepare to read a given comic for the first time, we experience a specific expectation for the narrative with which we are about to engage that is based on our prior knowledge and encounters with similar narratives. Someone who picks up *Love and Rockets Vol. 5* is primed in ways different from those of someone who picks up the same volume with no prior experience with reading comics is not thus primed.

In *Your Brain on Latino Comics*, Frederick Luis Aldama explores how Latino/a comics artists, through careful design of storyworld, can "create pleasing and even shocking effects in the brain" of the reader (82), engaging a reader's "cognitive and emotive architecture" (84). While Aldama is motivated to uncover how comics can alter and manipulate readers' affect in *Your Brain*, I am interested in the cognitive mechanism than can enable the triggering of powerful emotions in the first place. Memory can be the trip-hammer for the engagement of the "emotive architecture" Aldama mentions. In fact, discussions of universals and prototypes by Aldama, Patrick Colm Hogan, and others hinge on the brain's capacity for memory. That is to say, a reader's ability to recognize a prototype narrative, even innately, suggests that he or she has encountered it sometime in a past experience, perhaps without realizing it. Hogan has discussed how personal memories are triggered by prototypical narratives in *The Mind and Its Stories*.

Yet we must remember that memories are triggered by a multitude of elements within any given narrative, not just the type of narrative. Further, not only are personal memories of concern in how narratives engage emotions within a reader, but memories as they relate to the experience of reading a narrative are consequential as well. While in no way do I discount Hogan's and Aldama's employment of prototypes as a means for understanding how narratives can trigger very real emotions within a reader, I simply wish to complicate their model by offering up the cognitive operations of memory as an additional, related means by which narratives can impact readers' emotive architecture.

But this brings me to the issue of why graphic storytelling can so powerfully engage the memory functions of readers. There is a permanence associated with the visual, so much so that people often speak about not being able to forget certain images to which they have been exposed. Quite often, for example, verbal narration of a sexual act—even one that is explicitly rendered—does not raise the same level of controversy among audiences as a comic that visually depicts the same sexual act. Much of this has to do with the fact that images are unmediated: the viewer can do less in co-creating the image than, say, when reading a narrated passage. Or, as Jeffrey M. Zacks suggests, the brain's segmentivity function, coupled with the recursive nature of a particular segmented event, may cause us to habituate to this state and lessen the degree of encoding. In such cases we have become "desensitized" to certain segmented events. Alternative comics and their storyworlds work with this aspect of reader memory in mind.

Hernandez make full use of the visual power of comics in order to design a complex narrative blueprint. Indeed, one of my assertions is that Hernandez's craftsmanship, in a medium that has historically been viewed as lowbrow pulp art in society (i.e., underground comics), evinces what Aldama terms "will to style," a commitment to designing a narrative in ways that move audiences and break conventions or simplistic stereotypes. In other words, though *Love and Rockets* looks like an Archie-like comic for adults, it is actually doing very sophisticated work at the level of narrative form as it asks its audience to perform cognitively demanding work. Unlike many graphic novels that may ultimately be printed in one or two volumes, such as Art Spiegelman's *Maus*, *Love and Rockets* is so vast that its publisher, Fantagraphics Books, has continually found new ways of collecting and marketing the stories. For example, *High Soft Lisp* is a collection featuring the character Rosalba "Fritz" Martinez. Her stories appeared sporadically throughout *Love and Rockets*, as she is a tertiary character in the Palomar storyworld. Yet Fantagraphics, with Gilbert's collaboration,[2] packaged this single volume into what looks like a graphic novel. In point of fact, *High* is more akin to a short-story cycle, as all of the collected stories are interconnected.

The composite nature of *Love and Rockets*, its sprawl of time and space, make it a rare work of literature.[3] If we consider *Love and Rockets* as a single

---

2. I do not mean to suggest that Fantagraphics produces "new" collections of *Love and Rockets* without the involvement of Los Bros. In this case, the author and the publisher are very much unified in such a collection, as is evident from the copyright statement in *High*: "Most of this material was previously released in the comics series *Love and Rockets* Volume II and *Luba's Comics and Stories*; a few pages have been added, and some have been altered." Thus, a volume such as *High Soft Lisp* is not exactly a collection. One might say, then, that *High Soft Lisp* is a slightly revised version of the original Fritz narratives.

3. In attempting to identify texts with similar scopes of space and time, both the Bible and *The Simpsons* come to mind. The Bible ostensibly spans the initial creation story in Genesis to The Revelation. *The Simpsons*, on the other hand, is the longest-running scripted show in television history at twenty-eight seasons as of 2017. However, *The Simpsons*, unlike *Love and Rockets*, does not have a chronological progression over its history. Each episode is mostly independent from the others, with only the rare moment of continuity. An example here would

text broken into smaller parts, we begin to identify the challenges in reconstructing the overarching storyworld Hernandez has rendered on the page over the course of thirty-plus years. The challenging nature of *Love and Rockets* is revealed in how difficult it is to provide an effective summary for it. There are so many divergent storylines throughout a multitude of time-spaces that providing a plot summary of *Love and Rockets* is nearly futile. Thus, rather than attempt to encapsulate this vast storyworld, I will concentrate on a handful of major characters and storylines within *Love and Rockets*, using relevant parts of the narrative as demonstration texts for different challenges related to the time and space of the storyworld. In particular, I will examine the long-suffering Palomarian character Jesús Angel as well as Luba's origin story, *Poison River*.

THE DEVIL OF SERIALIZATION

My chief claim in this book is that Latino/a authors have steadily expanded audience expectations of what Latino/a literary and cultural production can look like. Along the same lines, Hernandez has created his comics by breaking from a priori adherence to narrative form and content that ascribes a certain aesthetic or mode of storytelling to Latino/a authors.[4] Additionally, the comics form itself imposes its own constraints on authors even if we do not consider specific audience expectations. Indeed, the business of creating comics is both a time-consuming and labor-intensive endeavor. This fact has forced the majority of graphic artists to adopt a specific business model: the model of serialization.[5] As Charles Hatfield and others have noted, most of the hand-

---

be the death of Ned Flanders's wife, Maud in "Alone Again, Natura-Diddly." Her death in this episode impacted subsequent episodes, particularly the character of Ned Flanders. So, while *The Simpsons* continues to develop stories that are unaffected by long-term continuity, its overarching narrative progression is unlike what we find in *Love and Rockets*, where we find characters growing old, fat, or dying. In that sense, *Love and Rockets* displays a continuing and ever-growing storyworld without a discernible teleology—much like our own lives.

4. Hernandez's work is an excellent example of how Latino/a authors can and do write narratives that do not foreground issues of Latino/a identity. His stand-alone graphic novels such as *Chance in Hell* (2007) have non-Latino protagonists.

5. I recognize that many comics are not true serials in the sense that they do not present a continuing narrative that is broken into contiguous parts. For instance, the *Love and Rockets* comics are not serial but episodic. While *serialization* may not be the most accurate term for such comics, I will continue the tradition of other scholars such as Charles Hatfield and Derek Parker Royal who use the term to indicate the publishing of shorter comic narratives over a given length of time rather than the publishing of a graphic novel that may take many years to bring to fruition.

some, book-like objects that are described as graphic novels are created serially over a length of time. With the book-length project as the perceived goal of the graphic artist, the necessity of serialization becomes a necessary evil—what Hatfield calls the "devil of serialization" (*Alternative* 153). Regarding the 2003 definitive collection of the Palomar stories into one volume, Hatfield notes:

> Yet the collected *Palomar* in effect denies its own origins, for it hides the way serialization both enabled and constrained Hernandez's creative process. The growth and eventual contraction of *Heartbreak Soup*, the series, epitomize the challenges faced by long-form comics. Though Hernandez successfully exploited serial publication to give his stories a broader canvas, and in the process developed radical new ways of evoking space and time in comics, serialization also curbed and directed his work, forcing him to confront, in the novel *Poison River* and subsequent efforts, the limits of periodical publishing. The story of *Heartbreak Soup*, in short, is the richest, also one of the most complex and problematic, examples of alternative comics in the long form. (69)

For Hatfield, the process of serialization is an inescapable consequence of what he terms "long-form comics"—one that benefits an artist such as Gilbert Hernandez because he is able to steadily grow his storyworld while seeing his work published periodically. Yet there are limitations to the process of serialization, limitations that are linked to the audience's memory capacity.[6]

I indicated above two types of audiences that must be considered in reading comics. The first are those readers who read each new installment as they appear, suffering through weeks, months, or perhaps years as they loyally wait for the next issue to appear in print. The second are ex post facto readers who are able to read the serialized installments as a collection, perhaps even in one sitting. Readers of the first kind perhaps bear their "original reader" status as a sort of badge of honor, a loyalty rooted in the fact that these readers have patiently followed each issue of a particular comic. Yet this raises two intriguing questions: Are there advantages or disadvantages to reading serials upon

---

6. Hatfield does an excellent job of identifying the sorts of challenges presented to loyal readers of *Love and Rockets*: "this loyalty was sorely tested by the brothers' innovative approach to long-form narrative. As it evolved, *Love & Rockets* demanded much of its audience, as its storylines were often serialized over many issues, creating long, sometimes novel-length, narratives of unprecedented depth and scope. In fact the stories grew in length and complexity throughout the eighties, climaxing between 1990 and 1993 as *Love & Rockets* ran no less than three serialized graphic novels at once—a period Gilbert has described in hindsight as 'crazy'" (70).

publication versus waiting until they have all been collected? Are the reading experiences different in some significant way?

While many scholars of serialized literature recognize this issue of how reading practices may differ, a preponderance of the scholarship focuses on the production side of the text. In other words, these studies address the author's potential gain or loss from serializing his or work. By contrast, the effect of serialization on readers has only been hinted at. Derek Parker Royal has acknowledged how serialized graphic novels, specifically the comics of Gilbert Hernandez, "impact reader affect" (263). For example, Royal notes that readers of self-contained or collected graphic novels (or the ex post facto readers mentioned above) have a greater sense of control over "the means of narrative acquisition" (265). I agree with Royal's take, for it is certainly less challenging to read a long work when all installments are available in one space and time. Conversely, because of the rich intratextuality of the *Love and Rockets* storyworld, there can be the tendency for information overload as the multilayered interconnectivity of these comics potentially overwhelms readers. And both Royal and Hatfield have noted how Gilbert's narratively complex graphic novel *Poison River* frustrated readers when it originally appeared in serialized installments. Hatfield's characterization of *Poison River* is that it "represents the apogee of Hernandez's art to date, a dense, aggressive, and disturbing novel that weds formal complexity to thematic ambition. (Collected in 1994, it remains notorious among fans as his most tangled and difficult work.)" (*Alternative* 86). Though *Poison River* is a notably complex text by any measure, its serialized nature tells us something about the limits of serialized graphic narrative in terms of its creation and its readership.

Serialized literature has particular implications on reading practices that differ from those of novels, though I recognize that some novels, such as nineteenth-century novels, were published serially. The reading of serialized literature, at least at the time of its creation, is a much more dynamic reading process. Not only is there a lack of closure (the "tune in next time" phenomenon), there can be a substantial measure of time between the publication of installments. This is especially critical in comics such as *Love and Rockets*, where there was not always a regular publication schedule of the sort that one might expect from, say, Marvel or DC superhero comics. In fact, though it ran in a serialized publication format, the various storylines in *Love and Rockets* are by and large episodic in nature. This distinction is key, for such narrative worldmaking influences how readers reconstruct storyworlds. Additionally, the process of serialization gives the Palomar stories, despite their Latin American hamlet setting, a panoramic quality due to their breadth of time and space. Further, in large measure, it is the ensemble cast that lends this sense of sprawl and immensity to the Palomar stories. There are so many characters that Gilbert often provides a page of dramatis personae that allows the reader to see how characters relate to one another. Third, as a result of the dozens of characters that inhabit the Palomar storyworld, some characters are necessarily foregrounded (such as Luba) while others remain mostly in the background and only occasionally enter into the narrative, such as the character of Jesús Angel. However, there are times when a background character carries the weight of the narrative, as in Fritz's coming to the fore in *High Soft Lisp*. These moments of enriching a tertiary character are particularly insightful in understanding how Hernandez quickly and efficiently takes a backdrop character and makes it the narrative focus—something of vital importance for the serial reader.

I am interested in how both types of readers I have identified above (ex post facto and serial readers) reconstruct the storyworld, that is, the global mental model of the situations and events within the text. However, not only is this ability dependent on how an author constructs the narrative blueprint with the reader in mind; it is also time sensitive, for the reconstruction of storyworlds as a cognitive function tied with memory has the capacity to degrade over time. Further complicating the reconstruction of the mental model of the storyworld, many of the competing Palomar storylines overlap. Due to the nature of serialized and episodic stories, the reader must reconstruct and maintain a mental model of the overarching storyworld. This places an extreme cognitive demand on both types of readers, but particularly the serial reader, and thus Hernandez must conduct his narrative worldmaking with this in mind. Here I turn to an examination of Jesús Angel, a character who typically inhabits the background in the Palomar stories.

CONSEQUENCES OF FOREGROUNDING A TERTIARY CHARACTER

A typical Gilbert Hernandez tertiary character, Jesús Angel (hereafter Jesús) features in two stories and provides the impetus for a third in *Love and Rockets*. The first of these stories comes in two parts and is titled "The Laughing Sun." The events of this story have implications for Jesús's second story, published over a year later, similarly titled "Holidays in the Sun." "The Laughing Sun" concerns an altercation between Jesús and his wife Laura that culminates in Jesús's inadvertent harming of his infant daughter. Fearing the consequences of what he has done, Jesús strikes out for a local mountain range, and his childhood friends (Heraclio, Israel, Satch, and Vicente) attempt to bring him back unharmed. Further, "The Laughing Sun" is, in truth, a serialized narrative; its plot continues into a second installment.

But as with all other aspects of *Love and Rockets,* in order to reconstruct the storyworld for "The Laughing Sun," a reader must already have some familiarity with the overarching Palomarian storyworld. Indeed, Hernandez does not provide the setting; nor does he give overviews of the over twenty characters with speaking parts in the twenty pages of text. He does not provide moments of orientation for the reader, even readers who may be familiar with Palomar. Thus, as an episode of one of Palomar citizens, "The Laughing Sun," though not specifically anchored to another storyline, is understood best if the reader has a preexisting mental model of the overarching Palomar storyworld. With it, a reader understands the significance of the character Diana Villaseñor, or recognizes Jesús's relation to both Diana and Luba, or sees why Heraclio is willing to risk his life and reputation to help his childhood friend at all. In other words, Hernandez does not seem to be concerned with whether a reader will understand the intricate interconnectivity that gives Palomar its vitality. Here we have an example of a constraint of the serial form that Hatfield identifies. Part One of "The Laughing Sun" is only eight pages long. The form itself is a constraint, and that constraint has a consequence on a reader's ability to comprehend and reconstruct the storyworld. Hernandez must then rely on the resourcefulness of the reader to consult earlier issues of *Love and Rockets,* for even serial readers would be challenged to remember every salient issue that arises in "The Laughing Sun." This is a significant risk when it comes to the ultimate reception of Hernandez's comics, as the reception of *Poison River* demonstrates.

However, Hernandez is not oblivious to the challenges that a compressed serial narrative places upon the reader. By granting the reader access to the thoughts of Jesús's childhood friends, Hernandez allows for the emotional component of the narrative to have its greatest impact on the reader. Even so, with only an adequate mental model of the storyworld, emotional engagement with the narrative is difficult at best. Indeed, this is one of the hallmarks of postmodern and avant-garde literature. Such texts are so difficult for readers that they often stop reading, if they pick it up at all. Generally speaking, if the cognitive demands of a text are too high, the predominant emotion will be one of frustration. This sort of reaction, of course, is reader specific.

Though he is essentially absent from the story, "The Laughing Sun, Part One" cannot take place without Jesús. He has become mentally unhinged, and the thought of having inadvertently killed his infant daughter literally

FIGURE 1. © Gilbert Hernandez, image courtesy Fantagraphics Books

drives him to the hills. While we are aware of his state of mind (his blank stare in Diana's house, the threatening manner in which he holds his dagger in figure 1), the visual narration[7] never objectively shows what happened between Jesús and his wife. We see Chelo holding the baby with "a nasty bruise on its head," and in the next panel, the reader gets a view of the devastated home (figure 2). A close-up of Laura gives us her account of Jesús: "He's crazy, that's all . . . tried to kill me . . . I swear, he tried to kill—wrecked the whole house . . . grabbed a steak knife and ran . . . ." Now we have a con-

---

7. In *Your Brain on Latino Comics*, Frederick Luis Aldama posits a distinction between what he terms the "visual narrator" and the "verbal narrator," which correspond to the visual elements and verbal elements of a graphic narrative, respectively (97–101). According to Aldama, despite there being two narrators, the visual and verbal narration is perceived by the reader as a gestalt (98). It is possible, however, that Aldama's conception of the visual and verbal narrator are, in fact, two distinct aspects of a single narrating presence. Despite Aldama's proposal for two narrators who operate within a comic, I rely on the term "visual narration" to convey the visual mode of narrative as an element distinct from the verbal mode. *Verbal narration* seems an apt term whether one does or does not support a single or dual narrator model in graphic narrative.

FIGURE 2. © Gilbert Hernandez, image courtesy Fantagraphics Books

text for Jesús's blank stare at the story's opening when he wandered, as if in a fugue state, to Diana's house (figure 1). Thus, "The Laughing Sun, Part One" opens after Jesús and Laura's altercation, but in medias res.

Hernandez creates a mystery in the opening page of "The Laughing Sun," and the reader, along with the rest of the characters in the story, must attempt to solve this mystery. Yet despite the clarity of the aftermath, there are no clues to lend insight into what might have forced Jesús to act so violently. His childhood friends are left with nothing but their own recollections and memories to draw upon to find some reasonable answer. Hernandez uses thought bubbles to represent memories, but entire panels have "bubbled corners," to represent cognitive function. And it is not simply memories, for dreams and hallucinations are rendered similarly in both parts of "The Laughing Sun." In one panel featuring Vicente, the reader is privy to his memory of himself and Jesús as children, both of whom are having a shared vision of what they imagine hell to be like. This panel is an example of Hernandez's ability to collapse time efficiently from one panel to the next. However, although the serial form at times compels Hernandez to perform such contextualizing moves in his storyworld design, he does so only when it suits the narrative, not as a device to make things easier on the reader (figure 3).

While Vicente is in the narrating now, he recollects his childhood. In that memory of his childhood, he and Jesús are contemplating "where little boys and girls go when they die," that is to say, they are contemplating their future. And in another sense, there is the specter of what Jesús has just done as well as what his future holds—all of this without the use of one written word. Though a greater familiarity with Jesús enriches this story, Hernandez's design allows for the serial reading experience without acquiescing to the desire of (some) readers for contextualization. By having Jesús vacate the story, Hernandez

FIGURE 3. © Gilbert Hernandez, image courtesy Fantagraphics Books

allows the rest of the cast to provide textual cues that allow for the reconstruction of the storyworld. What is more, Hernandez has the dramatis personae use their own memories in order to either refresh the memories of serial readers or to provide details about events that a reader may lack (figure 4).

Having the cast collectively sift through their memories of Jesús for some indication or rationale that explains his actions mirrors what readers must do in order to make sense of Jesús's actions, which is a deft demonstration of the importance of memory for understanding narrative. As the various characters reach into their memories of Jesús, the reader is invited to do the same. The reader has become a de facto member of the Palomar cast, and he or she is invited to use their own store of memories to account for why Jesús has gone temporarily mad. The ability to do so allows an emotional response from the reader, mostly because Jesús's history in the Palomar storyworld is relatively bland. His one life-changing incident is that he once offered to carry Luba across a river when he was younger but dropped her when he began to get an erection. That moment of humiliation and sexual frustration haunts Jesús throughout the remainder of the Palomar stories. And in Part Two of "The Laughing Sun," Hernandez depicts this pivotal event in Jesús's life through Heraclio's memories of the incident. Again, it is telling that Hernandez, rather than use unambiguous analepses to fill in the gaps for readers, instead uses the memories of Jesús's four childhood friends to help account for how Jesús could have fallen so low. Moreover, the character memories are not narrated by the characters themselves. Rather, the memories are depicted first as thought bubbles, until the bubbles themselves essentially become the panels. And it is not until the penultimate page of "The Laughing Sun, Part Two" that we hear Jesús's version of the events that led up to the altercation

FIGURE 4. © Gilbert Hernandez, image courtesy Fantagraphics Books

with Laura. Unlike the various memories that are visually depicted throughout "The Laughing Sun," this final panel is overburdened with text. Jesús's final words in the panel underscore the preoccupation with memory in this two-part series: "Don't remember much after that . . . not 'till I hear Israel yelling at me like always" (127). Hernandez's use of depicted memories as well as his economical use of textual space yields a wonderfully rich albeit fragmented character sketch of Jesús, one that not only challenges his characters but his audience to piece together the narrative.

On the other hand, "Holidays in the Sun" takes place many years after "The Laughing Sun" and was published over a year later. "Holidays in the Sun" shows Jesús on an Alcatraz-like Prison island where his only respite from his daily misery comes from his memory and his imagination. Though clearly connected to "The Laughing Sun," "Holidays in the Sun" is simply another episode in the multitude of Palomar stories. In this story there are no thought bubbles to designate characters accessing memory as they do in "The Laughing Sun." Instead, Jesús must contend with his horrible reality on an island prison while tempering his mind's desire to conjure the woman Jesús has always desired: Luba. He indulges in these escapist fantasies in order to keep his mind from contemplating Laura and his child. Yet his mind comes back to the night of his fight with Laura, and in a sequence of eighteen panels the reader is thrust back to that moment as well, and for the first time we actually sees the events that have only heretofore been hinted at. While in "The Laughing Sun" the reader must construct the scene via the character narration of both Laura and Jesús, and via the varying speculations of the rest of the characters, in this sequence a series of images corresponding to Jesús's memories and unaccompanied by words takes the reader through the entire timeline from the argument to the narrating now, where Jesús sits on his prison bunk.

In effect, Hernandez's eighteen-panel spread over two pages is a strategy that cues the serial reader (figures 5 and 6). "Holidays in the Sun" is a meditation on memory and imagination as both a means of escape and a means of torture. Jesús can master his imagination only so much before the unconscious force of memory imposes itself on him. When two fellow inmates invite Jesús to participate in a ménage à trois, he declines, saying, "Naw . . . not tonight . . . Got things on my mind" (202). This is the only preview that Jesús's mind in is a contest with itself. Two panels later, it appears that someone calls to Jesús from within a room. "Hey there, boy. I think you'd better have a look at this . . ." a voice says. The adjacent panel reveals the voice to be that of Luba, who is sexily dressed in a corset and fishnet hose.

This moment of disorientation that Jesús experiences is shared by the reader. The shock of seeing Luba in an island prison for men destabilizes the reader, even if only momentarily (figure 7). Luba's appearance is not immediately cued as a figment of Jesús's imagination. The two panels at the bottom of the page first show Jesús in a sexual act with Luba as he vows to marry her, and next reveals that Luba has transformed into Laura, his wife. What intensifies reader disorientation is that the reader believes he or she is seeing actual events within the storyworld. But from the moment Jesús hears Luba speak from within the room, the reader is experiencing the world of Jesús's mind. Yet Hernandez does not alert the reader to prepare for this shift beforehand and instead allows the reader the opportunity to tease out what is being depicted. But just in case readers linger in their confusion, Hernandez has an overt narrator stabilize the storyworld (figure 8): "Though Jesús Angel has never had relations with Luba, he has indeed indulged in over fifteen thousand different sexual fantasies of the woman from the moment he first set his eyes

FIGURE 5. © Gilbert Hernandez, image courtesy Fantagraphics Books

FIGURE 6. © Gilbert Hernandez, image courtesy Fantagraphics Books

FIGURE 7. © Gilbert Hernandez, image courtesy Fantagraphics Books

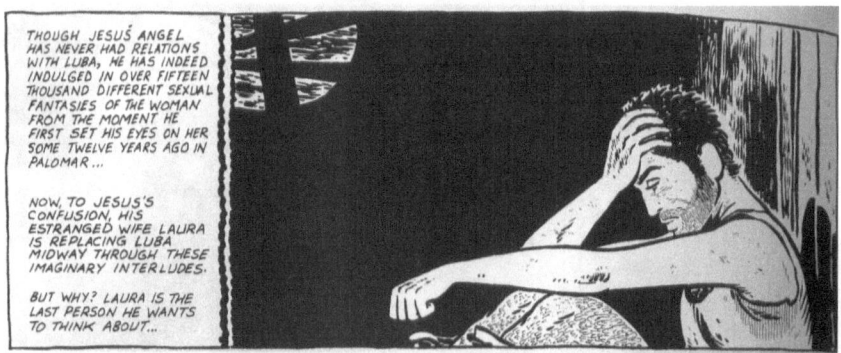

FIGURE 8. © Gilbert Hernandez, image courtesy Fantagraphics Books

on her some twelve years ago in Palomar . . . / Now, to Jesús's confusion, his estranged wife Laura is replacing Luba midway through these imaginary interludes. / But why? Laura is the last person he wants to think about . . ." (204). This intrusive narrator is superfluous for a reader who has read any of the prior Palomar stories that concern Jesús. Yet the shift between the represented storyworld and the world of Jesús's creation is so seamless that it threatened to

FIGURE 9. © Gilbert Hernandez, image courtesy Fantagraphics Books

confuse readers. The result is that Hernandez allows a small moment of narration to clear up any confusion.

A similar situation occurs only a few panels later, when Jesús again has a fantasy concerning Luba. Here he forces himself to think of another woman, for he realizes that his mind links Luba to Laura (figure 9): Hernandez uses this device in order to account for gaps in reader knowledge or memory of the Palomarian storyworld. Without the binding strip of narration, Hernandez's ideal readership instantly recognizes that the woman is Tonantzín, and it remembers her complex history in *Love and Rockets*. But as Sperber and Wilson's Principle of Relevance[8] suggests, Hernandez assumes his ideal readership will be able to fill in gaps for what is relevant to the narrative at hand. How-

---

8. Dan Sperber and Dierdre Wilson's Principle of Relevance, otherwise known as Relevance Theory, states "Every act of ostensive communication communicates a presumption of its own optimal relevance" (158). In other words, insofar as comprehension of communication operates with a high degree of efficiency, comprehension readily disambiguates information in a manner deemed most relevant to the receiver of the communication. Further, Sperber and Wilson's model suggests that the Principle of Relevance is automatic; we unconsciously seek the most relevant contexts for our interpretation.

ever, it is the type of concession that Hernandez makes at times in his work of the early 1980s, the type that begins to disappear from his later comics. As the series goes on, Hernandez's later work leaves out important contextualizing material, despite its relevance. Hernandez delegates more responsibility to the reader to discern the relevance of a given panel relative to the panels that come before and after it. However, in much of Hernandez's later work, the gaps in information are large enough that relevance is quite hindered. Indeed, Hernandez's aim of creating formally complex narratives coincides with the development of similarly complex Latino/a literature in the late 1990s and early 2000s.

Despite a reader's ability to concentrate on the relevant material from a panel or a particular issue of Hernandez's work, the accumulation of narrative events, character arcs, and story interconnectivity demands that readers track an ever-growing number of significant aspects of Palomar. As each of these stories is only a part of an even larger story, the text necessitates that a reader move fluidly between Jesús's stories in order to reconstruct a fully realized storyworld. Jesús's story requires an overarching perspective. Hernandez only partially overcomes the difficulties in reading these seemingly closed stories that are published irregularly. And in even more recalcitrant texts such as *Poison River*, his movement toward a more experimental and challenging narrative structure essentially repulsed attempts at reading it in serialized form.

Indeed, there is a high cognitive demand on the reader who reconstructs the Palomar storyworld. For a reader to establish the stable storyworld required by the narrative, there must be a sustained engagement with an overarching storyworld that gradually becomes more complex the further one reads into the Palomar stories. However, I assert that this cognitive scaffolding is networked to a reader's capacity to remember and recall significant narrative elements. Just like any function of memory and recall, this intricate latticework of narrative is finite and tends to decay over time. Royal is correct in noting the difficulties in rereading and cross-checking the various issues of a serialized graphic novel when compared to having the stories collected in a handful of volumes (264). As a result, though serialization may be a profitable means for a graphic artist to be able to do the work he or she needs to do, as Hatfield has shown, readers stand the best chance of recreating a mental model of the Palomarian storyworld with the entire set of stories at their disposal.

Of course the only way for readers to engage with the narrative on an emotional level is if they can successfully reconstruct the global mental representation encoded within the text. Memory function plays a large role in the mental scaffolding of a storyworld in the reader's imagination. Hernandez, through the medium of comics, accounts for both serial and ex post facto readers. This is not to say that serial readers will always have fewer challenges than other types of readers. Indeed, everything seems to suggest these cognitive demands might simply be insuperable for some readers no matter what. In the case of serialized literature, it would seem that time is the crucial issue. Building an overarching storyworld at the snail's pace of serialized publication is nearly impossible for readers, mostly because of the degradation of working memory of the reader. This necessitates reading and rereading as new installments are released. Waiting until all of the stories are collected into a "graphic novel" format has the least amount of short-term memory degradation, allowing for a more stable mental model of the storyworld. In the end, it seems that the ideal reading experience of the graphic novel comes at the culmination of the project.

Time is at the crux of the debate on the saliency of the graphic novel enterprise: if you have to wait until the end of the artist's project in order to achieve the sort of storyworld that allows for an emotional connection to the work, who will be around to purchase the individual installments as they are released and thereby financially keep the artist in business? On the other hand, if specific installments of serialized literature are so experimental and avant-garde that readers become frustrated and annoyed, the artist may be unable to finish the project due to financial constraints, as the purchasing audience may give up in frustration. Thus, some graphic artists who adopt the serial model can take narrative technique and experimentation only so far, as demonstrated by Hernandez's tour de force, *Poison River*.

THE LIMITS OF NURTURING A READERSHIP

Many of the challenges that *Poison River* presents to readers are manifest even when all of the serial installments are assembled in one volume. Thus, these challenges are only intensified when the novel is read serially. As scholars have noted, *Poison River* eschewed specific orienting devices for readers, devices later added when the serials were collected. For example, the chapter openings that appear in the collected version feature a specific character depicted in various stages of his or her life, complete with their name and chapter number. These chapter title pages were notably absent in *Poison River*'s original serial run. The utility of these chapter openings, however, is somewhat misleading. As each chapter is advertised with a specific character, readers might expect the chapter to be concentrated *on* that character. But the reality is that *Poison River* uses such a sprawling cast that the chapter titles are ultimately a bit misleading, which is understandable, for Hernandez added them much later.

I dwell on this issue as a sign of the frustration experienced by both readers and Hernandez during the publication of *Poison River*'s serial run. In short, Los Bros had cultivated a readership by that point which had specific expectations when picking up an issue of *Love and Rockets*. Though the respective storyworlds of Los Bros are contiguous, as noted above, many of the issues are short and self-contained. Hernandez's handling of the Jesús Angel storyline, which is similar to Jaime's handling of Speedy Ortiz, represents the default method of narration in *Love and Rockets*. Los Bros have mastered the art of expansive storytelling that is told within compressed space on the page. Again, I point to Hernandez's ability to move through great stretches of time in only a handful of panels. This technique is motivated in large degree by the richness of the *Love and Rockets* storyworld, especially as the series grew larger and larger. Los Bros could rely on the resourcefulness of the audience to bridge the gaps either by consultation of previous issues or through sheer force of memory recall from prior readings of *Love and Rockets*. As a result, in situations such as the Jesús Angel storyline where there are moments where the reader may be thwarted, Hernandez makes use of a device (such as an intrusive narrator), or instead the visual narrator blasts through years within the space of two pages (as in figure 6). These devices are evidence that Hernandez is acutely aware of the challenges his comics present to his audience. Thus, *Poison River* can be seen as the result of Hernandez's removal of these orienting devices that make the reading experience easier for the reader.

Before the publication of *Poison River*, Hernandez presented readers with his singular creation, Luba—a woman who is a force of will in Palomar—as a Latin American version of Athena, sprung fully formed upon the unsuspecting village to irrevocably alter the lives of its inhabitants. But as a result of the episodic and serial comics form used by Los Bros, there is rarely closure within the *Love and Rockets* storyworlds. That is to say, the story is never definitively "over." Unlike a self-contained novel that may provide closure without revealing subsequent events within the lives of the characters, Los Bros have the habit of taking up bits of the *Love and Rockets* narrative at any point, irrespective of what has happened to a character in an earlier episode.[9] This working method distinguishes the work of Los Bros from something that utilizes pre-

---

9. Gilbert's character Tonantzín Villaseñor is an excellent example of the fluidity of the *Love and Rockets* timeline. Though she publicly immolates herself as a demonstration of her political convictions in "Human Diastrophism," Tonantzín appears in a later issue of *Love and Rockets* that depicts the lead-up to her self-sacrifice.

quels such as *Star Wars*, which unfolds chronologically from earliest events to more recent. The prequels (Episodes I, II, and III), despite occurring before the events of the original trilogy of films, also follow a chronological structure, which provides Lucas's saga a significant dimension of tension as the audience awaits the outcome. *Love and Rockets*, by contrast, has never had a devotion to a chronological unfolding of events, precisely because there is no superordinate plot (or James Phelan's global instability) that motivates the narrative. Instead, the major locales (e.g., Palomar, Hoppers) anchor these patches of narrative that are woven together to create the larger fabric of the storyworld.[10]

COMPLEXITIES IN *POISON RIVER*

Poison River, at its core, is Luba's origin story that takes the reader from her early childhood (Luba is a newborn on the first page) to her arrival at Palomar on the final page. As Luba is arguably the central figure in Hernandez's comics, her origin story was poised to be of great interest to readers. This fact helps us understand the risks in storytelling that Hernandez takes in creating *Poison River*. In effect, he has a captive audience that will stay with him to the end because they want to see how this very popular character, Luba, came to be in Palomar. Heretofore, Luba's past had been an utter mystery to both readers and most of the inhabitants of Palomar. Because Hernandez had cultivated such a following among his readers, he had essentially earned the ability to push his art into areas he would not have early in his career.

Hernandez's opportunity to create such a complex serial comic tell us much about constraints and affordances that originate from the reader and how they affect an author's craft or will to style. Here it would seem that we have an excellent example of an audience with hospitable imaginations, a loyal readership that is, at least at the outset, willing to engage with a narrative on its own terms. But a closer inspection reveals not that Hernandez's reader-

---

10. Umberto Eco describes this type of narrative as a "loop": "Usually the loop series comes to be devised for commercial reasons: it is a matter of considering how to keep the series alive, of obviating the natural problem of the aging character. Instead of having characters put up with new adventures (that would imply their inexorable march toward death), they are made continually to relive their past. The loop solution produces paradoxes that were already the target of innumerable parodies. Characters have a little future but an enormous past, and in any case, nothing of their past will ever have to change the mythological present in which they have been presented to the reader from the beginning" (86). While I mostly agree with Eco here, I do wish to point out that while delving into Luba's past is ostensibly a commercial move on Gilbert's part, his execution of the narrative suggests that his desire to push himself and his art in *Poison River* superseded his motivation to sell many issues of his comics.

FIGURE 10. © Gilbert Hernandez, image courtesy Fantagraphics Books

ship was willingly receptive of his complex narrative, but rather that his own readership had a priori expectations for his comics that Hernandez himself had established. Thus, in the case of *Poison River*, Hernandez had nurtured his audience all too well, and they had become too accustomed to the narrative methods that he had already established. When he deviated from that form, his readership balked, unwilling to rise to Hernandez's challenge.

Interestingly, as *Poison River* entirely predates Luba's arrival to Palomar, reader memory is engaged differently than in Hernandez's other, highly intratextual, Palomarian comics. In other words, one requires no prior knowledge of Palomar in order to read *Poison River*, though there are moments when detailed knowledge of Hernandez's prior work enriches Luba's origin story. For example, in Palomarian comics published before *Poison River*, it is never explained why Luba's cousin, Ofelia, suffers from such awful back pain. Indeed, Ofelia's back pain seems to function as a characterizing device that enriches her as a personality. In *Poison River*, the reader who is familiar with Ofelia's back problems now comes to terms with the origins of this chronic, debilitating condition: a roadside attack that also results in the rapes and murders of her two friends, Gina and Ruben (figure 10).[11]

In this sequence, Gina and Ruben, late for Ruben's niece's baptism, offer to give Ofelia and the toddler Luba a ride to the movie theater. What happens next is no less horrific than the similarly styled violence that appears in both the novel version and the film adaptation of James Dickey's *Deliverance*.[12] Ofelia's back pain looms so large in Hernandez's comics that now that readers understand the violence imbued within the lingering pain Ofelia must bear for the rest of her life, Hernandez retroactively casts this shadow of violation on Ofelia's (and by extension, Luba's) story. Thus, although readers do not have to draw on their memories to supply the gaps in details, *Poison River* does supply further information about the Palomar with which he or she is already familiar. Hernandez demonstrates how his storyworld continually accretes and must be consistently revised by serial readers as more comics are introduced. Hatfield is correct when he says, "Everything is connected in *Poison River*, though not one single character realizes this: to movers and shakers like Garza, Salas, and Peter, the identities of such victims as Gina, Ruben, and Ofelia are beneath notice" (*Alternative* 88). But I go further when I state that everything in *Poison River* is connected to Palomar, even though everything in it predates what readers know about it. This shift in how readers view what they have already read, this revision of the memories of what they think they know, highlights the ever-evolving Palomarian storyworld and how reader experience shapes that world.

However, if a lack of prior reader experiences with Hernandez's work is not the source of the challenging nature of *Poison River*, whence does the recalcitrance originate? *Poison River* taxes readers' capacity for working memory and its ability to manage an overabundance of discrete bits of information. Working memory, as cognitive research has shown, is a crucial aspect of our ability to recall information. Specifically, episodic and semantic memory operations are in play to a large degree in reading a text such as *Poison River*. According to John J. Ratey, episodic memory "is the capacity to place facts and events in

---

11. Hatfield calls this event in *Poison River* a "terrorist attack." While technically he is correct, I dislike the connotation that the term carries in contemporary discussions, for it often suggests the U.S. so-called War on Terror. Incidentally, this attack sequence in *Poison River* may well be the most disturbing moment in the series for its shocking and senseless violence.

12. It is very likely that *Deliverance* is an intertext here. Both acts of violence befall unsuspecting travelers. Also, the settings for both scenes take place in what appears to be an isolated, heavily wooded area. Further, there is a depiction of male sodomy in both scenes, along with several murders. In one sense, then, Ofelia's survival of this attack and subsequent guardianship of Luba becomes a sort of deliverance within *Poison River*.

time and to refer to them freely" (201), and semantic memory as "detached from personal experience [...] allow[ing] for the retention of facts and everyday functions, including categories of events, objects, spatial knowledge, and symbolic description" (202). The two types of memory are related, and what seems to be one important difference is the emotional connections (or lack thereof) to the memories in question. Further, episodic memory appears to be tied to the creation of narrative, especially in weaving discrete events into a story. The two types of memory, it would seem, are responsible for our ability to recall our connection to personal experiences (episodic) as well as the ability to categorize and generalize information gathered by rote exposure.

In *Narrative Comprehension,* Catherine Emmott articulates the two memory categories as general knowledge (semantic) and text-specific knowledge (episodic). Both types of knowledge are crucial if a reader is to comprehend a text, and Emmott's study shows how research on text-specific knowledge helps shed light on the substantial body of work on general knowledge. In short, there is knowledge that is used by the reader "not only to 'fill in' missing parts of a script or to show the links between objects, but to deduce connections such as cause and effect" (27). A text "may also encourage the reader to draw on his/her general knowledge to create certain special effects or to contribute to the overall plot or themes of a book" (29). But there is also text-specific knowledge that the reader gains through the experience of reading a text, "information which applies only within a particular text (or related group of texts), such as accumulated knowledge about specific characters, about which characters are related to each other, and about which characters live in a particular place, as well as a record of the events that have occurred" (35). Because the store of text-specific knowledge that is accumulated when reading *Love and Rockets* is ever growing, storylines by Hernandez which rely heavily on text-specific knowledge present formidable challenges to readers. With these two types of memory function and knowledge in mind, we can further understand why *Poison River* is such a challenge to serial readers who must wait for long stretches of time between published issues.

There are nearly forty named characters who play significant roles in *Poison River.* Of these characters, only a few appear in earlier issues of *Love and Rockets.* As a result, even loyal readers are presented with a great deal of new materials to encode and track. And though *Poison River* is ostensibly Luba's story, she quite often recedes to the background. There is a palpable lack of an intrusive narrator, and, unlike in earlier episodes of Palomarian comics, characters do not convey crucial orienting material to the reader via dialogue with another character. The visual/verbal narrator goes to great pains to show the interconnections among the characters without making said interconnections unambiguous. More importantly, it is the introduction of Peter Río that pushes *Poison River* to its frustrating level of complexity.[13]

Before Peter is introduced, the storyline takes Luba from a newborn to a young girl of around eight years old, with several global instabilities that motivate the narrative progression: the discovery that María and Eduardo are Luba's parents; Eduardo's leaving Luba with his sister Hilda and niece Ofelia; and the attack on Ofelia, Gina, and Ruben that forces Ofelia to leave. These events follow in chronological order and are very much in line with the mode of storytelling Gilbert has established heretofore: the storytelling is very much what readers expect to find in a Palomar-related narrative. Thus, if Peter Río can be seen as a complicating, fracturing force in Luba's life, it is evident that he does the same for the narrative form in *Poison River*. In essence, Peter Río is poison within the storyworld, and his disruptive nature manages to bleed into the very design of Hernandez's comic.

Peter Río makes his entrance into the narrative in chapter 5 as the conga player and manager to Los Fritos, a third-rate musical act. With the introduction of Peter into Luba's world, Hernandez by default introduces all of Peter's salient relationships that will carry great weight in the remainder of *Poison River*. Río proves to be a catalyst for Luba's discontent, and soon after Peter fetishizes Luba's bellybutton,[14] she instantly gains a heightened sense of self-worth. She breaks off her relationship with her first boyfriend, Pino, and then assaults Omo with a hammer[15] when he makes sexual advances on her. Peter thus destabilizes Luba's world and, obliquely, his own. For at the end of chapter 5, when we see Peter and Luba leaving town together in his car, the last two frames introduce Isobel, the mother of Peter's child, Arjelia.

Peter's dealings as a small-time gangster quickly expand the cast in *Poison River* as he ascends to the top of the criminal underworld. Peter's grab for power comes to a head in chapter 10, a chapter that also provides an excellent example of the complexity of *Poison River*. Hernandez deploys several simultaneous storylines that depict differing events whose consequences will

---

13. It is clear that Peter Río (whose last name means "river" in Spanish and whose initials he shares with the title) is the poison river to which the title alludes. Hatfield has pointed to this fact, but no one has yet observed that the novel's complexity originates with Peter Río or why Río places such a strain on readers.

14. Peter's sexual fetish of choice is to masturbate while gazing into a woman's bellybutton.

15. Readers familiar with Gilbert's Palomar comics will immediately see the significance of this moment. Throughout *Love and Rockets*, Luba is often depicted holding a claw hammer, an object that becomes a metonym for her strength and stubbornness. Thus, the moment she defends herself from Omo with a hammer, we have another origin story.

FIGURE 11. © Gilbert Hernandez, image courtesy Fantagraphics Books

result in Peter's unchecked power.[16] However, there is a great deal of temporal compression in the last few pages of chapter 10 (figures 11, 12, and 13). Capitan Ortíz forces himself on Luba, and five panels later there is an image of a tiny fetus—the product of Luba's rape.

Garza and Salas have a meeting, and Blas is sent along to see if he is a spy. At the same time, Peter's father, Fermin, moves to strangle Isobel, while Luba is raped by Ricky, the organist for Los Fritos. Gorgo, a hit man long associated with Luba's family, is beset by thugs sent by enemies at the same moment

---

16. This scene in *Poison River* owes a great deal to a similar scene in Francis Ford Coppola's *The Godfather*, wherein Michael Corleone orchestrates the murders of the heads of the Five Families at the exact moment he literally becomes godfather to his nephew in a christening ceremony in a church. Just as those separate murders (and the child's christening) all occur simultaneously, Peter is in the presence of Capitan Ortíz and thus has an unassailable alibi.

FIGURE 12. © Gilbert Hernandez, image courtesy Fantagraphics Books

everything else occurs. Panels flash between events, and readers must work to keep track of all of the various relationships between the characters and the separate yet simultaneous events. Peter's ascension to power is realized as he is conspicuously absent from the final page of chapter 10, with the exception of the ubiquitous black-faced cartoon character Pedro Pacotilla, who, despite Peter's protests, is associated with him.[17] The close-up of Pedro smiling subsequent to the rape and carnage that closes the chapter serves as a stand-in for Peter himself (figure 13).

Peter's world crashes upon the Palomarian storyworld that readers have come to cherish and expect in ways that ratchet up the complexity of the nar-

---

17. Peter's given name is Pedro, but he insists on being called Peter because he vehemently dislikes the racist cartoon character of the same name.

FIGURE 13. © Gilbert Hernandez, image courtesy Fantagraphics Books

rative discourse. Often Gilbert moves freely amidst the chronology as it suits his narrative, as in chapter 12, when we see Luba's mother María in the heyday of her youth. But even here, we see the connections to Peter and Fermín Río, and so the narrative complexity is not lessened in this chapter. This analeptic chapter, appearing in the second half of *Poison River*, only indirectly impacts Luba. Instead, the chapter reveals something heretofore hidden regarding both Fermín and Peter Río—that they both had a sexual relationship with María and that both of them have known full well who Luba is for quite some time. Hernandez then takes the reader back to the moment Peter and Luba are introduced in chapter 5 and reveals the first actual meeting between the two, now in the context of not only his gangster ties but his ties to Luba's mother as well. Hernandez, as he did in comics such as "Holidays in the Sun," leaps forward many years in the space of one page. In this case, he opens the page with a top-left panel that shows Luba and Peter's marriage and efficiently moves to the moment after the birth of Luba's son as they both lie in bed, when it is revealed that Peter has had a stroke during the night. The moment Luba wakes up is the moment just subsequent to the extended analepsis that comprises chapter 11 and most of chapter 12.

Again, it is important to remember that Hernandez does not provide clear signposts during these temporal shifts but rather allows the reader to make clear sense of the intricate connections of time and character. At the height of *Poison River*'s complexity, Peter has a stroke. Accordingly, as he begins a slow deterioration, the cognitive challenges to the reader begin to recede. Similarly, Luba is forcibly extricated from Peter's world, and her character comes full circle as she reconciles with Pino and Omo. Ofelia's attackers encounter mob justice, providing some semblance of closure for her. As both Luba and her daughter, along with Ofelia, see Palomar in the distance, the serial reader is once more in familiar territory.

Unlike previous Palomar stories, *Poison River* is rigorously complex, which is fitting for its most complex character. Even without Luba's origin story, a reader has many indications that she has been through hell and back even before she set one foot in Palomar. Hatfield characterizes *Poison River* as a "supreme test of readers' loyalty" (*Alternative* 88) because of its experimental storytelling style. As with all of the examples I have raised in this book, the attempt at challenging audiences, even loyal ones, through the design of storyworlds may be even more important whether such challenges are accepted or not. It is the challenge that opens audiences to the possibilities that Latino/a authors have a wealth of narrative devices at their behest when creating storyworlds.

Though comics have been disparaged and derided as unimportant, juvenile, and even dangerous, they have also proven to be a highly imaginative and unrestrained mode of storytelling. And while there have been similar constraints placed on comics authors by publishers, there has also been a greater opportunity to publish work in the comics genre, thanks in large part to underground and alternative comics. Within this tradition, Latino/a authors such as Gus Arriola, Frank Espinosa, Lalo Alcaraz, and Los Bros Hernandez have made the most of this visual and verbal medium of storytelling. These and other Latino/a comics artists have cultivated large audiences who follow their often serialized works with passion and zeal. Yet even with such a devoted audience, authors such as Gilbert Hernandez have found that narrative design is still highly influenced by audience reception. Not only does Hernandez's work, and specifically *Poison River*, show the relationship between an audience's ability to work through a cognitively challenging text, but it also suggests how serial publication can intensify such reading challenges due to the burden of remembering salient features of the narrative. Still, the rise of Los Bros Hernandez and the ever-growing complexity of their craft parallel the development of Latino/a literature in general and the ability of Latino/a authors to make use of any and all tools of narrative worldmaking.

The next chapter examines two works of postmillennial Latino/a literature that feature complex narrative structures that force readers to move beyond the text in order to see the interconnectedness of history, literature, and popular culture not just within the United States but also within a global context.

CHAPTER 4

Paratextual Play

Intertextual Interventions in Sandra Cisneros's *Caramelo* and Junot Díaz's *The Brief Wondrous Life of Oscar Wao*

AS THE TWENTY-FIRST century opened, two novels by Latino/s writers received high acclaim and significant critical praise. Sandra Cisneros, long admired for her contribution to Chicana feminism with her book *The House on Mango Street*, and Junot Díaz, a Dominican American writer whose first collection of short stories, *Drown*, created noteworthy anticipation for his first major work, each wrote a novel whose respective scope aligns itself with the epic, spanning both time (as evidenced through generational links within the narrative) and geographic space.

While their heavy use of autobiographical material and genealogical narrative continues this tradition in Latino/a literature, both Cisneros and Díaz inflect this tradition with a postmodern spin, creating fictional, self-reflexive writers who are distinct from autobiographers such as Richard Rodriguez, Oscar Acosta, and Gloria Anzaldúa in several ways.[1] This turn in Latino/a

---

1. Again, the anomalous nature of Acosta's books in Latino letters comes to the fore. As Frederick Luis Aldama has pronounced in *Postethnic*, and as I have outlined in chapter 1, Acosta's books are *mostly* based on historical fact. Because of this dominance of Acosta's life history within his books, I am here including his works as very much entrenched in the autobiographical arc traced by most Latino fiction. Despite my claim that Cisneros and Díaz move toward a different type of writing than Latinos who have come before them, they—along with others such as Salvador Plascencia and Daniel Alarcón—continue to use personal life history within their fiction. Arguably, all writers of fiction do this to some degree, following the ubiq-

letters signals a changing readership, which has provided Cisneros and Díaz with the affordances to write in this postmodern mode with such confidence and success—affordances Latino/a writers of the twentieth century did not have to such a degree.

Unlike Acosta and Anzaldúa, who both create textual counterselves in order to use narrative as a means of understanding the self and the self-within-community, as I showed in chapter 1, in *Caramelo* and *The Brief Wondrous Life of Oscar Wao* (hereafter *Oscar Wao*), Cisneros and Díaz each create a fictional writer-as-protagonist who chronicles the lives of others as a means of indirectly (or vicariously) understanding the self. This inventing of a writer-as-protagonist who shapes the narrative world is momentous in Latino literature. It allows the reader to see more transparently how these sorts of narratives have been constructed *and* received by their contemporaneous audiences. In short, while Acosta and Anzaldúa project themselves into their storyworlds, Cisneros and Díaz create fictional protagonists who claim to have written the books *Caramelo* and *Oscar Wao*. Writing, which is often seen as an act of empowerment, is not used here under the guise of documenting but as an act of creation posing as documentation. It is a postmodern masquerade of the highest order.

If we consider the two types of narrators in question here, that is, a narrator who purports to write autobiography and a narrator as a chronicler of other lives, we can see how the demands of creating worlds with a particular ontological structure place constraints on the devices available to these narrators. These ontological structures, in turn, are embedded within audience expectations for the literature in question. For example, an author of an autobiography or memoir has a certain burden of truth when creating his or her narrative world. This standard of veracity nearly derailed the writing career of the infamous James Frey, when his egregious contortion of the facts came to light regarding his supposedly factual account of his struggles with addiction in *A Million Little Pieces*. Subsequent to the Frey scandal, John D'Agata was also accused of bending fact to his own narrative devices, particularly in his *About a Mountain*. And most recently, there is the case of Greg Mortenson's *Three Cups of Tea*, an arguably fictionalized account of the aftermath of his failed attempt to summit K2.

A *60 Minutes* exposé revealed Mortenson's narrative as a marketing tactic with the aim of moving readers beyond an emotional threshold that would make them donate their own money to Mortenson's charity—a charity which,

---

uitous dictum to "write what they know"; minority writers are often compelled to talk about this characteristic of their writing in interviews. It is as if ethnic writers are only able to write fiction rooted in life events, which is clearly not the case.

as Jon Krakauer maintains, functions as Mortenson's personal bank account that pays his travel arrangements for his paid speaking engagements. In the cases of Frey and D'Agata, and especially Mortenson, a desire to move creatively beyond the sheer facts (ostensibly to render a more compelling narrative and thus reading experience and, some would explain, to increase personal wealth) has been met with vociferous challenges from readers who feel they have been fooled.[2]

But what happens when we have fiction that poses as a true account—as autobiography or biography? How do audiences engage with creations that claim to chronicle true things that never happened? This metafictional ploy goes back as far as Cervantes, who in *Don Quixote de la Mancha* features a narrator posing as Cervantes who claims to translate an account of Don Quixote written by the Moor Cide Hamete Benengeli. *Don Quixote,* Daniel Defoe's *Robinson Crusoe,* and Jonathan Swift's *Gulliver's Travels* are all works of fiction that operate under the aegis of nonfiction. This mode of fictional storytelling that assumes a mask of truth is apparently as old as the novel itself. Why then have Latinos only recently written narratives using this well-established form?

Insofar as Piri Thomas worked to give an account of how difficult life on the streets is, the argument runs, he must therefore adhere strictly to the events as they happened. Realism in this case is a snapshot of the gritty realities of life, and so anything that undermines the factuality of this representation is to be avoided. Latino/a literature has grown out of a need to document the social contexts which its authors put on full display within their narratives. The use of social realism can give a voice for those whose stories are often unheard, and this narrative mode is one that often lends a sense of power to groups of disenfranchised people living in the liminal spaces of our society. Putting it another way, it is difficult to communicate a social commentary if an author decides to design formally complex narrative structure.

This is not to say that Cisneros and Díaz are unconcerned with the sociopolitical valences of their novels. History, as something to be unearthed and examined, is at the center of their texts. In addition, *Caramelo* and *Oscar Wao* are concerned with movement: with social, cultural, and national boundaries that are invariably crossed again and again. Each novel features a narrator who is the purported writer of the text we encounter, writers who are using the process of narrative worldmaking in order to make sense of some-

---

2. Each of these cases demonstrates in extremis just how certain narratives can powerfully move readers. Thus, when readers discover that their emotions have been falsely engaged in the cases of Frey, Mortenson, and to some degree D'Agata, other powerful emotions are then directed at the authors, who seem like purveyors of cheap tricks and manipulators of readers' trust.

thing very personal—something that remains hidden from them. However, in order to make sense of their experience and history, each narrator feels moved to invoke a multitude of intertexts in order to express his- or herself fully. It is as if they can only indirectly recreate the narratives they have experienced by implying a sense of what it's like—through allusion and analogy. Yet the heavy use of analogies, metaphors, and intertextual material presents significant challenges to audiences, for it assumes a shared base of knowledge. Without that shared base, the use of intertextual material is ineffectual at best, alienating at worst.

In addition to creating a dense network of intertextual references, Cisneros and Díaz make heavy use of footnotes. Footnotes are primarily used in works of scholarship to provide helpful, contextualizing material for the reader, and authors have relied on footnotes to shape their narrative worlds in a manner that rises above what may be called typical *paratextual material*.[3] In this final chapter, I want to examine how readers must cognitively move through these issues of intertextuality and paratextuality and negotiate the particular challenges these narrative issues raise. I also consider how these features of Cisneros's and Díaz's texts contribute meaningfully to their narrative designs.

Along with the authorial decision to make use of intertexts and paratexts within my case studies, the narrators themselves play a part in this narrative design, for they purport to be the ones writing the text that comprises the respective novels of Cisneros and Díaz. In other words, the fact that these narrators so readily move to intertexts and use footnotes denotes something very particular about them and their assumptions of audience. These narrators have information, often arcane bits of knowledge and history, readily at their disposal. It is as if they have encyclopedic memory as they casually refer to esoteric

---

3. While many authors have used this device, David Foster Wallace is generally acknowledged as having made particularly rich use of the footnote within his fiction. His massive *Infinite Jest* includes over one hundred footnotes, and several of these footnotes have footnotes themselves. But unlike many scholarly footnotes that may be superfluous depending on the reader's knowledge of the material, the footnotes in *Infinite Jest* are an integral part of the narrative architecture and cannot be disregarded by the reader, no matter how tempting it may be to do so. Similarly, Mark Z. Danielewski's *House of Leaves* presents a fractured narrative that is only reconstructed, in part, by the reader's stitching together of the small pieces—including the many footnotes—that lie strewn throughout the text. These purveyors of the fictional footnote all bear a great debt to Vladimir Nabokov's *Pale Fire*, which is essentially a compendium of footnotes to a 999-line poem written by the fictional poet John Shade. In all of these works, the reader must oscillate between the primary narrative and the secondary footnote. However, in each of these works the footnotes rise above being secondary material, especially in *Pale Fire*. In fact, one might easily profess that the 999-line poem in *Pale Fire* is the secondary material, not the notes that follow it.

facts. The result is that these narrators express themselves and their narrative in expansive ways—ways for which actual readers may not be prepared.

Rather than adhere to Kellman's dictum of educating the audience on matters of Latino/a culture as mentioned in chapter 2, Cisneros and Díaz make no such concessions to their audiences. In designing their storyworlds, these authors constantly reach beyond the text in order to "borrow" from other works of literature, moments in history, popular culture, and so on. In turn, these moments force the readers to engage with intertextual and paratextual materials by moving externally from the text proper to what appears to be secondary material. What happens, cognitively speaking, when a reader must engage with such "external" material? What occurs when a reader is presented with an intertext with which he or she is unfamiliar? What happens when the narrator has encyclopedic recall (seemingly) of a wealth of intertexts that readers do not? In pursuit of answers to these questions, I will first articulate how I am using the term *intertextuality*; then I will turn to examine these issues in Cisneros's *Caramelo* and Díaz's *Oscar Wao*.

While the high degree of intertextuality and use of footnotes in Cisneros's and Díaz's novels are significant moments in the arc of Latino/a literature, these novels also make equal use of these narrative devices. Indeed, Cisneros's intertexts and footnotes are not as tightly integrated within the narrative proper as are Díaz's, yet they still provide meaningful shape to the storyworld. Both novels use intertexts and footnotes as a means of granting a global and historic feel to what is, in both cases, a narrative about one Latino family. At issue in the present chapter is the degree to which the intertexts and footnotes in each respective novel contribute to storyworld design. Without question, the external material is meaningful to each novel. However, for reasons I will articulate below, Cisneros's intertexts and footnotes function more as traditional, ancillary material, while Díaz's are grafted in such a way that the narrative cannot be what it is without them.

INTERTEXTUALITY AND THE READER

Julia Kristeva is credited with coining the term *intertextuality* in her essay "Word, Dialogue and Novel." Other scholars, such as Graham Allen, have further expanded the issue of intertextuality, to the point that it may be that any and all texts are inherently intertextual, as T. S. Eliot claimed in "Tradition and Individual Talent" (4–5). At a base level, I also take this to be the case. That is to say, I agree that all writers are bound to the writers who have come before them; all writings are bound to the writings that have preceded them. Without a discernible lineage of forms and language among texts, certain texts would be devoid of meaning. Again, as Eliot maintained, all texts are born within a tradition of other writings. Further, it is the experiences of readers with these forms that "lend" meaning to any text we encounter for the first time. Simply put, a reader relies on his or her memory to help give context and shape to the newly encountered text; the reader does not encounter a text de novo.

Of course, Roland Barthes famously seized upon this rather patent notion and declared that the author was not the master of the text but instead that the author was subservient to other texts that preceded him or her. Thus, Barthes proclaimed the "death of the author." However, whether an author cannot truly create something deemed ex nihilo does not impinge on whether the author can rely on these prior forms or intertexts to create the semblance of something new when readers encounter it, as Barthes suggests with his concept of the scriptor. In fact, the newness of a text or its subject is hardly the point, as Shklovsky admirably demonstrated. Instead, the author enstranges the reader by presenting the familiar in new ways.

But if Kristeva, and Bakhtin before her, are correct in maintaining that a given text is intelligible based on a conglomeration of other texts that lend nuance and meaning and thus becomes something greater than the text at hand, what are we to make of a readership and its access to these conglomerate texts? For example, it seems to me that an author, conceived of as Barthes's scriptor, is fully aware of his or her use of intertexts. I agree that Cisneros may use Rita Hayworth or Raquel Welch, or Díaz may use the *Fantastic Four* or *Akira* as intertexts, as literary and/or cultural markers that provide further texture and nuance to the narrative world they create, and in deliberate ways.[4]

In other words, Cisneros introduces Hayworth and Welch into her novel as a means of conveying Hollywood's desire to whiten actresses of Latino/a ancestry as well as these actresses' apparent willingness to erase their Spanish surnames in order to gain entry into the Hollywood system. The use of Hayworth and Welch as intertexts is in alignment with Cisneros's will to style. Yet what happens when a reader encounters the name Rita Hayworth without the knowledge of her racial passing in Hollywood? In the case of Welch, Cisneros provides a sarcastic footnote that provides the reader with this biased take on

---

4. It may seem odd to refer to human beings as intertexts, but here it is useful to note that "Rita Hayworth" was the Hollywood persona of Margarita Carmen Cansino, who also functions as a major intertext in the Argentinian author Manuel Puig's novel, *Betrayed by Rita Hayworth*. Regarding Welch, Cisneros writes in a footnote: "According to the *Star*, Raquel Welch's real name is Raquel Tejada, and she's Latina. We would've cheered if we'd known this back then, except no one knew it except Raquel Tejada. Maybe not even Raquel Welch" (317). In both instances, Hayworth and Welch provide visual embodiments of the concept of passing.

Welch's name change. But Cisneros introduces Rita Hayworth ever so briefly with no context whatsoever. So, while the author here has a particular intent in introducing Hayworth as an intertext, there is the possibility that Cisneros's readership may be unaware of the significance of Rita Hayworth.

This potential unawareness of intertexts on the part of the reader is important, for it tells us something about the intelligibility and degree of difficulty of certain narratives. The saliency of a given intertext may vary, and the author may ameliorate the distancing effect of intertextual material through the narrative itself or through the use of footnotes. For instance, the *Fantastic Four* series of comics, for Díaz, is a crucial intertext in understanding *Oscar Wao*. Not only does the novel open with a quote from Galactus, an important antagonist in the *Fantastic Four*, but also the *Fantastic Four* storyworld is referred to again and again throughout the narrative and in footnotes. Díaz intuits that his audience may not have the specialized knowledge of the *Fantastic Four*. Thus, Díaz at times provides the barest reference material regarding this type of intertext so as to not "lose" his readership. On the other hand, there are many occasions where Díaz does not contextualize his intertext. It is an important example of the author's awareness of particular challenges his or her created narrative may present to readers, as well as his or her decision to force the reader to fill in their gap of knowledge without relying on the author to do it for him or her.

Arguably, there are at least three types of readers of narrative as far as intertexts are concerned: those who are intimately aware of the intertextual reference, those who are obliquely aware of the intertext, and those who are mostly unaware of the intertext. For each of these readers, the reconstruction of the storyworld yields a different result, leading to a difference in engagement with the narrative. If narrative comprehension is an aspect of storyworld reconstruction, and if storyworld reconstruction is a significant goal for the reader, the reader will then make certain attempts at understanding allusory intertexts. In either case, the reader must leave the narrative text proper in order to consult an external source, whether that source be a footnote, an online source, or experiential memory.

Consultation of these external sources presents a significant challenge for readers, especially if they are the kind of reader with no experience of a specific intertext. If the intertext is of the minor variety (i.e., a reader can comprehend the narrative without knowledge of the intertext), the reader can move through the narrative only slightly hindered by this lack of knowledge. On the other hand, if the intertext is crucial to narrative comprehension, the author will either provide the reader with the requisite textual support or will demand that the reader make the effort to uncover the value of the intertext in question. Intertexts, then, play varying roles within a narrative and are not equal.

I rely on Gérard Genette's definitions for intertextuality and paratexuality, which essentially come in the form of allusion and quotation, and texts that lie beyond the text proper, respectively. At issue, then, are the relationships between the various texts as they form a contiguous network that contributes to a reader's narrative comprehension. As many, if not all, narrative texts are intertextual in some form, I am concerned with those narratives by Latino/a authors whose narrative structure relies on a high level of intertextuality.

Cisneros's novel often uses historical intertexts in order to uncover the personal histories of the characters within *Caramelo* and also as a means of engaging with and contesting history. Díaz, conversely, uses a wide array of intertexts (both actual and fabricated) in a pastiche of pop culture and the historical record. Moreover, what is important here is the deliberate use of intertexts within the fiction of Latino/a-identified authors. What does it tell us that two major works of Latino/a literature with a greater degree of intertextuality than previous texts in this tradition appeared only after the turn of the twenty-first century? Or rather they are novels within the Latino/a tradition that make conscious, deliberate use of intertexts in their narrative designs. What does it tell us that these two novels were not only well received by audiences and critics but that each won highly prestigious literary awards?[5] Finally, what does it say that these two novels, whose thematic focus is on how genealogical history can provide new ways of understanding the present, must extend into historical and popular intertexts with a vigor and intensity not hitherto seen in Latino/a letters?

SANDRA CISNEROS'S *CARAMELO* IN CONTEXT

In a work that is at once expansive and faithful to Cisneros's vignette-style of narrative, one that purports to simultaneously document the lives of the sundry cast of Chicanos in the narrator's life while confessing to being "*puro cuento,*" a term that can also be likewise translated as "only story" or "pure fabrication," *Caramelo* foregrounds the epistemic issues involved in attempts to write or document the lives of the family. The narrator Celaya "Lala" Reyes begins with an annual trip south from Chicago to Mexico as the impetus for her recovery project that concerns her father's mother (whom she calls the "Awful Grandmother"), her father's father ("Little Grandfather"), and the

---

5. Cisneros won the American Book Award for *Caramelo*. Díaz won the Pulitzer Prize for Literature for *The Brief Wondrous Life of Oscar Wao*.

events in their lives that inform the moment that ends part one when Celaya's father must choose between his love for his wife and his loyalty to his mother. The remainder of the novel is Celaya's coming to terms with her hidden family history, a history that spans many generations and nations. In divining the past and reconstructing the significant moments in the histories of her family members as well as the nations of the United States and Mexico, Cisneros often relies on the footnote as a contextualizing and historicizing apparatus in her narrative.

The many footnotes that appear in *Caramelo* help distinguish it from prior works of Latino/a literature. In spite of my claim, the footnotes in *Caramelo* have also had a mixed reception among critics, as Eva Paulina Bueno has noted, appropriately enough, in a footnote (47–48). The general thrust of the reviewers Bueno cites is that while they recognize the effort that must have gone into accumulating and documenting the sundry material contained in the footnotes, they are ultimately too cumbersome and add to *Caramelo*'s unwieldy bulk. Ilan Stavans, too, is perplexed at Cisneros's use of footnotes (*A Critic's Journey* 58). Such reviewers are of interest because of their expectations that are rooted in the Latino/a literary tradition as well as Cisneros's own prior narrative excursions.

As I mentioned at the beginning of this section, Cisneros characteristically writes vignettes and, as Stavans maintains, is quite accomplished in this brief narrative form. Her novella *The House on Mango Street* is essentially a series of interconnected vignettes, as is *Caramelo*. Also, her narrative prose prior to *Caramelo* is often straightforward and localized within the narrator's immediate experience; only rarely does the narrator reach into intertextual material during the narrative. But that is not all. The expansiveness that is created with the significant usage of footnotes is rare in Latino/a letters, and the only major novel by a Latino that uses footnotes and appeared prior to *Caramelo* is Oscar Hijuelos's *The Mambo Kings Play Songs of Love*, which incidentally also won the Pulitzer Prize for Literature.[6]

Jordana Finnegan views the footnotes in *Caramelo* in this way:

> Moreover, the novel often locates these "epic" figures and events in footnotes at the end of chapters, which minimizes their importance in relation to the Reyes family history. *Caramelo*'s unconventional footnotes, marked by conversational language and references to popular culture, subvert the traditional use of footnotes to substantiate academic claims. Yet even as Cisneros revises

---

6. I must make it clear that in no way do I assert that the use of footnotes or other paratextual material somehow elevates the literariness (or at least prize-worthiness) of Latino/a literature. It just so happens that several of the notable novels written by Latinos have used footnotes in interesting ways.

the function of the footnote in scholarly studies, the very presence of footnotes in the novel positions *Caramelo* as an alternative kind of history. (131)

While I agree that the use of footnotes in fiction is unconventional in a general sense, they do have precedent in U.S. fiction written at around the same time—novels that I have mentioned in footnote 3 of this chapter. But the footnotes in *Caramelo* are even more unconventional if we only consider Latino/a literature, and that is the salient concern here. Perhaps this is what Finnegan means when she says that Cisneros uses footnotes to subvert the ways in which academic claims are often made.

I maintain, however, that this is a rather limited view of how the footnotes in *Caramelo* enrich the reading experience. Clearly, many reviewers found the footnotes to be challenging, if not superfluous. Further, we do not need the footnotes to view *Caramelo* as an "alternative kind of history" as Finnegan remarks. The fact that Celaya reconstructs her family history under the auspices of the spirit of Awful Grandmother lets us know that we are not getting a so-called accurate reconstruction of historical events, footnotes or no. In other words, the footnotes are not in the novel simply to provide the semblance of historical heft to the narrative, and they do not function only to minimize historical figures while exalting Celaya's family. The significance of the footnotes in *Caramelo* is rooted firmly in the imaginations of the reader.

THE SIGNIFICANCE OF FOOTNOTES IN *CARAMELO*

In a seminal essay that appeared in *PMLA* in 1983, Shari Benstock grapples with the issue of the footnote in the fictional text:

> Footnotes in fictional texts do not necessarily follow the rules that govern annotation in critical texts: they may or may not provide citation, explication, elaboration, or definition for an aspect of the text; they may or may not follow "standard form"; they may or may not be subordinate to the text to which they are affixed. Most significant, they belong to a fictional universe, stem from a creative act rather than a critical one, and direct themselves toward the fiction and never toward an external construct, even when they cite "real" works in the world outside the particular fiction. (204–5)

For Benstock, the issue of authority within the work of fiction is of particular interest and specifically the ways readers account for the varied voices that often appear in footnotes—voices that are often not the same as the narrative proper. If this is a matter of authority and its consequent subversion of authority, as Finnegan asserts, then we have a case of an author using these prior expectations of readers in support of specific effects in the narratives in which footnotes appear.

In essence, an author such as Cisneros is acutely aware that readers have been conditioned to recognize footnotes as being authoritative, as being the external verification apparatus upon which the reader can rely when texts become difficult or present unfamiliar material that must be glossed. The questions then become: Does Cisneros use her footnotes in an authoritative way, or does she use them to subvert academic claims? Also, does Cisneros employ a different voice from the narrative proper? Another way of thinking of this issue is to ask how the footnotes change the reading experience of *Caramelo*.

There are forty-one footnotes in *Caramelo*. The first two footnotes appear as a footnote within a footnote, and already they display how Cisneros will deploy the footnotes throughout her novel. The first footnote gives the reader an explication of the Maxwell Street flea market Celaya invokes on page 7. When reading the first footnote, one can see why it is not a part of the main narrative; it is a tangential aside that gives a nostalgic opinion of the flea market on Maxwell Street in Chicago: "It was a filthy, pungent, wonderful place filled with astonishing people, good music, and goods from don't-ask-where" (9). The writer of the footnotes remarks on how the flea market (the actual flea market) no longer exists in the manner recalled in the narrative.

There is a dislocation of space and time, and the reader experiences this firsthand when reading the footnote. Though the first mention of the Maxwell Street flea market in the novel occurs when Celaya is eight years old, the footnote is written well after the flea market has moved to a different street. Like the photograph of the family that hangs above Celaya's father's bed in the novel's opening, the allusion to the Maxwell Street flea market is preserved in the amber of memory. The author of the footnote accuses the University of Illinois of forcing the relocation of the flea market, making obvious how the gentrification and eminent domain of the educational elite conflicted with the purveyors of modest goods at a flea market.

Yet the second footnote is significant for different reasons. First, it provides further commentary on something mentioned in the first footnote: Jim's Original Hot Dogs, "founded in 1939, stands where it always has, a memorial to Maxwell Street's funky past" (9). Second, it suggests that the narrator of the footnotes is Sandra Cisneros: "Alas! While I was busy writing this book, Jim's Original Hot Dogs was gobbled up by the University of Illinois [. . .]."[7] This self-reflexive moment announces the generally tacit fact regarding novels that they are lengthy projects that take time to complete. During the completion of *Caramelo*, the University of Illinois had basically swallowed up another icon of this early period of Chicago's history, and this second footnote confirms what was hinted at in the preceding one: "tidy parks and tidy houses for the very very wealthy, while the poor, as always, get swept under the rug, out of sight and out of mind" (9). Having Cisneros's authorial voice at the helm of the footnotes is a momentous authorial intrusion within the text. Could Celaya, the ostensible writer and narrator of *Caramelo*, also have written the footnotes? I think there is reason to believe that Celaya could have written the footnotes, but instead Cisneros comes to the fore as the true author of the footnotes over the course of the novel.

To press this point further, if Cisneros is indeed the narrator of the footnotes, why does she employ the first person except when she is clearly referencing herself, as in the thirteenth footnote: "This song was actually written by the author's great-grandfather, Enrique Cisneros Vásquez" (123)? Why does Cisneros use the third person in this case? Why not simply say that the song "was written by my great-grandfather"? It is a curious moment that shows the sort of ambiguous narrative situation created by the introduction of footnotes in a fictional narrative.

Perhaps it is here that we should examine the different ways Cisneros uses footnotes in her novel. I have already demonstrated how the footnotes serve to provide texture to specific intertexts with which readers may be unfamiliar. This characteristic of Cisneros's footnotes can be arguably described as extraneous. That is to say, it is not vital to narrative comprehension or storyworld reconstruction that the reader be aware of the specific history of the Maxwell Street flea market, for instance. If the footnotes are voiced by Cisneros, then it is fascinating that Celaya does not give the flea market the same sort of attention that Cisneros does. While Celaya casually mentions the flea market in her narrative, Cisneros uses the flea market as an occasion to raise a particular political issue, invoking the name of Chicago's Mayor Daley and pairing it with the University of Illinois's gentrification of the city. Here, Cisneros appears to press the issue of gentrification in her city of Chicago—an issue that is not addressed by the novel's narrator Celaya. In the case of the first two

---

7. Of course, Cisneros is the author of the entire book, footnotes and all. But while the novel is narrated by a fictional character, the footnotes are narrated by Cisneros herself. It is as if, after writing her novel, Cisneros went back and inserted commentary in strategic locations in the book.

footnotes, the information regarding the Maxwell Street flea market provides texture to Celaya's storyworld and her remembered Chicago, but the notes overtly force the reader outside of Celaya's specific storyworld and into the personal musings of Sandra Cisneros regarding Chicago. The footnotes force the reader to do double work.

Cisneros makes other digressions at the prompting of certain intertexts. For instance, in characterizing her father, Celaya recounts how at times, while suffering from migraines, her father would sit "on his La-Z-Boy watching Mexican *telenovelas.—¿Qué intentas ocultar, Juan Sebastián? ¿Qué intentas ocultar?*" (15). At the prompting of the quoted *telenovela*, a footnote provides further examples of similar melodramatic statements typical of the *telenovela* format of storytelling:

—¿Qué intentas ocultar?
—¿Por qué eres tan cruel conmigo?
—Te encanta hacerme sufrir.
¿Por qué me mortificas?

Say any of the above, or say anything twice, slower and more dramatic the second time 'round, and it will sound like the dialogue of any telenovela. (15, italics in original)

The purpose of footnoting the quoted lines from a typical *telenovela* would appear to be an explication of this genre of Spanish-language television for a reader unfamiliar with these examples of over-the-top dialogue. In reality, the footnote not only provides three more examples of untranslated lines of dialogue that encapsulate *telenovelas*, but it also provides sarcastic commentary on the *telenovela* form itself. The footnoted comment, in turn, renders the example lines of dialogue moot by claiming that anything said slowly and more dramatically the second time actually sounds like *telenovela* dialogue.

Such footnotes as this one concerning the type of dialogue found in a *telenovela* does not contribute in any meaningful way to the characterization of Celaya's father. Instead, this footnote appears to be the author indulging herself in a moment of humor at the expense of a television serial form of narrative that is wildly popular in many places around the world. The tone of the footnote is mocking and sarcastic, and it indirectly mocks Celaya's father—the man who is watching this melodramatic television genre. Here, the reader leaves Celaya's reminiscence of her father's fondness for a favorite chair—his place of refuge when he suffered from migraines—only to have the footnote mock *telenovela* dialogue. Thus, the footnote disrupts this picture of Celaya's father at his most vulnerable only to offer a glib comment on something that only tangentially concerns the primary narrative. The incongruity tacks from an overindulgence in sentimentality by pointing to a popular narrative form that has melodrama as one of its primary ingredients.

Footnotes of this type—those that comment so obliquely with regard to the narrative as to be nearly non sequiturs—occur in only a few instances in the novel. When they do appear, they destabilize the storyworld and the reader's engagement with the narrative. For instance, there is the sarcastic comment regarding the Reyes family's delusion that they are high cultured: "The truth was they had only recently learned to eat with knives, spoons, forks, and napkins" (163); or the pithy discussion on "the Mexican obsession with cleaning" (298). There are only a few such footnotes that leave the reader wondering at the impetus of these authorial intrusions and disruptions within *Caramelo*. In these instances, Cisneros seems to indulge her own sense of humor as she displays a backbiting wit that strips any supposed grandiosity the Reyes family may have for themselves. More important, these intrusions also have the effect of destabilizing the author as an authority figure and instead present her as someone who is opinionated and struggles with the frustrations she grapples with in the narrative. It is as if Cisneros cannot help herself from articulating her disgust about the changes on Market Street or her feeling that the Reyes family's haughty attitude dishonors the realities of their personal history, or that Mexicans can go too far in their devotion to cleaning. Rather than provide texture to the storyworld proper, this type of footnote provides texture to the implied Cisneros, so much so that we may think of her as explicit rather than implied.

Yet not all of the footnotes in *Caramelo* are so indicative of Cisneros's overt attitudes toward the narrative. The vast majority of the footnotes, and ostensibly all of the footnotes to some degree, are concerned with history. The footnotes reach into the recesses of history and bring little-known events or personages to light. From smaller events significant to major events in world history to minor figures that had only limited local impacts on their immediate surroundings, the footnotes include an expansive repertoire of historical and popular cultural moments that allows the Reyes story to be situated alongside historically important figures such as Pancho Villa, Emiliano Zapata, Emperor Maximiliano, and Empress Carlota. In doing so, the footnotes consistently yoke the fictional world with the ontologically separated actual world of the reader. Unlike the footnotes in *Oscar Wao* that are at times unreliable if not factually inaccurate, the footnotes in *Caramelo* have been carefully and painstakingly researched.[8]

---

8. In her acknowledgments page at the end of *Caramelo,* Cisneros thanks several individuals for "research assistance," as she puts it. In particular she thanks "Mr. Eddie López for

The result is that the historical accuracy of the footnotes is occasionally undone by Cisneros's idiosyncratic musings on Celaya's narrative. Despite this, the footnotes anchor Celaya's story within the historical record without being history itself. Indeed, the entire novel turns on the long tradition and historical import of the *rebozo* or "shawl" that is one symbol of Mexico. In a concise but informative footnote, Cisneros makes the history of the *rebozo* a global history:

> *The* rebozo *was born in Mexico, but like all* mestizos, *it came from everywhere. It evolved from the cloths Indian women used to carry their babies, borrowed its knotted fringe from Spanish shawls, and was influenced by the silk embroideries from the imperial court of China exported to Manila, then Acapulco, via the Spanish galleons. During the colonial period, mestizo women were prohibited by statutes dictated by the Spanish Crown to dress like Indians, and since they had no means to buy clothing like the Spaniards', they began to weave cloth on the indigenous looms creating a long and narrow shawl that slowly was shaped by foreign influences. The quintessential Mexican rebozo is the* rebozo de bolita, *whose spotted design imitates a snakeskin, an animal venerated by the Indians in pre-Columbian times.* (96, italics in original)

This footnote serves as a historical mini-lesson that has a different objective than does Celaya's narrative. Celaya, as an American-born Latina, uses the writing process of the narrative to uncover her genealogical history as a means of understanding herself. Using the actual movements across geographical terrain as well as through family history, Celaya herself does not understand the import of the unfinished caramel-colored *rebozo* she first sees as a child in Awful Grandmother's home in Mexico.

This particular unfinished *rebozo* is the dominant symbol in *Caramelo*, and part of Celaya's purpose of uncovering her family history is linked to this specific Mexican shawl, for several reasons. First, Celaya reveals that Awful Grandmother was orphaned as a child, and consequently her own mother was unable to pass down the specific knowledge of *rebozo*-making to her.

---

sharing his personal papers on World War II, and to his wife, la Sra. María Luisa Camacho de López, for her invaluable knowledge on *rebozos*. Mario and Alejandro Sánchez assisted on library research. The historian Steven Rodríguez reviewed my historical references. [. . .] Thanks to María Herrera Sobek for song research" (443). This paratexual material confirms the degree to which Cisneros wishes her fictive narrative to chafe against and be shaped by historically accurate events. The result of these overt acknowledgments reassures the readers as to the validity of the historical record as represented in the novel. In effect, the statements provide tacit reassurance to the reader that Cisneros's "facts" can be trusted, which is another means of establishing the authority of the footnotes.

Thus, this one memento, or *recuerdo,* as Little Grandfather calls it, is both a reminder of the past while simultaneously signifying an interruption of family history. There can be little doubt that the process of making *rebozos* is not unlike the process of storytelling for Celaya, whose Awful Grandmother, now dead, continually influences Celaya as the novel progresses.

This brings me to the purpose of the *rebozo* footnote I cited above, and I approach it with a few questions in mind. Does Celaya herself understand the rich, global history of the *rebozo*? Perhaps more important, why is this history worthy of a footnote but not worthy of inclusion in the narrative proper? Again, we are confronted with the uses of footnotes to begin with. The information revealed in the footnote regarding the *rebozo* is exactly the type of information one would expect to find in an academic text.

Edith Grossman, one of the preeminent contemporary translators of Spanish-language literature into English, has an interesting take on the use of footnotes in translations. In her translator's note to her lauded translation of *Don Quixote,* Grossman states, "I debated the question of footnotes with myself and decided I was obliged to put some in, though I had never used them before in a translation (I did not want the reader to be put off by references that may now be obscure, or to miss layers of intention and meaning those allusions create)" (xviii). Grossman's apprehension at using footnotes in her translations tells us something about her understanding of the apparatus of the footnote in the process of reading. Is it that the footnotes, obtrusive and unavoidable, somehow disrupt or distract from the reading process? As a translator, Grossman does not want anything bound to the text to disrupt the reader of the translation if a similar device is not encountered by the reader in the source language. However, understanding the potential obscurity of certain references and how they might undesirably thwart readers of her translation, Grossman intervenes with a carefully measured footnote.

It would seem that Cisneros uses historical footnotes in a manner similar to Grossman's. However, upon further examination, the mini-lessons of history are seemingly superfluous. Ostensibly, Cisneros includes this footnote regarding the *rebozo* as a way of enriching the reader's understanding of this specific article of clothing that is a symbol of the Mexican nation and reflects its history. Yet if we identify the impetus for the footnote, we see that Celaya (with the constant interruptions of Awful Grandmother's spirit) narrates her grandmother's childhood—how Soledad descends from a family of famed *rebozo* makers.

Along with the craft of making *rebozos,* Celaya gives other examples of Mexican items that were as black as the black *rebozos* made by her family: "as black as Coyotepec pottery, as black as *huitlacoche,* the corn mushroom, as true-black as an *olla* of fresh-cooked black beans" (92), leading her to meditate on the art of *"las empuntadoras"* or the women who complete the *rebozos* by knotting the intricately patterned fringe at their ends. Celaya claims that this technique for knotting the silk strands of a *rebozo* may have Arabic or Asian origins: "Perhaps, as is often the case with things Mexican, it comes from neither and both" (93). The footnote regarding the *rebozo* corresponds to Celaya's untenable claim of belonging simultaneously to both and to neither. Thus, the footnote is not a recitation of the origins of the *rebozo* but rather an opportunity to highlight the *mestizo* nature of the Mexican people and how it is made manifest in this symbolic garment. The footnote is not there to educate someone unfamiliar with *rebozos*. It is there to show the history of Mexico as interwoven with other grand traditions of the world.

Further, the timing and placement of this footnote is curious.[9] For a contextualizing history of the *rebozo*, it appears nearly one hundred pages into the novel. Its placement begs the question: if the history of the *rebozo* is footnote-worthy, why not deploy the footnote when the *rebozo* is first mentioned on page 26? If we turn to the academic uses of footnotes, we would expect the footnote to appear when the reference to the *rebozo* is first made. However, Cisneros, as Finnegan suggests, is determined to upend this academic convention by balancing the historical legitimacy and authority of the footnote with a rather quixotic and arbitrary use of it. Further, the *rebozo* footnote is a clear example of what critical reviews mention when discussing *Caramelo*. We might imagine the text without footnotes quite easily with little lost of Celaya's story from beginning to end.

The excess number of footnotes in *Caramelo* is rooted in the disjointed purposes of Celaya the narrator, and Cisneros the author. What's more, the footnotes do not appear to be part of the organic whole of the novel but rather an ex post facto device that suits Cisneros's purpose beyond the storyworld blueprint of the novel. Unlike *House of Leaves,* where the footnotes are required in order to piece together the fragmented narrative, or unlike *Pale Fire,* where the secondary footnotes are inextricable from narrative comprehension, all of the footnotes of *Caramelo* can be excised without disruption to storyworld proper and its reconstruction. Still, the footnotes in *Caramelo* will yield a more nuanced storyworld within the reader's imagination. By anchor-

---

9. Ilan Stavans, commenting on the general placement of the footnotes in *Caramelo,* cannot see the logic in having the footnotes placed at the end of the chapter. The result of this is that the footnotes often appear several pages after they are indicated in the novel. While reading, a reader must either wait until the end of the chapter is reached to read the footnote, or the reader must leap forward to the end when the symbol for the designated footnote is reached. If nothing else, the footnote *placement* contributes to a disruption of the reading process (*Critic's* 58).

ing her novel to historical footnotes, Cisneros attempts to provide her family drama with historical heft. But the historical heft from which Cisneros borrows is only tangentially of import to Celaya's narrative. One final example will illustrate this point.

In what appears to be the most superfluous footnote in all of *Caramelo*, Cisneros provides a brief history of the dance known as the Charleston. Celaya, in the narrative proper, states:

> The condition of Prince Narciso's feet did not improve during the seven years he lived with his Uncle Old. They were as abused at the end of his U.S. stay as they were in the beginning, not from the labor by then, but from pleasure. Narciso danced all weekend at the black-and-tan clubs on South State Street. This was during the time the Charleston was outlawed in some U.S. cities. (140)

The corresponding footnote reads:

> *The Charleston was named "the Dance of Death" after a Boston tragedy that claimed 147 lives when a Charleston-throbbing dance floor collapsed in a heap, causing the building to do the Charleston too. Variety reported: "The offbeat rhythm of the Charleston, reinforced by the indulgence in things alcoholic is said to have caused the Hotel Pickwick to sway so violently that it fell apart."* (142, italics in original)

If Cisneros is subverting the academic convention of the footnote here, then there is no better, unequivocal example in all of *Caramelo*.

It is as if the footnotes in *Caramelo* insist on a reader different from the reader of the primary narrative. While the footnote regarding the Charleston may help readers understand more about this allusion, it is clear from Celaya's narration that the Charleston was a dance that was outlawed in certain U.S. cities. What *Variety* reported on the dance is only peripherally related to Celaya's narrative, and because there are dozens of allusions that would better serve the reader were they contextualized, one cannot help noticing the apparent arbitrariness of the footnotes.

Cisneros's strategy challenges understandings of history, authority, and narrative. Her decision to introduce footnotes as a narrative device in her fiction is a significant move within Latino/a letters. Though she is manacled to the traditional Latino/a narrative in U.S. fiction that is genealogically based, as Stavans complains, she also is one of the first Latino/a authors to move toward the use of narrative devices that complicate a conventional reading experience.

By introducing footnotes within her fiction, as well as inserting a myriad of historical and cultural intertexts, Cisneros expands what readers may expect from Latino/a literature.

Her use of footnotes opened the door for paratextual playfulness within Latino/a literature—something that must be explored further if Latino/a literature is ever to be considered as having all of the devices for narrative worldmaking at its disposal. Further, Cisneros makes the attempt in *Caramelo* to put the reader in a position of having to work at understanding the narrative she is creating. It is a difficult cognitive move to read the primary narrative only to have to cross an ontological border and inhabit an entirely different rhetorical style and narrative objective. I maintain that readers and critics would not have reacted so negatively if Cisneros's footnotes were clearly bound to Celaya's ontology and put to the service of texturing her storyworld. On the other hand, Cisneros exquisitely reveals that she is poised to write the kinds of narratives that she envisions, rather than write according to the constraints of others' expectations.

But the footnotes are only one part of a larger postmodernist move on Cisneros's part. Celaya's metafictional and self-reflextive narration, her narrative collaboration with Awful Grandmother's spirit, her extensive use of intertexts, and her interweaving of her narrative with Cisneros's footnotes all bespeak of an expansive rather than constrained presentation of narrative design and will to style of Latino/a authors. This bold move would help provide Junot Díaz with the opportunity to make further use of postmodernist fiction devices while challenging notions of Latinidad his breakthrough novel, *Oscar Wao*.

THE SIGNIFICANCE OF JUNOT DÍAZ'S *THE BRIEF WONDROUS LIFE OF OSCAR WAO*

Amidst a growing body of scholarship on Junot Díaz's fiction, several recent articles have examined a number of critical aspects regarding the narration in his work—particularly his 2007 Pulitzer Prize–winning novel, *The Brief Wondrous Life of Oscar Wao*. For instance, Monica Hanna describes the interweaving of genres as a means by which Díaz's novel aims for "resistance history" (500), the result of which she calls a "historiographic battle royal" (504) between historical events and the narrator's (and the reader's) attempt to reconstruct history, making *Oscar Wao* a clear example of Linda Hutcheon's concept of historiographic metafiction (5). Indeed, it often does appear that Díaz's project is to void a biased historical record while simultaneously supplanting it with his own. Daniel Bautista has investigated Díaz's use of what

Bautista terms "comic book realism"—an irreverent mix of realism and popular culture (42) as a salient feature of Díaz's novel. For her part, Anne Garland Mahler makes the important argument that in Yunior, Díaz has constructed a superhero

> who creates the zafa—or counterspell—to the evil forces of the fukú, as a writer who uses the pen to shed light on the existence of the violent structures of power that have been concealed [...] that Díaz promotes a writing that does not repress its own inherent violence but rather exposes it in order to disarm tyrannical power of perhaps its most effective weapon: the written word. (120)

All of these takes on Díaz's narrative style help elucidate the richness and complexity of his novel. Yet two issues have yet to be examined in light of Díaz's novel: his use of intertexts and footnotes and his empowerment of a narrator to highlight issues of race. These two issues arise from the multifarious use of texts to fill gaps in understanding or to give rise to the architecture of Díaz's storyworld.

Díaz contributed a virtuosic narrative worldmaker to Latino/a letters, a linguistically unrestrained *author* who unabashedly foregrounds the African ancestry of his panoply of characters—an ancestry that has traditionally been under erasure throughout Dominican history, to say nothing of this legacy upon the Dominican émigré to the United States. Díaz's contribution remains a significant aspect of his novel. Rather than simply writing against hegemony, Díaz, through Yunior, etches the African legacy of Dominicans by speaking for the many artists, scholars, journalists, and mythmakers who are silenced repeatedly in *Oscar Wao*. Moreover, Yunior reaches beyond his localized, experiential self and into the narrative worlds created by other authors. It is as if he is unable to narrate Oscar's story without the aid of these other possible worlds. Reading this novel necessitates specific knowledge of these intertexts, for unlike Cisneros, Díaz goes to great lengths to keep from assuming an authoritative historical voice in his novel. What is more, Díaz draws upon the intertexts in ways that are crucial for the execution of his novel.

In this section, I address Díaz's deft use of intertextuality in *Oscar Wao*. Due to its highly intertextual nature, Díaz's novel is wide-ranging in its subject matter, seamlessly interweaving world history, languages, comic-book lore, literary knowledge, and science fiction and fantasy in order to construct his own narrative worlds. Yet what strikes me as more significant, and indeed what provides the impetus for these issues I am set to explore, is how Yunior as an author sets about the business of narrative worldmaking in order to render his story. Indeed, Díaz's characters and narrators all strive to actuate their differing (and at times competing) agendas as Afro Latinos in both the

United States and the Dominican Republic. In doing so, Díaz creates fictional Afro Latinos (as opposed to Piri Thomas's representation of himself in his autobiography, *Down These Mean Streets*) who are written into existence by another Afro Latino (i.e., Yunior). Attending to Díaz's creation of an author/narrator, with his particularized renditions of Afrolatinidad, illuminates how Díaz seeks to inscribe the African *página en blanco*[10] of Dominican culture with a significant instance of Afro Latinos in U.S. fiction. What is interesting, however, is that Díaz uses both historical accounts related to the African ancestry of Dominican Americans and fictional works in order to tell the story of his tragic hero, Oscar de León.

Besides the history of the slave trade in the Americas, two specific intertexts loom large in the structure of *Oscar Wao*: J. R. R. Tolkien's *Lord of the Rings* and Stan Lee and Jack Kirby's *Fantastic Four*. Without the historical record that reveals the depths of African and dictatorial enslavement, and the completely imagined storyworlds of comics and speculative literature, recounting Oscar's narrative is impossible for Yunior. Díaz's manufacture of Afro Latino characters with the power to inscribe the many *páginas en blanco* of both global and local history with the story of *other* Afro-Latinos, as well as to reach into an array of intertexts as an aid to narrative worldmaking, affirms the power of an author, and fiction more generally, to bring to light what the restrictive historical record omits. If Cisneros's *Caramelo* shows the limits of using history in an attempt to rectify history, Díaz's novel suggests that plumbing the depths of history is ultimately untenable, in part because it is often the case that truth is stranger than fiction. Hence his use of both historical and speculative intertexts.

"THE *PÁGINA* IS STILL *BLANCA*"

Central to my argument is Díaz's use of the *página en blanco*. This phrase, which Díaz invokes several times in *Oscar Wao*, works as a double entendre. In a literal sense, *página en blanco* refers to a page that is either blank or white, which suggests at least two things: the page is blank because the text that was inscribed has now been erased, or the page is blank because the page has yet to be written. Thus the blank page can indicate a violation or a promise yet to be fulfilled. However, in a more provocative sense, Díaz views the

---

10. Literally, "blank page." The term tends to represent an omission or erasure in the historic record. In Díaz's novel, there are several such gaps in the narrative, as well as lost manuscripts and letters that purport to have significant answers—such as the manuscript Oscar promises to send Yunior, which never arrives. Díaz's novel itself can thus serve as an attempt to redress, however imperfectly, an omission in the historical record.

white page as a direct reflection of the history of the Dominican Republic to insist upon a whitened citizenry—the government going to such lengths as to "import" individuals from Europe with a distinctly Anglo phenotype. For Díaz, inscribing the white page with the African legacy of all Dominicans is a necessary move.

Díaz often uses the motif of blankness or erasure as a recurring feature in his fiction. In *Drown* the character Ysrael is forced to wear a dingy mask in order to hide his facial disfigurement, and his mask serves as a source of both curiosity and poignancy in the stories "Ysrael" and "No Face." In *Oscar Wao*, Oscar's mother, Beli, often gazes at a man without a face during the most traumatic events of her life and later dreams that her foster father, who scarred her back with a skillet of hot oil when she was a child, had a face that "turned blank at the moment he picked up the skillet" (261). Indeed, there is an evident link between a personified blankness and trauma throughout *Oscar Wao*.

Also in the same novel, Yunior, in a lengthy footnote, recounts the events surrounding a Columbia graduate student named Jesús de Galíndez, who writes a doctoral dissertation on the dictatorial era of Rafael Leónidas Trujillo Molina. Subsequently, Galíndez disappears, and Yunior intimates that Galíndez was presumably murdered by the Dominican dictator himself. Perhaps not surprisingly, Galíndez's dissertation vanishes as well. Abelard Cabral, Oscar's maternal grandfather, is tortured and later erased out of existence because of a book he was supposedly writing on Trujillo, along with the only extant copy of Abelard's exposé that Yunior hints revealed Trujillo's supernatural origins. Near the end of the novel, Oscar writes a manuscript that purports to explain "everything" to Yunior only to have it go missing after Oscar is murdered, never having reached Yunior. Finally, Yunior has dreams years after Oscar's death in which Oscar wears "a wrathful mask that hides his face but behind the eyeholes I see a familiar pair of close-set eyes" and has hands that "are seamless" as he invites Yunior to examine a book he is holding for him to see, until Yunior realizes "the book's pages are blank" (325). Thus, Díaz's continual allusions to these and other instances of erasure, these examples of *páginas en blanco*, remind the reader that there is always some aspect of Díaz's fiction (and consequently Dominican history) that keeps full knowledge just out of a reader's reach. As a result, Yunior consistently struggles to supply narrative material to fill these lacunae.

One of the methods that Díaz, through Yunior, uses to address these blank pages is to rely on external sources to provide a precedent for his attempt to narrate what has been forgotten, or erased, or ignored. Yunior consistently works to invoke analogues for the often improbable moments in his narration, and it does not seem to matter from where these intertexts originate. He is just as apt to draw upon an iconic Japanese animation film such as *Akira* as he is rumor and hearsay many times removed. In fact, one of the significant achievements of *Oscar Wao* is the patent disregard of narrative convention and constraints. Yunior's account of what befalls Oscar, were this an attempt at biography or nonfiction, is so based on speculation and speculative intertexts that it would most likely be disregarded, if it ever even found its way into print. Yunior writes Oscar's story as a means for his own therapy that endeavors to get to the truth of the matter. Though Yunior often unambiguously invokes an unseen narratee, I maintain the distinct possibility that Yunior is actually writing for himself. In short, Yunior is his own ideal audience.

Additionally, Yunior is fascinated by both writers and writing. This is unsurprising, as he himself has taken on the craft of creating narrative, and his self-reflexive musings on the process of writing provide him with an additional dimension for critical analysis. In other words, Yunior is not just a narrator who recounts events he's witnessed or stories he's heard. It is clear that he is constructing a narrative by putting words onto the page—often a figurative blank page—a fact of which he is acutely aware. This fact becomes especially significant as he provides repeated examples of the silencing of writers related to Oscar's story. Despite the frustrating inability of these articulate personages and characters to write a final product, there is one writer who does manage to write, and write prolifically—a writer whom Yunior discusses at length in footnote 9, namely, Dominican Republic President Joaquín Balaguer:

> Although not essential to our tale, per se, Balaguer is essential to the Dominican one, so therefore we must mention him, even though I'd rather piss in his face. [. . .] In the days of the Trujillato, Balaguer was just one of El Jefe's more efficient ringwraiths. Much is made of his intelligence (he certainly impressed the Failed Cattle Thief) and of his asceticism (when *he* raped his little girls he kept it real quiet). [. . .] It was he who oversaw/initiated the thing we call Diaspora. Considered our national "genius," Joaquín Balaguer was a Negrophobe, an apologist to genocide, an election thief, and a killer of people who wrote better than himself, famously ordering the death of journalist Orlando Martínez. Later, when he wrote his memoirs, he claimed he knew who had done the foul deed (not him, of course) and left a blank page, a página en

blanco, in the text to be filled in with the truth upon his death. (Can you say *impunity*?) Balaguer died in 2002. The página is still blanca. (90)

Several key points in Yunior's footnote regarding Balaguer can help focus our understanding of the dynamic between power, writing, text, and race in *Oscar Wao*. The historical record shows that Balaguer was a productive writer who wrote in many genres, including poetry, narrative fiction, biography, and autobiography. In short, unlike Trujillo, who carefully crafted a persona that gave the impression of cerebral prowess, Balaguer was a true intellectual. Yet, because of his close affiliation to Trujillo and his own rise to Dominican power, Balaguer represents, for Yunior, the powers of writing at their worst. According to Yunior, Balaguer, insecure in his own writing, ordered the murder of other writers. Further, Balaguer provided the impetus for Dominican diaspora, which of course has a direct bearing on Oscar's family, specifically his mother Beli, who was forced to flee the Dominican Republic so that her life might be spared. And, hypocritically in Yunior's eyes, Balaguer self-censures his own memoir by silencing himself in order to appear as a more sympathetic figure. The deliberate act of leaving a blank page in his memoir signals how those in power have the ability to reveal facts but choose not to do so. The blank page here is more than Balaguer covering misdeeds, so to speak. When Yunior decries the cowardice of leaving the page blank, he reveals his own aim to inscribe such pages whenever and wherever he can. Balaguer's blank page denotes the hegemony of power as an inherent aspect of writing itself, simultaneously denying access to information while challenging others to inscribe the page with information if they can.

As a result, the two great antagonists in *Oscar Wao* are not the local bullies that Oscar encounters throughout his brief wondrous life, but Trujillo and Balaguer. Additionally, these two powerful men, like Sauron in *Lord of the Rings,* hover above the narrative without ever explicitly engaging in the events of the narrative. Despite already being dead when Yunior begins the narrative, Trujillo and Balaguer are depicted as evil incarnate, with the ultimate power to make living bodies disappear without a trace and to act with, as Yunior says, impunity. The result is that the two brutal dictators described in *Oscar Wao* silence writers while promoting their own Negrophobic agendas. Within the novel, the dictators' ability to obliterate lives and texts equally coincides with expunging the Dominican record of its African roots. Indeed, one of Yunior's charges is to substantiate the African legacy of Dominicans as well as to create the narrative of Oscar's family by proxy.

According to Yunior, Abelard, Oscar's maternal grandfather, initiates the fukú curse—a curse according to the culture of the Dominican Republic—that will plague his progeny. Yunior attributes Trujillo's violence against Abelard to one of two things: (1) Abelard did not readily offer up his beautiful daughters when Trujillo desired it or (2) Abelard had written a book that claimed Trujillo's supernaturalism. That Trujillo would go to such lengths in order to punish a rebuke was a commonly held belief among the Dominican community. On this subject, Yunior states, "There's one of these bellaco tales in almost everybody's hometown. It's one of those easy stories because in essence *it explains it all*. Trujillo took your houses, your properties, put your pops and your moms in jail? Well, it was because he wanted to fuck the beautiful daughter of the house! And your family wouldn't let him!" (244).

Yet Yunior is not interested in "easy stories." He, like his "*compañero*" Oscar, is attracted to the "speculative genres" (43). For Yunior, the sheer might and vigor of the Cabral/de León fukú curse suggests that it is the result of more than simply another *bellaco* tale. Rather, Abelard's "*grimoire*" (as Yunior describes it) was set to expose Trujillo's other-worldliness. Thus, just as Balaguer ordered the death of Orlando Martínez, Trujillo imposes a fukú upon Abelard and his family because of a book:

> Sometime in 1944 (so the story goes), while Abelard was still worried about whether he was in trouble with Trujillo, he started writing a book about—what else?—Trujillo. By 1945 there was already a tradition of ex-officials writing tell-all books about the Trujillo regime. But that apparently was not the kind of book Abelard was writing. His shit, if we are to believe the whispers, was an exposé of the supernatural roots of the Trujillo regime! A book about the Dark Powers of the President, a book in which Abelard argued that the tales the common people told about the president—that he was supernatural, that he was not human—may in some ways have been true. That it was possible that Trujillo was, if not in fact, then in principle, a creature from another world! (245)

Thus, "The Lost Final Book of Dr. Abelard Luis Cabral" (246), along with Cabral's entire library and every bit of his handwriting, vanishes, leaving Yunior and Oscar wishing they could have read Cabral's grimoire. Instead, Yunior sets about to create his own book that bridges Abelard's project with Oscar's longing to be the "Dominican Tolkien." Despite the many writers who have been silenced, Yunior strives to have his story fill the void created by dictators and curses alike. By incorporating the redacted legacy of Africa, along with the speculative genres, Yunior is now empowered to tell Oscar's story.

NARRATION IN *OSCAR WAO*

As I discussed in chapter 1, post-1972 Latino literature is dominated by the presence of homodiegetic narrators who narrate autobiographically, often in the bildungsroman mode. Next in order of frequency, we find the use of heterodiegetic narrators who remain, as Gérard Genette would describe it, extradiegetically positioned with respect to the narrative situation. What appear less often in Latino/a literature are homodiegetic narrators who purport to have written the text one holds when reading the novel—in the modes specific to fictional autobiographies as well as fictionalized biographies. This is a significant narrating stance adopted by narrators of Latino/a literature, for it highlights the recognition of worth (at least in narrative value) of another Latino/a, one who is not the narrator.

These narrators document the life experiences of another person as an epistemic venue for the exploration of the self. Thus, it is a kind of self-exploration by narrative proxy. Throughout much of Latino/a literature, narrators often weave their narratives around their personal experiences. Rare are the narrators in Latino/a literature that narrate the lives of other Latinos. Despite their few numbers in Latino/a literature, this kind of narrator features prominently in other world traditions of literature, such as the fiction of twentieth-century authors Philip Roth and J. M. Coetzee, to name but two. If we set about identifying trends in the development of Latino/a literature, the use of specific narrators, their narrating functions, and their narrative subject all allow us to recognize how authors and their fictive authors set about creating narrative worlds.

For instance, Rudolfo Anaya's *Bless Me, Ultima* (1972) uses a narrator named Antonio who tells the story of his youth while using the eponymous Ultima as a foil for the undesirable position he finds himself in: whether he should embrace the indigenous folk practices of his people or leave them to wither on the vine upon Ultima's death. However, the narrator essentially shuts out the world beyond the text throughout the novel. Though his brothers go off to fight in World War II, this seismic world event seems somehow false to the world of Ultima's making. A close examination of the novel reveals that the narrative is located in a very specific space-time, and the text never urges the reader to move beyond that inscribed storyworld. Antonio's narration always seeks an internal movement, staying away from the calamitous events on the European or Pacific fronts, or the contemporaneous and volatile political civil rights and labor issues that energized the Chicano movement set within a nation fighting (and losing) the war in Vietnam.

Anaya's novel seeks to block these issues out of the text. As a result, there is an almost timeless quality to *Bless Me,* as if a reader is observing an artifact of nature captured beneath a bell jar. Though there are identifiably deictic shifts within Anaya's novel, there is little if any use of intertexts throughout the narrative. Not only does *Bless Me, Ultima,* along with Acosta's *The Autobiography of a Brown Buffalo,* help locate the post-1972 period of Latino literature; it also remains an exemplar of this type of narrative in Latino literature. In terms of apocalypse, *Bless Me* seems to work toward a homeostatic resolution, one in which actual apocalyptic world events such as World War II are pushed to the limits of the textual boundary. The reader is also urged to set these moments of terror to the side while considering the storyworld. Indeed, Díaz's *Oscar Wao* consistently seeks to move the reader beyond the narrative proper and into marginalia, in the form of both footnotes and intertextual allusions.

Yunior de las Casas, the narrator of Díaz's novel, is a Dominican American who teaches creative writing and has set about to detail the events surrounding the life (and death) of his friend Oscar de León. As he reveals near the novel's conclusion, Yunior is compelled to write the book because he continues to be tormented by dreams of Oscar, dreams in which Oscar shows Yunior a book that is composed of pristinely blank pages. In order to stop the dreams, or perhaps symbolically to allow Oscar to rest in peace, Yunior writes his book. Indeed, *Oscar Wao* is a work of metafiction par excellence, with Yunior constantly reflecting on his creation of his book. Yet his book is a testament to an apocalyptic view of the world, and, further, his book reveals that there is not one apocalypse but rather a series or cycle of apocalypses going all the way back to the transportation of Africans as slaves to the Caribbean and tracing that line of endings to the moment when Yunior writes his book. Within the pages of his writing, Yunior hopes to find a positive outcome to all of the tragedy that he has purportedly documented.

In *Oscar Wao,* Yunior—who has become Díaz's narrator of choice[11]—narrates the tragic events that surround the family of Oscar de León, the Oscar "Wao" of the novel's title. Oscar is the ultimate outcast figure, an outsider even among his Dominican compatriots. Yunior, who, despite his penchant for womanizing, is in love with Oscar's sister Lola and recounts the various circumstances that lead to Oscar's demise. Yunior is unable to do so coherently, however, without piecing together the personal history of Oscar's mother, Beli, which in turn necessitates an exploration of Beli's parents, Abelard and

---

11. Yunior is the narrator of several stories in *Drown,* the majority of *Oscar Wao,* and most of Díaz's uncollected stories.

Socorro Cabral, a prominent couple in Dominican society during the dictatorship of Raphael Trujillo. Beli appropriately links the Dominican Republic at the height of Trujillo's power to her son Oscar, the lowly American-born Dominican outcast who fancies himself to be a self-appointed Dominican mythmaker like J. R. R. Tolkien, a master of genre fiction like Stephen King.

Among Yunior's few desirable traits[12] is his yearning to construct narrative worlds. Throughout Díaz's many stories that concentrate on Yunior in some significant way, the one activity that seems to make Yunior a more palatable person is his desire to tell stories and, specifically, to become what Oscar calls a "real writer" (30). While *Drown* features stories that recount either Yunior's childhood or the experiences of his young adulthood, in *Oscar Wao* readers discover that Yunior's project is to bring Oscar's life and genealogy into a larger, perhaps less transient, existence through the careful scaffolding of the book he has written—the book we hold in our hands when we read *Oscar Wao*.

Yunior is a character narrator, but unambiguously he is a narrator actively engaged in the writing process. In other words, Yunior claims to be the author of *Oscar Wao*. Yet for Yunior, his book is not a novel; it is more of a testimonial or tribute in hagiographic support of another personage.[13] The result is that Yunior belongs to a relatively small group of similar characters in American fiction—a group that most famously includes F. Scott Fitzgerald's Nick Carraway, Ken Kesey's Chief Bromden, and Philip Roth's Nathan Zuckerman, as Ben Railton has noted.[14] Each of these character narrators desires to tell someone else's story, and each of them has a different reason for doing so. Nick believes that he alone understands Gatsby, and he certainly cannot understand

---

12. Though charming, Yunior is, to a large extent, unlikable. While he is often a sympathetic character in short stories such as "Fiesta, 1980," "Nilda," "Edison, New Jersey," and "The Pura Principle," one gets the sense that he would have nothing to do with Oscar were it not for Yunior's desire for Lola. His decision to document Oscar's story, then, is stunning. Ironically, Yunior is more like Oscar than he would care to openly admit.

13. Yunior's claim that he has written the book makes for an interesting narrative situation. Depending on the reader's perspective, one might read *Oscar Wao* as a novel by Junot Díaz or as a work of nonfiction by Yunior de las Casas.

14. Specifically, Railton concentrates his investigation of what he terms "meta-realism" on four such narrators: Carraway, Zuckerman, Willa Cather's Jim Burden, and Yunior. However, Railton casts Yunior as a "novelist-narrator," when Yunior has clearly written a work that, if he were an actual person, we would call nonfiction—a significant detail that makes Yunior's document stand out in American fiction. Within U.S. Latino literature, the narrative style in *Oscar Wao* has a progenitor in Oscar "Zeta" Acosta's two novels, *The Autobiography of a Brown Buffalo* and *The Revolt of the Cockroach People*. Both Díaz's and Acosta's texts feature unfettered narrators who set about the task of documenting historical events. One crucial difference, however, is subject: Acosta testifies to the "Brown Buffalo" (i.e., himself), while Díaz (through Yunior) testifies to Oscar and his family.

how Gatsby's greatness went ignored by so many people. There is a certain mystery that leads Nick to narrate the events surrounding Gatsby's final days. Similarly, Randall Patrick McMurphy is a mystery to Bromden as well, but for Bromden, McMurphy stands as a testament to the power of resisting institutional authority. Thus, Bromden's narrative is both a memorial and a narrative monument for the sacrificial McMurphy.

However, while both Nick and Bromden have in common with Yunior the need to memorialize through narration, it is with Nathan Zuckerman that Yunior has the strongest affinity. Both Zuckerman and Yunior are writers devoted to the craft of narrative worldmaking (Zuckerman, like his creator Philip Roth, is a successful novelist; Yunior is a creative writing teacher), and in both *American Pastoral* and *The Human Stain*, Zuckerman cannot resist weaving a narrative around a certain charismatic figure (Seymour "Swede" Levov and Coleman Silk, respectively) in an effort to understand how these great men fell from such lofty heights. Zuckerman uses narrative in order to plausibly fill in the gaps created by the historical record surrounding both Levov and Silk.

Yet there is a key difference between Zuckerman's desire to explore a great man's fall from grace and Yunior's compulsion to write the story of an utterly unremarkable person. Levov and Silk are near-mythic figures, and even after their personal downfalls their story continues on in the stories of their respective communities. But one gets the sense that no one is going to continue telling Oscar's story. Both Zuckerman and Yunior want to reconstruct the events of particular lives, but it is Yunior that apotheosizes Oscar. Like any good writer of speculative fiction, Yunior casts Oscar as his hero from humble origins who is pitted against dark forces that are almost unimaginable in scope, just as Tolkien does with Bilbo Baggins and, later, Frodo Baggins.

As a result of his significant use of intertexts, part of Yunior's repertoire in creating his narrative is to digress beyond the primary narrative into footnotes. But unlike Cisneros's *Caramelo* where the footnotes appear to originate from the author's position (as opposed to the narrator's), Yunior also narrates the thirty-three footnotes in *Oscar Wao*. The distinction here between the two novel's use of footnotes is key here, for the distinction rests in the presumed authority of the footnote itself. Whereas Cisneros assumes the footnotes as a sort of quality control within her novel, Yunior maintains the same level of authority whether he narrates in the primary narrative or from the position of the footnote. In *Caramelo*, the difference in narrators of the primary text and the secondary footnote compels the reader to wonder at the authorial intrusions of the footnotes. Rather than use the footnote as a device simply to clarify or expand upon material originating from the primary narrative,

Yunior often introduces intertexts that enrich Oscar's narrative in a meaningful way that is an ingrained aspect of the narrative progression. The reader, in turn, must be willing and able to make sense of the intertextual allusion when it is deployed within the narrative. It is a significant challenge, one that is not found in the initial rise of Latino/a literature.

For instance, in his prologue wherein Yunior establishes the import and significance of the fukú curse, he introduces his two most important intertexts from speculative fiction: "It's doom-ish in that way, makes it harder to put a finger on, to brace yourself against. But be assured: like Darkseid's Omega Effect, like Morgoth's bane, no matter how many turns and digressions this shit might take, it always—and I mean always—gets its man" (5). Darkseid is Jack Kirby's creation, an overarching villain of Kirby's Fourth World. Darkseid is, as Charles Hatfield describes, "the über-fascist [. . .] whose plans to enslave all life were opposed by a motley group of demigods and heroes" (*Hand of Fire* 10). Yet there is no indication of who or what Darkseid is in *Oscar Wao*'s prologue; no context or footnote is provided. Also, Jack Kirby's created comic worlds become a dominant intertext in Díaz's novel. As for Morgoth's bane, a footnote is provided:

> I am the Elder King: Melkor, first and mightiest of all the Valar, who was before the world and made it. The shadow of my purpose lies upon Arda, and all that is in it bends slowly and surely to my will. But upon all whom you love my thought shall weigh as a cloud of Doom, and it shall bring them down into darkness and despair. Wherever they go, evil shall arise. Whenever they speak, their words shall bring ill counsel. Whatsoever they do shall turn against them. They shall die without hope, cursing both life and death. (5)

The footnote consists of a single, uncontextualized, uncited quotation. From a reader's perspective, this footnote is extremely recalcitrant, refusing to provide the reader with further explanation as to the relevance of the quote to Morgoth's bane.

In fact, the quote actually provides more material that might also beg a footnote: "Melkor," "Valar," "Arda," and so on. Yunior cites neither the narrator of this bit of quoted speech nor the author of the text. It is a challenging reading situation of the first order for several reasons. First, while Morgoth is a character in the Tolkien legendarium, Morgoth is only a referential character in *Lord of the Rings*. Morgoth's quoted speech is found in Tolkien's *The Silmarillion*, a paratext that is essentially the mythology that operates in *Lord of the*

Rings. Second, the footnote is Morgoth's quoted speech, but it does not reveal what Yunior means by "Morgoth's bane."[15] This third difficulty that arises in this footnote, the identification of what Morgoth's bane actually is, encapsulates how the footnotes generally function in *Oscar Wao*. That is to say, while they provide insight into the primary narrative, they don't always provide said insight in an easy manner.

Because Yunior is such a free-flowing narrator who is unconcerned with making storyworld reconstruction easy for readers, he is freed to intersperse a wide array of allusions and intertexts—references that can be grappled with, as the previous footnote demonstrates—only with serious research that wields the power of Google. In fact, it may be that *Oscar Wao* is the first true Latino/a novel of the Internet generation and that its design anticipates the usage of computer algorithms to aid in storyworld reconstruction and narrative comprehension. Not only must the reader move from primary narrative to secondary footnote, but he or she may often be forced to leave the confines of the material book altogether and forage through the Internet for reference material.

Díaz's first novel suggests how intertexts can be used not merely as a postmodernist device that self-reflexively calls attention to itself but also as a means of providing significant layers of meaning to the narrative proper. While Cisneros's *Caramelo* makes a stunning move to use such postmodernist techniques such as multitudinous intertexts and use of footnotes in fiction, Díaz's *Oscar Wao* reveals a more organic use of these devices in Latino/a fiction. Both Cisneros and Díaz make little concession to their readerships, and by placing the onus of working through intertextual material (some often obscure), they reflect the developing nature of Latino/a literature. After many decades of consistently shaping their narratives to conform to a particular structure with a readership unwilling to deal with narrative challenges of language, structure, or content, Cisneros and Díaz have made it clear that their works are highly interconnected to other aspects of human cultural production. If a reader does not understand a specific intertext, it is now up to the

---

15. Several websites have taken up the challenge of accounting for this particular footnote in *Oscar Wao*. Wayne G. Hammond and Christina Scull's website, *Too Many Books and Never Enough*, has an entry on the use of "Morgoth's bane" in *Oscar Wao*. Hammond maintains that what Yunior means is that "Morgoth was the bane of Arda, but 'Morgoth's bane' = 'the bane (or doom) of Morgoth,' just as the balrog of Moria was 'Durin's bane.'" I disagree that Yunior intends to say that Morgoth is the bane of Arda. Clearly, "bane" belongs to Morgoth. If *bane* refers to something that results from Morgoth, and based on Yunior's constant references to him, I maintain that Morgoth's bane is the dark lord Sauron himself, the chief antagonist and source of ubiquitous evil in *Lord of the Rings*.

reader to make sense of it. Again, I maintain that it is certainly possible that Díaz and Cisneros envisioned writing their respective novels for their own tastes rather than for a particular readership. If so, this is a sign of empowerment for the author's desire to construct narratives that are shaped in ways that comport with their own imaginations rather than those of a supposed audience. Latino/a authors are now poised to write not what others such as publishers and audiences would have them write but instead what they feel compelled to write based on their own imaginings of their storyworld design and will to style. The challenge has now been presented to readers. It remains to be seen whether such narratives, as Jorge Luis Borges hoped, "will continue to ramify within the hospitable imaginations of the readers" (485).

CONCLUSION

The Narrative Possibilities of Latino/a Literature

IN MY INITIAL curiosity on the topic that would later become this book, I wondered why it was that Latino/a literature seemed to come to complexly designed and challenging narratives relatively late when compared to, say, Anglo-American literature. Why was it that novels such as Díaz's *The Brief Wondrous Life of Oscar Wao* or Salvador Plascencia's *The People of Paper*, with their postmodernist tendencies and unconventional narrative structures, had not appeared earlier in the development of Latino/a literature? In my initial musings, I erroneously ascribed the possibility of a new aesthetic as far as Latino/a literature was concerned. At the turn of the twenty-first century, I thought, Latino/a authors had broken away from the dominance of the realistic narrative structures rooted in cultural tradition and history. Latino/a authors could now create any type of narrative that tickled their fancies—from sci-fi to melodrama, from postmodernism to formulaic thrillers.

While my initial hypothesis about the wide-open formal and generic possibilities now being embraced by Latino/a authors has remained intact, I realize that I had failed to consider the possibility that even the earliest Latino/a authors *were* already attempting to break from a priori expectations of what types of narratives they could create; what they lacked was narrative permissibility from their audiences. Barring idiosyncratic tendencies among cultures and nations when creating narratives, the human mind has the capacity to take aspects of our reality and use them as foundational pieces of imagined storyworlds. That certain narrative structures or devices "belong" to one nation, one culture, or one religion is untenable and does not hold up under close examination. While some narrative devices may or may not be used to different ends among disparate peoples, the devices themselves are available for all. Not only do authors from marginalized communities have the task of writing a viable and compelling narrative, but they must also get their audiences to acquiesce to narrative choices that do not easily fit within narrative schemas with which they have become accustomed and comfortable. Audiences have values, beliefs, histories, and experiences embedded within those schemas. When their narrative schemas are challenged, when their a priori attitudes are countered, it can become personal—as personal as the narrative in question is to the author, though in distinct ways. The author is invested in the narrative, but the audience must *accept* the narrative in ways that might contradict deep-seated values or beliefs. Narratives can flourish in the minds of audiences only if they are deemed permissible.

In the previous chapters, I made the case that narrative innovation is not a recent development in Latino/a literature—an argument that depends on how Latino/a narratives were (and are) received by both ideal and real readerships. Though my examination concentrates on the textual phenomena as it suggests an ideal readership, I acknowledge that publishers' expectations do operate as an unseen but omnipresent intermediary between the author and the reader. Indeed, it may be that the primary constraint placed upon Latino/a authors regarding the design of their narratives originates from editors and publishers. As I mentioned in my introduction to this book, Arturo Islas and the tortuous publication of *The Rain God* is an example of this phenomenon of Latino/a authors acquiescing to a publisher's demands, particularly in the early years of the development of Latino/a literature.

This is not to say that all publishers conspire to keep Latino/a authors in a tidy box. To be sure, smaller presses such as Arte Público Press, Bilingual Review Press, Quinto Sol, and Aunt Lute Books have published the bulk of the corpus of Latino/a literature. Without the efforts of these relatively smaller presses, there would be a dearth of Latino/a works available to the public, and their efforts ought to be lauded. However, despite the mission of these specialized publishers to bring Latino/a works to the public, they themselves have constraints for the types of literature they publish.

For example, Arte Público Press's submission policy states, "Please take time to familiarize yourself with our current and previous titles, as well as specialized fields, and send only the material relevant to our publishing needs" ("Manuscript Submissions"). As Arte Público Press "specializes in publishing contemporary novels, short stories, poetry, and drama based on U.S. Hispanic

(Cuban American, Mexican American, Puerto Rican, and others) cultural issues and themes," a writer such as Michael Nava who writes legal thrillers or John Rechy's famous *City of Night* might not be published by Arte Público Press. This is perfectly fine; I'm not indicting Arte Público or other specialty presses for the types of books they publish. Rather, I am highlighting the issue that publishers have specific tastes in terms of what they will publish—even presses that work to market Latino/a literature.

Thus my aim is not to excoriate publishers and presses for limiting the development of Latino/a literature. Far from it. Publishers, until recently, have been a necessary part of allowing an author's creative work to reach a real audience.[1] Nevertheless, publishers have played a significant role in the failed reception of Acosta's *The Autobiography of a Brown Buffalo,* as well as the soaring reception of Díaz's *The Brief Wondrous Life of Oscar Wao.* Indeed, part of Arte Público Press's most significant legacy, under the direction of Nicolás Kanellos, is its series Recovering the U.S. Hispanic Literary Heritage—a series that has brought forgotten works such as *The Adventures of Don Chipote, or, When Parrots Breast-Feed* by Daniél Venegas, *Dew on the Thorn* by Jovita González, and *The Squatter and the Don* by María Amparo Ruiz de Burton. But even here, Kanellos's stewardship of a series that seeks to bring to the fore works that have somehow fallen out of print or have been otherwise lost is a potent reminder that Latino/a authors in particular have not always benefitted from a committed publisher that would vigorously market Latino/a works or from purchasing audiences that keep such works in print. The role of the publisher in the development in Latino/a literature specifically, and U.S. ethnic literature generally, remains a rich topic yet to be explored.

Innovative narrative design in Latino/a literature is not a recent phenomenon but instead has been evident for decades. I use the term *innovative* with caution, and I am not suggesting that Latino/a authors were designing storyworlds in a manner altogether unseen up to that moment. That would be an extraordinary claim, for narrative necessarily is rooted in forms that are in some way recognizable *as narrative*. What I am positing, rather, is that Latino/a literature has posed significant challenges to its audiences—challenges that reside both in the narrative blueprint of specific works of Latino/a literature and in the imaginations of the audience. *Imagination,* as I define

---

1. Most notably, the online bookseller Amazon has enabled authors to sell their books directly to a buying audience without the need for a traditional publisher. Though there has been the option of so-called vanity presses that will publish anyone's manuscript sans the traditional marketing and editing infrastructure of large presses, many authors who are selling their books electronically through Amazon are making larger profits than they might even with traditional publishers.

it within the scope of my project, is the process of co-creating the narrative storyworld in the reader's mind. Moreover, the ideal readership/actual readership distinction is crucial for understanding the sorts of challenges manifest in Latino/a narrative storyworlds, and this potential difference between ideal and actual audience provides the impetus for my previous chapters.

As my book reveals, the types of challenging reading situations presented by Latino/a literature suggest the inherent complexity of this body of works. Additionally, these challenges arise out of historical, political, and national contexts. Latino/a literature interposes itself between reader expectations and the larger Anglo-American tradition of literature. This interposition, while bearing these specific contexts in mind, engages audiences at the level of narrative design. I stress that Latino/a literature presents a multitudinous set of challenges to audiences rather than one monolithic act of resistance, as some scholars in the field of Latino/a cultural studies have asserted in the past. Further, these challenges are not simply a matter of presenting thematics that problematize a hegemonic articulation of, say, patriarchy or nationalism. Rather, the challenges have the potential to resonate most powerfully within the mind of a novel's audience. I have attempted to demonstrate that it is the cognitive and emotional processes of audiences that are the specific sites where reductive assumptions of Latinos may be redressed.

So many of the challenges I have identified in *Permissible Narratives* all force the reader to contend with them. How the readership contends with these specific challenges tells us much about the development of Latino/a literature over the last fifty-plus years. Though readerships vary in how they respond to challenges in reading comprehension, we can begin to identify an actual audience's response by noting the challenging reading situation vis-à-vis an ideal readership. For example, one of the most overt challenges in my case studies from chapter 1, Acosta's *Autobiography* and Anzaldúa's *Borderlands,* remains the ontology of the text. That is to say, each respective text asks its ideal readership to recognize it for a fictional reality that in many ways reflects the actual world. Much of the complexity of each of these texts is rooted in this blurred ontological distinction. Yet in each case actual audiences have unproblematically cast Acosta's and Anzaldúa's texts as reflections and representations of their selves. These texts, despite their fictional status, have been received by audiences as documentary evidence at the expense of their more creative aspects as works of literature. The minimization of Acosta's work and the overdetermination of Anzaldúa's signal the inability of actual audiences to align with the ideal readerships for each text.

Not only is the very ontology of Latino/a literature a salient concern for audience, but reading comprehension, language, time, space, and intertexts all pose certain problems for actual audiences to some degree or another. Ostensibly, an ideal readership does not see these issues as challenges at all, which is precisely the point of my study. Latino/a authors, like other authors, work with a specific ideal readership in mind when designing their storyworlds. Piri Thomas's ideal readership for *Down These Mean Streets* does not need a glossary and does not really need to be proficient in Spanish, while Giannina Braschi's ideal readership for *Yo-Yo Boing!* is equally literate in both English and Spanish.

Though the challenge of bilingualism and code-switching I explored in chapter 2 arises out of a cultural context, Gilbert Hernandez demonstrates that challenging reading situations can arise from a purely narrative design perspective. The comics medium, despite its characterization as an illegitimate literary form for most of its history, has been a venue for diverse representations of culture and social concerns. Alternative comics have given artists such as Gilbert Hernandez a canvas on which to push their storytelling techniques in ways satisfying to themselves first and foremost. His use of time in challenging works such as *Poison River* suggests not an ideal readership that recognizes certain markers of cultural signification but an ideal readership that can itemize and reconstruct two highly fragmented storyworlds that continue to expand both on the page and within the minds of the audience. Most importantly, Hernandez took the opportunity to purposefully design a challenging reading experience irrespective of whether his work would be well received by his loyal readership. And Sandra Cisneros and Junot Díaz both make significant use of intertextual material so as to suggest an ideal readership that either has an encyclopedic type of knowledge or has access to a knowledge database in order to make sense of their intertextual storyworlds. In short, Cisneros and Díaz create a narrative blueprint that views the invocation of intertexts (some often quite abstruse) as a nonimpediment, as a device that enriches and provides specific texture to their narrative storyworlds.

This issue of the ideal readership as an orienting concept around which Latino/a authors design their storyworld blueprint is at the crux of this book. What is more, though the ideal readerships of my case studies can recognize a host of signifiers and referents within the narrative, the ideal readership may or may not be Latino/a. Unlike other ethnic groups in the United States, Latinos have multinational origins (Cuba, Dominican Republic, Mexico, and so on), *and* they span racial difference according to phenotype. Latinos are Spanish speaking and they are not. Latinos have African, European, Asian, and indigenous American ancestry. In sum, Latinos have a wide-ranging set of experiences, traditions, and histories. So if we suggest that an author such as Piri Thomas has a "Latino" readership in mind, we must be quick to ask what a Latino readership expects. Instead, the concept of the ideal readership allows us to examine works of Latino/a literature without an a priori expectation, which is, in effect, a liberating move in literary studies because we are no longer attempting to place Latino/a literature in a box but instead take it on the terms it establishes for itself.

If actual readerships are asked to step into the position of the ideal readership, if this is the heart of the challenging reading situation, then such a move is done only via a stringent cognitive effort. The actual readership is often asked to participate in knowledge and codes outside their purview—an often potentially alienating aspect of reading to which readers' comments on Amazon's website often attest.[2] Indeed, if the ideal readership is capable of comprehending all sorts of cognitively challenging narratives, then Latino/a literature ought to be limited only by an ideal readership rather than publishers or actual readerships' demands for certain types of narratives. The ideal readership necessarily dwells within the imagination of the author and illuminates the possibility of the storyworld design. Ultimately, it is the goal of the author to get actual readerships to move into the position of the ideal readership. In reality, this shaping of the actual readership takes place over many years.

Over the course of over fifty years, Latino/a literature has steadily worked to grow its readership. It is a process that can occur only when Latino/a authors engage in storyworld design across a multitude of genres that are articulated for low-, middle-, and high-brow tastes. In order for Latino/a literature to achieve full consideration as a "Literature," it must be allowed to express itself using all of the devices available in the endeavor of narrative worldmaking. For this to occur, Latino/a authors must move beyond the dominant tropes that have become so inextricably linked to Latino/a literature, such as magic realism, family epics, and barrio bildungsroman. They must also continue to venture into all forms of genre fiction, from chick-lit to fantasy to sci-fi and beyond. They must continue to work in graphic narrative forms and animation. There must be no form of storytelling that is beyond reach for Latinos, for there is no form of storytelling that is beyond the reach of the human imagination. Storyworlds, those rendered by Latinos or otherwise, must shape their readerships—not the reverse.

---

2. For instance, concerning Díaz's novel, most readers are confounded by his narrator's use of untranslated, uncontextualized Spanish, not his arcane citations of comic-book lore. The general sentiment of such comments that deride his use of Spanish is one of frustration and distraction.

WORKS CITED

Acosta, Oscar "Zeta." *The Autobiography of a Brown Buffalo*. 1972. New York: Vintage Books, 1989. Print.

———. *The Revolt of the Cockroach People*. 1973. New York: Vintage, 1989. Print.

Aldama, Arturo J. *Disrupting Savagism: Intersecting Chicano/a, Mexican Immigrant, and Native American Struggles for Self-Representation*. Durham: Duke UP, 2001. Print.

Aldama, Frederick Luis. *Dancing with Ghosts: A Critical Biography of Arturo Islas*. Berkeley: U of California P, 2005. Print.

———, ed. *Multicultural Comics: From Zap to Blue Beetle*. Austin: U of Texas P, 2010. Print.

———. *Postethnic Narrative Criticism*. Austin: U of Texas P, 2003. Print.

———. *The Routledge Concise History of Latino/a Literature*. New York: Routledge, 2013. Print.

———. *A User's Guide to Postcolonial and Latino Borderlands Fiction*. Austin: U of Texas P, 2009. Print.

———. *Your Brain on Latino Comics*. Austin: U of Texas P, 2009. Print.

Aldama, Frederick Luis and Patrick Colm Hogan. *Conversations on Cognitive Cultural Studies: Literature, Language, and Aesthetics*. Columbus: Ohio State UP, 2014. Print.

Allen, Graham. *Intertextuality*. New York: Routledge, 2000. Print.

Alonso, Sarah. "The Hispanic Market for Book Publishing." *Publishing Research Quarterly* 21.3 (2005): 46–76. Print.

Alvarez, Julia. *How the García Girls Lost Their Accents*. New York: Plume, 1992. Print.

Anaya, Rudolfo. *Bless Me, Ultima*. 1972. New York: Warner, 1999. Print.

Anders, Gigi. "Hispanic Literature: Many Authors, Few Agents." *Hispanic* 15.9 (2002): 50. Print.

Anonymous. Rev. of *Yo-Yo Boing! Publishers Weekly* 31 Aug. 1998: 49. Print.

Anzaldúa, Gloria, ed. *Borderlands/La Frontera: The New Mestiza*. San Francisco: Aunt Lute, 1987. Print.

———. *Making Face, Making Soul/Haciendo Caras: Creative and Critical Perspectives by Women of Color*. San Francisco: Aunt Lute, 1990. Print.

Aparicio, Frances R. "From Ethnicity to Multiculturalism: An Historical Overview of Puerto Rican Literature in the United States." *Vol. 1: Handbook of Hispanic Cultures in the United States: Literature and Art*. Ed. Francisco A. Lomelí. Houston: Arte Público, 1993. 19–39. Print.

Arellano, Gustavo. "No Comprendo." *Publishers Weekly* 26 Feb. 2007: 98o. Print.

Arteaga, Alfred, ed. *An Other Tongue: Nation and Ethnicity in the Linguistic Borderlands*. 2nd ed. Durham: Duke UP, 1996. Print.

Bakhtin, M. M. *The Dialogic Imagination: Four Essays*. Trans. Caryl Emerson and Michael Holquist. Ed. Michael Holquist. Austin: U of Texas P, 1981. Print.

Bautista, Daniel. "Comic Book Realism: Form and Genre in Junot Díaz's *The Brief Wondrous Life of Oscar Wao*." *Journal of the Fantastic in the Arts* 21.1 (2010): 41–53. Print.

Benstock, Shari. "At the Margin of Discourse: Footnotes in the Fictional Text." *PMLA* 98.2 (1983): 204–25. Print.

Berila, Beth. "The Radical Disruptions of *Borderlands/La Frontera*." *EntreMundos/AmongWorlds: New Perspectives on Gloria Anzaldúa*. Ed. AnaLouise Keating. New York: Palgrave Macmillan, 2005. Print.

Bhabha, Homi. *The Location of Culture*. New York: Routledge, 1994. Print.

Borges, Jorge Luis. *Collected Fictions*. Trans. Andrew Hurley. New York: Penguin, 1998. Print.

Braschi, Giannina. "Pelos en la lengua." *Hopscotch* 2.2 (2000): 50. Print.

———. *Yo-Yo Boing!* Pittsburgh: Latin American Literary Review Press, 1998. Print.

Bruce-Novoa, Juan. "Fear and Loathing on the Buffalo Trail." *MELUS* 6 (1979): 39–50. Print.

Bueno, Eva Paulina. "The Importance of Being Sandra Cisneros." *A Companion to US Latino Literatures*. Ed. Carlota Caulfield and Darién J. Davis. Rochester, NY: Tamesis, 2007. Print.

Carrasquillo, Marci L. "Oscar 'Zeta' Acosta's American Odyssey." *MELUS* 35.1 (2010): 77–97. Print.

Carroll, Julia. "Spanish Affect and Its Effects: Bilingual Process in Giannina Braschi's *Yo-Yo Boing!*" *Leading Ladies: mujeres en la literatura hispana y en las artes*. Ed. Yvonne Fuentes and Margaret R. Parker. Baton Rouge: Louisiana State UP, 2006. Print.

Carvajal, Doreen. "Of Hispanic Literature and Not So Equal Opportunities." *New York Times* 4 May 1996. Print.

Chatman, Seymour. *Story and Discourse: Narrative Structure in Fiction and Film*. Ithaca: Cornell UP, 1978. Print.

Christie, John S. *Latino Fiction and the Modernist Imagination*. Albuquerque: U of New Mexico P, 1998. Print.

Cisneros, Sandra. *Caramelo*. New York: Knopf, 2003. Print.

Cohn, Dorrit. "Signposts of Fictionality: A Narratological Perspective." *Poetics Today* 11.4 (1990): 775–804. Print.

———. *Transparent Minds: Narrative Modes for Presenting Consciousness in Fiction*. Princeton, NJ: Princeton UP, 1978. Print.

Contreras, Sheila Marie. *Blood Myth: Myth, Indigenism, and Chicana/o Literature*. Austin: U of Texas P, 2008. Print.

Cortázar, Julio. "Blow-Up." *Blow-Up and Other Stories*. Trans. Paul Blackburn. New York: Pantheon Books, 1985. Print.

Dalleo, Raphael. "Review of Frederick Luis Aldama's *A User's Guide to Postcolonial and Latino Borderlands Fiction*." *Camino Real* 1.2 (2010): 175–76. Print.

Dalleo, Raphael, and Elena Machado Sáez, eds. *The Latino/a Canon and the Emergence of Post-Sixties Literature*. New York: Palgrave Macmillan, 2007. Print.

Danielewski, Mark Z. *House of Leaves*. New York: Pantheon Books, 2000. Print.

Díaz, Junot. *The Brief Wondrous Life of Oscar Wao*. New York: Riverhead, 2007. Print.

———. "Pulitzer Prize-winning Novelist Junot Díaz interviewed by *The Progressive*." *The Progressive*. Sept. 2007. 10 Oct. 2011. Web.

Dickey, James. *Deliverance*. 1970. New York: Delta, 1994. Print.

Doležel, Lubomír. "Truth and Authenticity in Narrative." *Poetics Today* 1.3 (1980): 7–25. Print.

Du Bois, W. E. B. *The Souls of Black Folk*. 1903. Ed. Henry Louis Gates Jr., and Terri Hume Oliver. New York: Norton, 1999. Print.

Eco, Umberto. *The Limits of Interpretation*. Bloomington: Indiana UP, 1991. Print.

Eisner, Will. *Comics and Sequential Art*. Tamarac, FL: Poorhouse Press, 1985. Print.

Eliot, T.S. "Tradition and the Individual Talent." 1917. *Selected Essays, 1917–1932*. New York: Harcourt, Brace and Company, 1932. 3–11. Print.

Emerson, Ralph Waldo. *The Essential Writings of Ralph Waldo Emerson*. New York: Modern Library, 2000. Print.

Emmott, Catherine. *Narrative Comprehension: A Discourse Perspective*. Oxford: Clarendon Press, 1997. Print.

Faulkner, William. *The Sound and the Fury*. 1929. New York: Vintage International, 1990. Print.

Finnegan, Jordana. *Narrating the American West: New Forms of Historical Memory*. Amherst: Cambria, 2008. Print.

Fishkin, Shelley Fisher. *Feminist Engagements: Forays into American Literature and Culture*. New York: Palgrave Macmillan, 2009. Print.

Fitzgerald, F. Scott. *The Great Gatsby*. New York: Scribner's Sons, 1958. Print.

Foster, David William. Rev. of *Yo-Yo Boing! Review of Contemporary Fiction* 19.1 (1999): 202–3. Print.

Foster, Shesshu. *Atomik Aztex*. San Francisco: City Lights, 2005. Print.

Genette, Gérard. *Narrative Discourse: An Essay in Method*. Trans. Jane E. Lewin. Ithaca: Cornell UP, 1980. Print.

The Godfather. Dir. Francis Ford Coppola. Perf. Marlon Brando, Al Pacino, and James Caan. Paramount, 1972. DVD.

Gonzales, Rodolfo. *Yo Soy Joaquín; an epic poem*. New York: Bantam Books, 1972. Print.

Groensteen, Thierry. *The System of Comics*. Trans. Bart Beaty and Nick Nguyen. Jackson: UP of Mississippi, 2007. Print.

Grossman, Edith. "Translator's Note to the Reader." *Don Quixote*. By Miguel de Cervantes. New York: Ecco, 2003. Print.

Gumperz, John J. *Discourse Strategies*. Cambridge: Cambridge UP, 1982. Print.

Gutiérrez, Ramón A. "Reflections on 1972." *Aztlán: A Journal of Chicano Studies* 32:1 (2007): 183–90. Print.

Gutiérrez, Ramón, and Genaro Padilla, ed. *Recovering the U.S. Hispanic Literary Heritage*. Houston: Arte Público, 1993. Print.

Hammond, Wayne G. and Christina Scull. "William Reads." *Too Many Books and Never Enough.* 9 Feb. 2010. 2 Feb. 2012. Web.

Hanna, Monica. "'Reassembling the Fragments': Battling Historiographies, Caribbean Discourse, and Nerd Genre in Junot Díaz's *The Brief Wondrous Life of Oscar Wao.*" *Callaloo* 33.2 (2010): 498–520. Print.

Hatfield, Charles. *Alternative Comics: An Emerging Literature.* Jackson: UP of Mississippi, 2005. Print.

———. *Hand of Fire: The Comics Art of Jack Kirby.* Jackson: UP of Mississippi, 2012. Print.

———. "How To Read a . . ." *English Language Notes* 46.2 (2008): 129–49. Print.

Heredia, Juanita. "The Dominican Diaspora Strikes Back: Cultural Archive and Race in Junot Díaz's *The Brief Wondrous Life of Oscar Wao.*" *Hispanic Caribbean Literature of Migration: Narratives of Displacement.* Ed. Vanessa Pérez Rosario. New York: Palgrave Macmillan, 2010. Print.

Herman, David. *Basic Elements of Narrative.* West Sussex, UK: Wiley-Blackwell, 2009. Print.

———. *Story Logic: Problems and Possibilities of Narrative.* Lincoln: U of Nebraska P, 2002. Print.

———. *Storytelling and the Sciences of the Mind.* Cambridge, MA: Massachusetts Institute of Technology P, 2013. Print.

Hernandez, Gilbert. *High Soft Lisp.* Seattle: Fantagraphics, 2010. Print.

———. "Holidays in the Sun." 1988. *Heartbreak Soup.* Seattle: Fantagraphics, 2007. 199–212. Print.

———. "The Laughing Sun." 1984. *Heartbreak Soup.* Seattle: Fantagraphics, 2007. 117–28. Print.

———. "Poison River." 1989–1993. *Beyond Palomar.* Seattle: Fantagraphics, 2007. 7–189. Print.

Hernandez, Gilbert, Jaime Hernandez, and Mario Hernandez. *Love and Rockets* Series. Seattle: Fantagraphics, 1982–Present. Print.

Herrera Sobek, María. "Canon Formation and Chicano Literature." *Recovering the U.S. Hispanic Literary Heritage.* Ed. Ramón Gutiérrez and Genaro Padilla, 209–21. Houston: Arte Público Press, 1993. Print.

———. "Gloria Anzaldúa: Place, Race, Language, and Sexuality in the Magic Valley." *PMLA* 121.1 (2006): 266–71. Print.

Hogan, Patrick Colm. *Affective Narratology.* Lincoln: U of Nebraska P, 2011. Print.

———. "Literary Universals." *Introduction to Cognitive Cultural Studies.* Ed. Lisa Zunshine. Baltimore: Johns Hopkins UP, 2010. Print.

———. *The Mind and Its Stories: Narrative Universals and Human Emotion.* New York: Cambridge UP, 2003. Print.

———. *Understanding Nationalism: On Narrative, Cognitive Science, and Identity.* Columbus: Ohio State UP, 2009. Print.

Hutcheon, Linda. *A Poetics of Postmodernism: History, Theory, Fiction.* New York: Routledge, 1988. Print.

Inge, Thomas M. *Comics as Culture.* Jackson: UP of Mississippi, 1990. Print.

Islas, Arturo. *The Rain God.* 1984. New York: Perennial, 2003. Print.

Jauss, Hans Robert. *Aesthetic Experience and Literary Hermeneutics.* 1977. Trans. Michael Shaw. Minneapolis: U of Minnesota P, 1982. Print.

———. *Toward an Aesthetic of Reception.* 1977. Trans. Timothy Bahti. Minneapolis: U of Minnesota P, 1982. Print.

Johnson, Susan. "*Harry Potter*, Eucatastrophe, and Christian Hope." *Logos* 14.1 (2011): 66–90. Print.

Joyce, James. *Ulysses*. 1922. New York: Random House, 1986. Print.

Keen, Suzanne. *Empathy and the Novel*. Oxford: Oxford UP, 2007. Print.

Kellman, Steve G, ed. *Switching Languages: Translingual Writers Reflect on Their Craft*. Lincoln: U of Nebraska P, 2003. Print.

———. *The Translingual Imagination*. Lincoln: U of Nebraska P, 2000. Print.

Kesey, Ken. *One Flew Over the Cuckoo's Nest*. 1962. New York: Penguin, 2007. Print.

Kristeva, Julia. "Word, Dialogue and Novel." *The Kristeva Reader*. Ed. Toril Moi. New York: Columbia UP, 1986. Print.

Ley, David, and Roman Cybriwsky. "Urban Graffiti as Territorial Markers." *Annals of the Association of American Geographers* 64.4 (1974): 491–505. Print.

Loftus, Geoffrey R., and Elizabeth F. Loftus. *Human Memory: The Processing of Information*. New York: Wiley & Sons, 1976. Print.

London, Scott. "Crossing Borders: An Interview with Richard Rodriguez." *The Sun* August 1997. http://thesunmagazine.org/issues/260/crossing_borders.Web. Accessed 18 April 2017.

Lorde, Audre. "The Master's Tools Will Never Dismantle the Master's House." *Sister Outsider: Essays and Speeches by Audre Lorde*. Freedom, CA: Crossing Press, 1984. Print.

Lugones, María. "On *Borderlands/La Frontera*: An Interpretive Essay." *Hypatia* 7.4 (1992): 31–37. Print.

Madsen, Deborah L. *Understanding Contemporary Chicana Literature*. Columbia: U of South Carolina P, 2000. Print.

Mahler, Anne Garland. "The Writer as Superhero: Fighting the Colonial Curse in Junot Díaz's *The Brief Wondrous Life of Oscar Wao*." *Journal of Latin American Cultural Studies* 19.2 (2010): 119–40. Print.

Margolis, Mac. "Is Magical Realism Dead?" *Newsweek* 6 May 2002: 50–53. Print.

Martinez, Manuel Luis. *Countering the Counterculture: Rereading Postwar American Dissent from Jack Kerouac to Tomás Rivera*. Madison: U of Wisconsin P, 2003. Print.

Martín-Rodríguez, Manuel M. *Life in Search of Readers: Reading (in) Chicano/a Literature*. Albuquerque: U of New Mexico P, 2003. Print.

McCloud, Scott. *Understanding Comics*. New York: HarperPerennial, 1994. Print.

Milroy, Lesley and Pieter Muysken, eds. *One Speaker, Two Languages: Cross-Disciplinary Perspectives on Code-Switching*. New York: Cambridge UP, 1995. Print.

Mohr, Eugene V. "Piri Thomas: Author and Persona." *Caribbean Studies* 20.2 (1980): 61–74. Print.

Montagne, Renee. Interview of Gustavo Pérez Firmat. *Morning Edition*. Natl. Public Radio, 17 Oct. 2011. NPR.org. 8 Feb. 2012. Web.

Moraga, Cherríe. *Loving in the War Years: lo que nunca pasó por sus labios*. 1983. Expanded ed. Cambridge, MA: South End Press Classics, 2000. Print.

Moraga, Cherríe, and Gloria Anzaldúa, eds. *This Bridge Called My Back: Writings by Radical Women of Color*. New York: Kitchen Table, Women of Color Press, 1983. Print.

Nabokov, Vladimir. *Pale Fire*. 1962. New York: Vintage, 1989. Print.

O'Dwyer, Tess. "Grunting and Grooming in a Room of One's Own: On Translating Giannina Braschi's *Yo-Yo Boing!*" *Artful Dodge* 34–35 (1999): 70–79. Print.

Olliz Boyd, Antonio. *The Latin American Identity and the African Diaspora: Ethnogenesis in Conflict.* Amherst: Cambria, 2010. Print.

Paredes, Américo. *With His Pistol in His Hand: A Border Ballad and Its Hero.* 1958. Austin: U of Texas P, 2004. Print.

Pérez Firmat, Gustavo. *Life on the Hyphen: The Cuban-American Way.* Rev. ed. Austin: U of Texas P, 2012. Print.

———. *Tongue Ties.* New York: Palgrave Macmillan, 2003. Print.

Phelan, James. *Living to Tell about It: A Rhetoric and Ethics of Character Narration.* Ithaca: Cornell UP, 2005. Print.

Plascencia, Salvador. *The People of Paper.* San Francisco: McSweeney's Books, 2005. Print.

Portales, Marco. *Crowding Out Latinos: Mexican Americans in the Public Consciousness.* Philadelphia: Temple UP, 2000. Print.

Puig, Manuel. *Betrayed by Rita Hayworth.* 1971. Trans. Suzanne Jill Levine. Elmwood Park, IL: Dalkey Archive, 2009. Print.

———. *Kiss of the Spider Woman.* New York: Vintage Books, 1991. Print.

Rabinowitz, Peter J. "'Betraying the Sender': The Rhetoric and Ethics of Fragile Texts." *Narrative* 2.3 (1994): 201–13. Print.

Railton, Ben. "Novelist-Narrators of the American Dream: The (Meta-) Realistic Chronicles of Cather, Fitzgerald, Roth, and Díaz." *American Literary Realism* 43.2 (2011): 133–53. Print.

Ratey, John J. *A User's Guide to the Brain: Perception, Attention, and the Four Theaters of the Brain.* New York: Vintage, 2001. Print.

Rechy, John. *City of Night.* 1963. New York: Grove/Atlantic, 1984. Print.

Reuman, Ann E. "Coming into Play: An Interview with Gloria Anzaldúa." *MELUS* 25.2 (2000): 3–45. Print.

Richardson, Brian. "Singular Text, Multiple Implied Readers." *Style* 41.3 (2007): 259–74. Print.

Rivera, George, Jr. "Nosotros Venceremos: Chicano Consciousness and Change Strategies." *The Journal of Applied Behavioral Science* 8.1 (1972): 56–71. Print.

Rodriguez, Richard. *The Hunger of Memory: The Education of Richard Rodriguez.* 1982. New York: Dial, 2005. Print.

Roth, Philip. *American Pastoral.* Boston: Houghton Mifflin, 1997. Print.

———. *Deception.* 1990. New York: Vintage International, 1997. Print.

———. *The Human Stain.* Boston: Houghton Mifflin, 2000. Print.

Rothenberg, Albert. *The Creative Process in Art, Science, and Other Fields.* Chicago: U of Chicago P, 1979. Print.

Royal, Derek Parker. "To Be Continued . . . Serialization and Its Discontent in the Recent Comics of Gilbert Hernandez." *International Journal of Comic Art* 11.1 (2009): 262–80. Print.

Ryan, Marie-Laure. "Cognitive Maps and the Construction of Narrative Space." *Narrative Theory and the Cognitive Sciences.* Ed. David Herman. Lincoln: U of Nebraska P, 2003. Print.

Saldívar, José David. *Dialectics of Our America: Genealogy, Cultural Critique, and Literary History.* Durham: Duke UP, 1991. Print.

Saldívar, Ramón. *Chicano Narrative: The Dialectics of Difference.* Madison: U of Wisconsin P, 1990. Print.

Saldívar-Hull, Sonia. *Feminism on the Border: Chicana Gender Politics and the Border.* Berkeley: U of California P, 2000. Print.

Sánchez, Marta. "La Malinche at the Intersection: Race and Gender in *Down These Mean Streets.*" *PMLA* 113-1 (1998): 117-28. Print.

Shen, Dan and Dejin Xu. "Intratextuality, Extratextuality, Intertextuality: Unreliability in Autobiography versus Fiction." *Poetics Today* 28.1 (2007): 43-87. Print.

Shklovsky, Viktor. *Theory of Prose.* Trans. Benjamin Sher. Intro. Gerald L. Bruns. Elmwood Park, IL: Dalkey Archive, 1991. Print.

Sova, Dawn B. *Banned Books: Literature Suppressed on Sexual Grounds.* Rev. ed. New York: Facts on File, 2006. Print.

Sperber, Dan and Diedre Wilson. *Relevance: Communication and Cognition.* 2nd ed. Oxford: Blackwell, 1995. Print.

Stavans, Ilan. *Bandido: Oscar "Zeta" Acosta and the Chicano Experience.* New York: HarperCollins, 1995. Print.

———. *A Critic's Journey.* Ann Arbor: U of Michigan P, 2010. Print.

———. *The Hispanic Condition.* 1995. New York: HarperCollins, 2001. Print.

———, ed. *The Norton Anthology of Latino Literature.* New York: Norton, 2011. Print.

———. "Race and Mercy: A Conversation with Piri Thomas." *Massachusetts Review* 37 (August 1996): 344-54. Print.

Thomas, Piri. *Down These Mean Streets.* 1967. New York: Vintage, 1997. Print.

Tolkien, J. R. R. *The Lord of the Rings.* 1954-55. Boston: Houghton Mifflin, 1994. Print.

———. "On Fairy Stories." *Tolkien on Fairy Stories.* Ed. Verlyn Flieger and Douglas A. Anderson. New York: HarperCollins, 2008. Print.

———. *The Silmarillion.* Boston: Houghton Mifflin, 1977. Print.

Torres-Padilla, José. "When Hybridity Doesn't Resist." *Complicating Constructions: Race, Ethnicity, and Hybridity in American Texts.* Ed. David S. Goldstein and Audrey B. Thacker. Seattle: U of Washington P, 2007. Print.

Torres-Saillant, Silvio. "The Tribulations of Blackness: Stages in Dominican Racial Identity." *Callaloo* 23.3 (2000): 1086-1111. Print.

Versaci, Rocco. *This Book Contains Graphic Language: Comics as Literature.* New York: Continuum, 2007. Print.

Villarreal, José Antonio. *Pocho.* 1959. New York: Anchor Books, 1989. Print.

Wallace, David Foster. *Infinite Jest.* Boston: Little, Brown and Company, 1996. Print.

Waugh, Colton. *The Comics.* New York: Macmillan, 1947. Print.

Wright, Bradford W. *Comic Book Nation: The Transformation of Youth Culture in America.* Baltimore: Johns Hopkins UP, 2001. Print.

Zacks, Jeffrey M. "How We Organize Our Experience into Events." *Psychological Science Agenda* 26.4 (April 2012). http://www.apa.org/science/about/psa/2010/04/sci-brief.aspx. 21 Apr. 2012. Web.

Zunshine, Lisa. *Why We Read Fiction: Theory of Mind and the Novel.* Columbus: Ohio State UP, 2006. Print.

INDEX

accents, 68–69, 71, 86, 98
Acosta, 26, 28–29, 34–48, 53, 56–57, 65–66, 146, 171–72, 179; Oscar, 37, 52, 97, 145
aesthetics, 91–93, 106
Affective Narratology (Hogan), 25
African Americans, 13, 25, 45, 75, 109–10
African legacy, 164, 166, 168
Afro Latino characters, 165
Afro Latinos, 71, 75–76, 164–65
Aldama, Frederick Luis, 6, 12, 20, 22, 40, 43, 50, 109, 116, 123
allusions, 114, 148, 152, 155, 160, 162, 175
America, 8–9, 105, 107, 165
Anaya, Rudolfo, 5, 37–38, 47–48, 171
Angel, Jesús, 121, 127, 134
Anzaldúa, Gloria, 4, 29, 43, 48–52, 54–55, 58–69, 71, 145, 146
apocalypses, 171
a priori approach, 9
a priori expectations, 10, 136, 177, 182
art, 7, 54–55, 64, 100, 134–35, 161
Arte Público Press, 5, 13, 26, 178–79
artists, 16, 105, 119, 133, 164
Asian American, 10, 109
atavisms, 105–6
audience expectations, 73, 118, 146
audience reception, 29, 39, 75, 143
audiences, 3–5, 7–8, 10–11, 14, 22–23, 34–36, 52–53, 64–65, 82–83, 87–89, 104–7, 110–12, 133–36, 147–49, 176–81; actual, 22–23, 30, 44, 180–81; challenging, 143

authentication function, 99
author-artists, 108–9
authorial audience, 21
authorial counterself, 17, 29, 33–34
authorial intent, 21
authoritative historical discourses, 60
authority, 73, 78, 83, 98–99, 154–55, 159, 161–62
Autobiography (Acosta), 36, 52, 180; life history, 145; narratives, 47
autobiography genre, 40, 46
Awful Grandmother, 152, 154, 159–60, 163

Babel, 104–5
bilingualism, 17, 29, 67–68, 74, 82, 87–88, 93–96, 105–6, 110, 113, 181
biography, 147, 167–68
biological author, 23, 34, 37, 77
border, 4, 38, 53, 56–59, 61, 64, 73
Borderlands (Anzaldúa), 50, 52, 64, 180; mother, 69
brain, 20, 104, 109, 115–16, 123
Braschi, Giannina, 29, 66, 89–95, 99, 102–6

California, 11, 67, 69
caló, 71, 73
canon formation, 7, 13–14
categorial identities, 11, 17, 28, 30, 56–58, 62
Celaya, 153–57, 159–62
challenges, 10–11, 17, 20, 22, 28–29, 31, 35, 38, 77–78, 80, 88–89, 105, 118–19, 133–34,

190

179–81; narrative, 175; reading, 10–11, 29–30, 66, 89, 111, 144
challenging reading situations, 4, 10, 17, 20, 26, 28–29, 42, 62, 88, 174, 180–82
characterization, 85, 102, 157, 181
character narration, 98, 127
characters, 97–98, 101–2, 104–5, 110–11, 114–15, 118, 121–22, 124–27, 133–35, 138–39, 141, 143, 164, 172, 174
Chicana, 4, 24, 33, 51–53, 57, 62–63
Chicana Feminist, 4, 23, 28, 35, 48, 51
Chicano literature, 6, 9, 14, 45
Chicano movement, 1, 3, 16, 28–29, 34–35
Chicanos, 3–5, 12–14, 28, 32–34, 36–37, 39, 41, 44–45, 47–48, 52, 60–66, 69, 71, 73, 91
Cisneros, Sandra, 4, 30, 32, 47–48, 74, 145, 148–64, 173, 176, 181
Civil Rights Act, 75–77
code-switching, 17, 29, 60, 66–67, 70, 72, 74–75, 77, 106, 181
cognition, 113, 115
cognitive narratology, 17, 28
cognitive processes, 33, 114–15
cognitive sciences, 111, 113, 115
comics, 30, 107–12, 116–20, 132–37, 142–43, 151, 165; alternative, 109, 117, 119, 143, 181
comics medium, 108, 133, 181
comprehension, 113, 131; reading, 2, 7, 17–18, 112, 115, 180
consciousness, 28–29, 32–35, 41, 44–45, 51, 56–57, 60, 98, 101, 110; collective, 63; narrative, 60, 63
constraints, 5, 11, 29, 35, 44, 72, 75, 82, 94, 100–101, 109, 118, 122, 163, 167
counterself, 33–34, 102
creative process, 55, 64, 104, 119
Cuba, 67, 71–72, 181
Cuban Americans, 71, 179
culture, 7–8, 17, 28–30, 57, 63, 65, 67, 70, 104–5, 107, 168, 177–78, 181
curses, 79, 168–69

Dante, 105
Darkseid, 174
death, 104, 118, 135, 167–69, 171, 174
design, 17, 20, 22, 54, 59, 88, 93, 106, 116–17, 139, 143, 147, 175, 178, 181; textual, 20, 53

devices, 74–75, 83, 86–87, 89, 131, 133–34, 136, 146, 148, 160, 163, 173, 175, 178, 181–82; orienting, 133–34
dialogue, 72–73, 81, 102, 138, 149, 157
Díaz, Junot, 146–52, 163–66, 171–72, 174–77, 179, 181–82
Díaz's characters and narrators, 164; manufacture of Afro Latino characters, 165; narrator of choice, 171; storyworld, 164
dictators, 168–69
document, 33–34, 61, 74, 147, 152; social, 36, 42
Doležel, Lubomir, 99
Dominican Americans and fictional works, 165
Dominican history, 164, 166
Dominican Republic, 165–66, 168, 172, 181
dreams, 12, 90, 102, 113, 124, 166, 171

education, 11, 15, 26, 29, 45, 68–69, 93, 188; formal, x, 29
Eliot, T. S., 149–50
emotions, 43, 56, 58, 81, 116, 147
emotive architecture, 116
empathy, 24, 43, 57, 187, 190; narrative, 24
encoding, 113, 115, 117
engagement, 27, 29, 74, 114, 116, 151
English, 14, 29, 37, 66–73, 75, 78, 80, 82–83, 85–91, 94–95, 99, 101, 106, 160, 181
ethnicity, 11, 23, 42
ethnic literature, 10, 13, 44, 74, 179
ethnic studies, 44–45, 69
expectations, 2, 6, 9, 11, 27–28, 30–31, 35, 76, 91, 109, 116, 153, 163, 178, 180; horizon of, 26–27, 30
experience, 25, 27–28, 30, 32–34, 59, 61, 67–69, 72, 76, 110, 113, 116, 148, 151, 153

family, 67, 69, 74, 80, 82, 90, 95, 98, 152, 155, 160, 169, 171–72
Fantagraphics, 117; Books, xi, 117, 140–41
fiction, 16–17, 20–21, 24–25, 32, 34, 40, 42, 46, 88, 145–48, 154, 162–63, 165–66, 175; narrative, 115, 168; speculative, 173–74
fictionality, 34, 46, 62, 87
footnotes, 17, 30, 78, 148–51, 153–64, 166–67, 171, 173–75; designated, 161; fictional, 148; unconventional, 153; use of, 30, 149, 151, 153–54, 160, 163, 175

freedom, 16, 19, 28–29, 75, 89, 108–9
Frey, James, 147

gaps, 39, 94, 104, 113–14, 125, 131–32, 134, 137, 151, 164–65, 173
Gonzales, Rodolfo "Corky," 16, 36
gringos, 61–62
Grossman, Edith, 160
groups, 7, 11, 13, 15, 24–25, 33, 58, 62, 76, 98, 105, 138, 147, 172; control, 115; dominant, 1–2; social, 56–57

Hamlet, 105
Hatfield, Charles, 118–20, 122, 132, 137, 139, 143, 174
Hayworth, Rita, 150–51
Heartbreak Soup (Hernandez), 119
hegemony, 4, 62–63, 73–74, 91, 164, 168
Herman, David, 17–20, 23–25
Hernandez, 108, 112, 117–19, 121–22, 124–25, 127, 131–39, 142–43, 181; Gilbert, xi, 30, 106–7, 110–12, 119–21, 123–26, 128–31, 136, 140–43, 181
Herrera Sobek, Maria, 49
High Soft Lisp (Hernandez), 117, 121
Hijuelos, Oscar, 14, 153
Hispanic literature, 15
Hispanics, 13–15, 32, 85, 91, 110, 178; historical context, 27, 38, 76, 79, 85, 88, 93, 106, 114; historical marginalization, 50
Hogan, Patrick Colm, xii, 11, 17, 20, 25, 56–57, 116
"Holidays in the Sun" (Hernandez), 121, 126–27, 142
house, 12, 62, 96, 103, 123, 145, 153, 161, 169
hybridity, 92–94

ideal audience, 8, 17, 21–23, 34, 39, 43, 47, 52–54, 57, 89–90, 94, 105, 113, 167
ideal readership, 17, 20–28, 30, 43, 60, 63, 83, 89, 105, 112, 131, 178, 180–82
identity, 1, 8–9, 19, 23–24, 26–29, 32, 39, 41, 43, 50–52, 56–57, 65–67, 76, 80, 102
identity formation, 11, 42, 45, 56, 58
implications, 24–26, 40, 121
implied authors, 9, 21, 23, 33–34, 82, 86
interior monologue, 97, 99

intertexts, 30, 102, 137, 148–52, 156–57, 164, 167, 174–75, 180–81; deliberate use of, 152; obscure, 30–31
intertextuality, 31, 114, 148–49, 152, 164

Jauss, Hans Robert, 26–28

knowledge, 22, 24, 36, 53, 61, 131, 136, 138, 148, 150–51, 159, 164, 166, 181–82

languages, 29, 37, 47, 49, 54, 56, 66–73, 75–76, 78, 80–82, 84–87, 89–93, 95–97, 104–6; challenges of, 77, 89; use of, 66, 76–77, 80–81, 85, 89
Latinidad, 72, 75, 163
Latino/a, x–xi, 2–17, 22–23, 25–26, 28–33, 35, 67–78, 87–89, 93–99, 104–11, 143–45, 152–54, 162–64, 170, 174–82
Latino/a comics, 20, 109, 112, 116, 123
Latino/a literature, 9, 13, 17, 85, 88, 94, 146, 171–72
literature, x, 1–17, 22–23, 25–26, 28–33, 35–36, 72–73, 92–94, 96–99, 144–47, 152–54, 170, 177–80, 182; minority, 6, 13, 30–31; reading, 18, 27; serialized, 120, 133
Los Bros, 108, 110, 112, 117, 134
Love and Rockets (Los Bros), 111–12, 115, 117–22, 131, 134–35, 139
Luba, 121–22, 125, 127, 131, 134–35, 137, 139–40, 142–43

magical realism, 5–6, 10, 16, 51, 96
memories, x–xi, 11, 14, 27, 30, 38, 102, 107, 111–17, 121, 124–27, 131–32, 136–38, 150, 155; episodic, 137–38; personal, 116; working, 30, 111–12, 114, 116, 133, 137
memory function, 113, 115–16, 132, 138
mental cognitive impairment (MCI), 115
mental model, 89, 95, 114, 121–22, 132
mental representation, 19–20
metaphors, 1, 48–49, 56–60, 64, 70, 96, 100, 103, 148
Mexicans, 15, 37–38, 52, 62, 68, 71, 158, 161
Mexico, 35–36, 48, 64, 68, 152–53, 159, 161, 181
mind, 17–19, 22–24, 26, 33, 39, 41, 44, 52–56, 61–62, 64–65, 116–17, 121, 127; reader's, 19–20, 25, 58, 112, 180
Morgoth's bane, 174–75

Mortenson, Greg, 146–47

narrating, 58–59, 124, 127, 185
narration, 28, 61–63, 86, 96, 98, 131, 134, 163, 167, 170, 173
narrative blueprints, 17, 20, 33, 75, 88, 93–94, 106, 113, 115, 121, 179, 181; comprehension, 111, 113, 138, 151–52, 156, 161, 175; design, 2–3, 10, 39, 44, 53, 56, 87–88, 106, 112–13, 143, 148, 152, 163, 180; devices, 1–2, 16, 19, 30, 143, 146, 149, 162, 178; discourse, 29, 46, 76, 89–90, 94, 106
Narrative Encounters, 66–67, 69, 71, 73, 75, 77, 79, 81, 83, 85, 87, 89, 91, 93, 95
narrative features, 17
narrative form, 2, 5, 11, 16, 26, 51–52, 56–57, 66, 75, 92, 109, 117–18, 139, 153, 182
narrative innovations, 26, 178
narrative permissibility, 2–3, 177
narratives, 2–3, 19–20, 22–24, 28–29, 33, 35–36, 74, 76–77, 87, 92, 112–16, 118–19, 146–48, 151–52, 175–78
narrative schemas, 178
narrative theory, 2, 20, 22, 26, 50–51
narrative worldmaking, 17, 19, 51, 70, 95, 121, 144, 147, 164–65, 173, 182
narrators, 33–34, 58, 60–63, 82, 86, 96–102, 114, 123, 146–49, 153, 155–56, 161, 163–65, 167, 170–74
nations, 11, 55, 57, 70–71, 73, 105, 153, 177–78
neuroscience, 111–13, 115
novels, x, 5, 11, 16, 24, 30, 35–36, 120, 145, 147, 149, 152–54, 156, 172, 177
number, 6, 13, 75–76, 85, 133, 163, 170

objects, 60, 119, 138–39
ontologies, 29, 180
oppressors, 58–59, 62

pages, 77–78, 108, 112, 117–18, 121–22, 127, 134, 140, 142, 155, 161, 165, 167–68, 171, 181
páginas, 165–68
Palomar, 122, 130, 132, 134–37, 143
Palomar stories, 119–21, 125–26, 132, 143
panels, 123–27, 131–32, 134, 140
paradigmatic changes, 2–3
patriarchy, 42, 53, 55, 62–63, 65, 180
Phelan, James, 21, 86–87, 114

poetics, 73,
poetry, 4, 49, 54, 56, 58–59, 64, 73–74, 90–91, 96, 104–5, 168, 178
Poison River (Hernandez), 118, 120, 122, 132–40, 142–43, 181
politics, 4, 7, 55
position, 4, 7, 9, 21–22, 25, 27, 35, 39, 44, 58, 69–70, 163, 170, 173, 182
practical identity, 11, 24, 56
process of storyworld reconstruction, 17, 19, 25
prose, 49, 56, 59, 90–91
protagonist, ix, 34, 39, 77, 97, 100, 102, 104
prototypes, 60, 116
publishers, 3, 5, 11–16, 31, 72–74, 77–78, 80, 88, 92, 94, 109, 117, 176, 178–79, 182
Publishers Weekly, 90
publishing, 12, 26, 36, 110, 118, 178; houses, 5, 12–13, 15–16, 87; industry, 5, 8, 10, 12, 16
Puerto Rico, 13, 91–92, 94

Quixote, Don, 147, 160
quoted speech, 174–75

race, 4, 11, 23, 25, 29, 42–43, 49, 57, 67, 75–76, 102, 164, 168
readership, 3, 10–11, 14–16, 20, 29–32, 36, 39, 47–48, 88, 133–34, 136, 150–51, 175, 180, 182
rebozo, 159–61
Rodriguez, Richard, 13, 56, 67, 69–71, 74

San Francisco, 12, 16
self-translation, 74, 80–81, 84–85, 87
serialization, 30, 107, 118–20, 132; process of, 119–20
Spanish, 12, 29, 37, 52, 65–67, 69–73, 75, 77–78, 80–91, 94–96, 99, 101, 106, 139, 181–82
Stavans, Ilan, 13–15, 36, 47, 65, 76, 153
stories, ix–xi, 16–19, 102, 105, 111, 116–19, 121–22, 124, 126, 132–34, 137–38, 164–67, 169–73
storying the world, 17–19, 23
storytelling, ix, xi, 17, 34, 106, 108, 135, 139, 143, 157, 160, 182
storyworld, 17–26, 30–31, 33–35, 72, 74–75, 95–96, 98–99, 105–7, 109–13, 115–16,

118–22, 127, 133, 149, 151; blueprint, 28, 77, 89–90, 181; design, 2, 29, 75, 124, 149, 176, 182; reconstruction, 17–19, 25, 53, 70, 86, 88–89, 151, 156, 175

target audience, 52, 63

Theory of Mind, 33

Tolkien, J. R. R., 172–74

translation, 70, 72, 74, 78, 82–84, 86–87, 89, 102, 160

types, 22, 24, 106–7, 110–11, 113–14, 116, 119, 121, 132–33, 135, 138, 145–46, 151, 157–58, 177–80

United States, 1–4, 6–10, 13, 32–33, 36–38, 43–44, 64–65, 67–68, 70–71, 75, 85, 92, 94–95, 164–65

voices, 14, 46, 48, 50–51, 60, 96, 98, 127, 147, 155–56

Wao, Oscar, 3, 30, 35, 78, 145–47, 152, 158, 163–68, 170–75, 177, 179

World War II, 32, 38, 159, 170–71

Yo-Yo Boing (Braschi), 88, 90, 92, 94, 105, 181

"Zeta," 26, 28, 34–35, 47, 66, 172

Zuckerman, Nathan, 172–73

COGNITIVE APPROACHES TO CULTURE
FREDERICK LUIS ALDAMA, PATRICK COLM HOGAN, LALITA PANDIT HOGAN, AND SUE KIM, SERIES EDITORS

This new series takes up cutting edge research in a broad range of cognitive sciences insofar as this research bears on and illuminates cultural phenomena such as literature, film, drama, music, dance, visual art, digital media, and comics, among others. For the purpose of the series, "cognitive science" will be construed broadly to encompass work derived from cognitive and social psychology, neuroscience, cognitive and generative linguistics, affective science, and related areas in anthropology, philosophy, computer science, and elsewhere. Though open to all forms of cognitive analysis, the series is particularly interested in works that explore the social and political consequences of cognitive cultural study.

Permissible Narratives: The Promise of Latino/a Literature
　CHRISTOPHER GONZÁLEZ

Literatures of Liberation: Non-European Universalisms and Democratic Progress
　MUKTI LAKHI MANGHARAM

Affective Ecologies: Empathy, Emotion, and Environmental Narrative
　ALEXA WEIK VON MOSSNER

A Passion for Specificity: Confronting Inner Experience in Literature and Science
　MARCO CARACCIOLO AND RUSSELL T. HURLBURT

www.ingramcontent.com/pod-product-compliance
Lightning Source LLC
Chambersburg PA
CBHW030138240426
43672CB00005B/174